COMPUTER GRAPHICS

JOHN LEWELL

COMPUTER GRAPHICS

a survey of current techniques and applications

© 1983 MELVIN L. PRUEITT

VNR VAN NOSTRAND REINHOLD COMPANY

New York

First published in Great Britain by Orbis Publishing
Limited, 1985

Library of Congress Catalog Card Number
84-29076

ISBN 0-442-26045-8

Colour reproduction by Imago Publishing Limited
Printed in Italy

Van Nostrand Reinhold Company Inc.
135 West 50th Street
New York, New York 10020

16 15 14 13 12 11 10 9 8 7 6 5 4 3 2

Library of Congress Cataloging in Publication Data

Lewell, John.
    Computer graphics.

    Bibliography: p.
    Includes index.
    1. Computer graphics.   I. Title.
T385.L485   1985   001.64'43   84-29076
ISBN 0-442-26045-8

CONTENTS

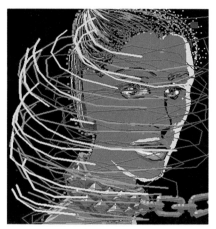

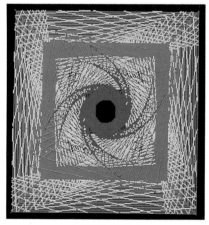

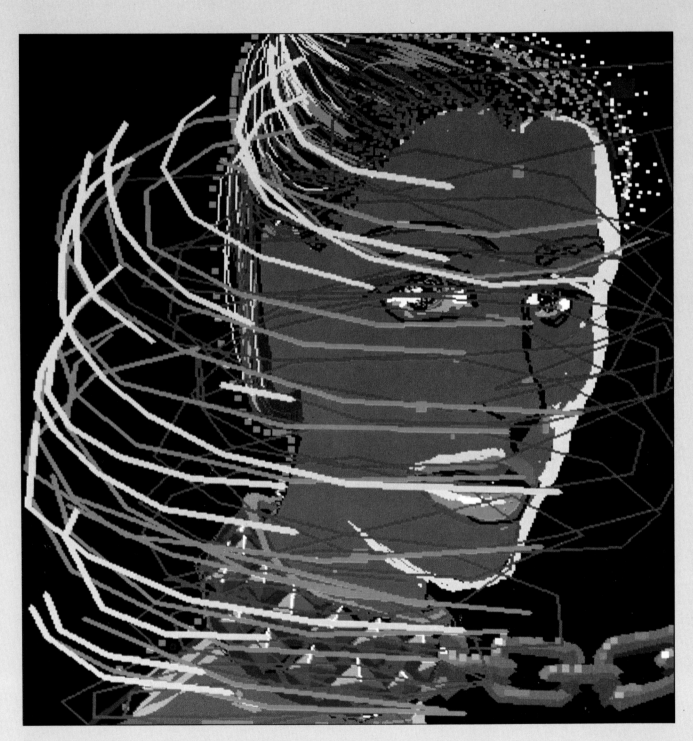

Computer-assisted painting *Electric Lady*, DEI/Mark Lindquist   *Digital Effects, Inc., New York, New York*

INTRODUCTION
TO
COMPUTER
GRAPHICS

In the 1980s, on a normal busy day in the working week, you might observe the following activities taking place at various points around the globe. A businessman in Frankfurt, Germany, examines a graph of his company's sales in fifty European cities. An architect in Houston, Texas, takes his client on a conducted tour of a building that does not yet exist. In New York, a choreographer plans a ballet, setting 'dancers' in motion and watching their movements even before anyone has arrived for rehearsals. An electronics engineer in Santa Clara, California, pieces together a complex labyrinth of circuits destined for a new microprocessor. An archaeologist in Oxford, England, deciphers writing on an ancient fragment of stone. And on the other side of the world, in Tokyo, Japan, an automobile engineer tests a new model on a rough surface, even though no prototype of the vehicle has been constructed.

All of this will sound very mysterious until we realize that there is a common factor linking these people and their diverse activities together. Each of them is using a powerful new tool to generate images. They are using a computer. The common factor is *computer graphics.*

Making, storing and manipulating pictures

During this decade, the image-making capability of the computer has reached a level of sophistication that allows people with little or no knowledge of computing to use an electronic system for manipulating pictorial data. At the same time, experts have pushed the techniques of computer imaging to new heights of realism, and manufacturers have introduced improvements to electronic displays that suddenly make the home television set appear to be wholly inadequate in quality, colour and resolution.

Not since the birth of photography in the nineteenth century has any technological development had such a profound impact on the way we make pictures. For it is with the *making* of pictures – not simply the recording or transmitting of them, as in film or television – that we are chiefly concerned in this book. Making a picture, storing it, and manipulating it on a computer: this is the essence of computer graphics.

The list of computer graphics users could be extended indefinitely. Dr Tony Diment, a graphics expert, has said: 'There now seems to be no area of human endeavour that cannot be enhanced by the application of computer graphics.' This is an extravagant claim, but it may not be as wide of the mark as one might at first suppose. While computer graphics is unlikely to enhance the writing of poetry or the composing of music it can certainly be applied to an astonishing range of tasks. Its users already include film makers and television designers, astronomers and biologists, artists and stock-brokers – and these are strange bedfellows indeed. But computer graphics, like the computer itself, is infinitely

▷ **Model of an interactive system**
The user completes the loop in this functional model of an interactive graphics system, indicating commands and reacting to the machine's responses

▽ **State of the art workstation**
The Dicomed Imaginator is a complete graphic design station for generating images intended for high-resolution (up to 8000-line) photographic slides. By moving the hand cursor around the digitizing surface an artist can select drawing functions which are represented as a menu on the screen. Inside the console is the hardware necessary to support several interactive design programs and provide mass storage for the picture data

Dicomed (UK) Limited, Ascot, Berkshire, England

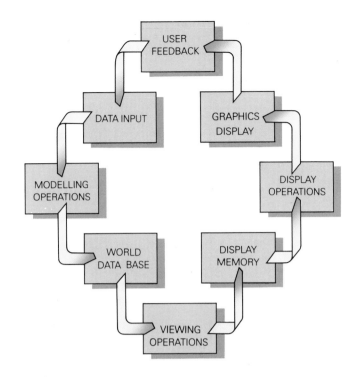

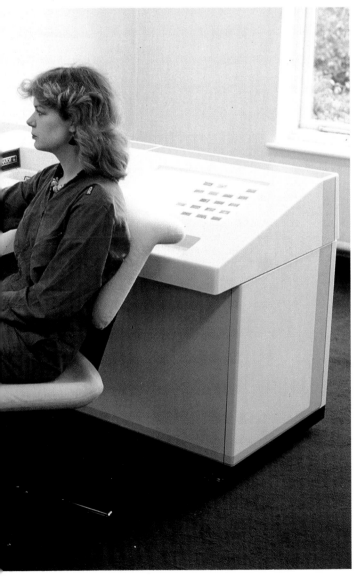

adaptable. Anyone who deals with moving or static images, or who compiles or refers to information that can be given graphic expression, will eventually have access to computer graphics in his (or her) daily work. Even away from the working environment we are already constantly exposed to computer-generated images: in press advertisements and posters, at the cinema, and especially on television.

Yet the new techniques are not familiar to everyone, despite the proliferation of the pictures they generate. In fact, never before have we been able specifically to *generate* images with any degree of sophistication. Pictures are normally drawn or painted, or perhaps constructed, or they are 'taken'. The idea of generating an image carries with it an implication of power – of the ability to make visible what would otherwise remain invisible.

To a great extent this is true. Nothing better demonstrates the power of the computer than operating a three-dimensional, high-resolution graphics display. To be able to 'fly through' a completely modelled DNA molecule, or across an artificial landscape, as real as though it had been filmed by a cameraman, and in each case to be able to control your flightpath as an aircraft pilot does, is an experience guaranteed to renew a sense of wonder.

Interactive graphics

The example of flight simulation introduces a concept that is fundamental to computer graphics. The majority of graphics systems are *interactive* in their design. Whether you are simply viewing a picture, or actually constructing a picture element-by-element, the system allows you to interact with it. You make a move – then you wait – then the computer makes a move – and it waits. The process is somewhat like a game of chess, except that it can be played so quickly that the user and the computer often appear to be performing simultaneously.

Suppose, for example, you are looking at an image that has already been made on a graphics system. It is displayed on a *visual display unit* (VDU) and may very well be such a highly realistic three-dimensional image, complete with a light source and shadows, that we can call it an 'object'. By moving a control lever (a *joystick*) you can rotate this object and look at the back of it. When you switch to another mode – 'pan' instead of 'rotate' – you can cause it to move from side to side.

The consequent movement of the object on the VDU will appear to be fluid and continuous, but it is not. If you were to slow down the process in order to examine exactly what is happening you would discover that the computer is carefully noting 'your turn/my turn/your turn ...'. By keeping pressure on the joystick you are sending a whole chain of repeated commands: 'move left, move left ...'. After each one the computer makes its move. In other words, the *analog* (continuous) movement of the control lever is being translated into *digital* (discrete) instructions, many times each second, and after each command the computer performs its task – such as calculating the new position of the object when it is moved a fraction to the left. Then it waits. After all, you might change your mind at any time and decide to move the object to the right.

This interactive process is particularly significant when the user wants to construct an image. By its ability to make millions of calculations in a very short time (and the most powerful computers can make over 100 million in a single second) the computer can act as a servant to the designer.

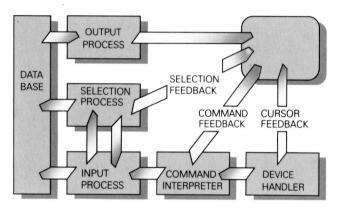

△ **Interactive processing**
Each stage of interactive processing provides feedback to guide the user. For example, moving the screen cursor in response to the user's hand movements is the computer's first task

Take, for instance, a simple task such as drawing a circle. If it is the user's turn to move he selects 'circle' from a *menu* of choices on the VDU. The computer makes its own move by calling up its circle-drawing routines; then it waits for the user to take advantage of them. In turn, the user places a dot for the centre of a circle somewhere on the displayed area. The computer, however, does nothing at this stage because it already knows that a circle requires at least two commands: one for the centre and one for the circumference. It waits until the user has indicated the size of the circle by placing a second dot, and then automatically switches into its circle-drawing routine, which is poised ready for action.

Each circle requires hundreds of calculations at a lower level of the program. This is because any curved line will actually consist of lots of very small straight lines. The computer, we must remember, is a digital machine, and at the lowest level knows only two things: 'yes' and 'no'. In this case, it is calculating 'line' and 'no-line' hundreds of times in order to draw the circle.

A slow machine will take longer to draw a shape than a fast machine, and the user will not get his turn in the interactive game until the whole circle has been drawn. Fortunately, since circle drawing is a relatively simple set of calculations, the shape will appear almost instantaneously. Now the interactive process can continue – and we can begin to see why computer graphics is becoming such an indispensable tool. For not only has the computer drawn a circle, but it *also 'knows' what it has drawn*. In its memory it

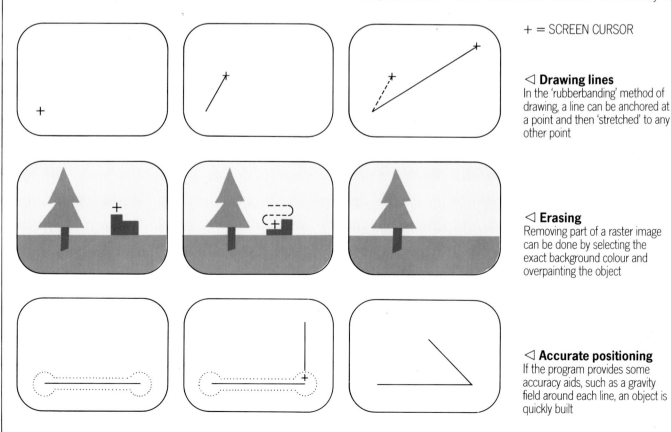

+ = SCREEN CURSOR

◁ **Drawing lines**
In the 'rubberbanding' method of drawing, a line can be anchored at a point and then 'stretched' to any other point

◁ **Erasing**
Removing part of a raster image can be done by selecting the exact background colour and overpainting the object

◁ **Accurate positioning**
If the program provides some accuracy aids, such as a gravity field around each line, an object is quickly built

has switched from one state to another: from 'no circle' to 'circle'. This means that the user can continue to interact with the machine at a higher level. Since the computer 'knows' that it is now displaying a circular shape, it is also able to treat this new object as a whole.

Thus the circle can be moved around the screen area, shrunk or expanded. The operator can move to a 'repeat' mode and replicate the circle as many times as he wishes. All of this process takes place interactively, with the computer making its calculations at great speed while the operator pauses briefly for the display to change.

Prior to the development of computer graphics, computing did not have this mode of interactive operation. Processing was carried out in *batches*. But the dramatic increase in the power and memory capacity of the computer has made interactive graphics possible. The experts refer to the 'higher-bandwidth man/machine communication' that has resulted from this development. In other words, we can now talk to the computer more easily and in more detail – using shapes as well as words – and its replies, too, have become more intelligent.

Non-interactive graphics

Not all of computer graphics is interactive. Non-interactive, or *passive*, computer graphics can be equally useful, depending on the application. In many instances, a picture can be made on an interactive system and then turned into passive computer graphics for viewing. The pictures in this book are a good example. They have been 'frozen' on to paper, where they permit only passive viewing by the reader. However, many of them still exist as electronic data. If you had the appropriate display system you could manipulate the image of, say, the fighter plane, rotating it on the VDU and perhaps zooming in to examine the detail of a wing section.

Since computer graphics is not restricted to the electronic medium it frequently takes on a non-interactive role. Whenever the electronic image is placed on paper or film for convenient viewing or projection it becomes non-interactive. Even on conventional video, frames follow each other in a sequential *linear* mode. Interactive systems always require a computer to calculate the display. If there are many different options, the data must be selected in a *non-linear* fashion. Non-linearity is the chief characteristic of the new technology, and it is lost when pictures are frozen into the older and more conventional media.

One advantage of non-interactive graphics is that all the processing power of the computer can be devoted towards providing the highest picture quality. By calculating one line at a time, a *film recorder* will produce an image with a higher *resolution* (finer-grained detail) than can be obtained on an electronic display. Likewise, *plotters* and *printers*, which draw the images on paper, can show detail that would not be readable on the screen. In architecture and engineering, the portability and convenience of non-interactive graphics are essential, while back at the computer all the interactive techniques can still be employed to create the images.

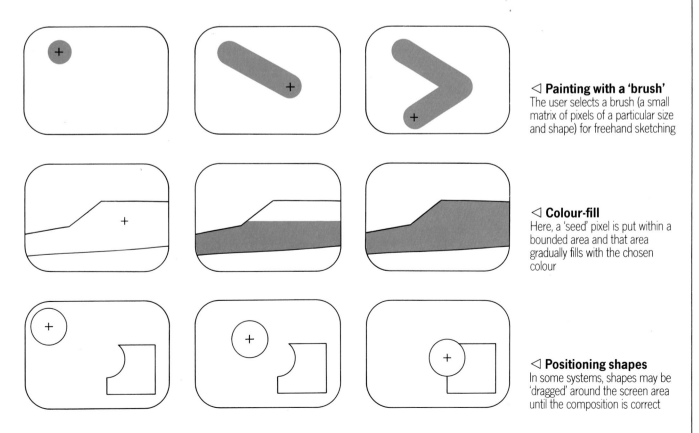

◁ **Painting with a 'brush'**
The user selects a brush (a small matrix of pixels of a particular size and shape) for freehand sketching

◁ **Colour-fill**
Here, a 'seed' pixel is put within a bounded area and that area gradually fills with the chosen colour

◁ **Positioning shapes**
In some systems, shapes may be 'dragged' around the screen area until the composition is correct

The role of computer graphics

Users of computer graphics can be divided into two groups: those whose primary concern is with the image itself (such as graphic designers, film makers or illustrators); and those for whom the image is merely a carrier of information (scientists, engineers or business graphics users). This is a most important distinction to make. The majority of computer graphics applications have been adopted by the second group of users. For the scientist or engineer the picture is not an end in itself, but a means to an end.

A physicist, for example, may very well be studying subatomic reactions. When he creates a simulation of these reactions on a computer his chief concern is that the system accurately simulates his concept of the reaction. If he has a graphics display to help with the task he is using it as an *interface* (mediating device) between himself and the *application data base* of the computer (the store of data relating to the task in hand). The graphics system is merely the 'front end' of the whole computer system. It provides a way of communicating with the machine.

Similarly, the businessman who wants to see an analysis of his company's performance will expect the computer to provide him with the latest figures in a convenient and easily-readable format. Again computer graphics can be a means to an end. The alternative would be a list of figures that would require long and careful scrutiny before market trends could be spotted. With graphics, the information is presented to be seen at a glance. A market trend is immediately recognizable when figures have been translated into a graphic format.

Computer graphics for such purposes has enjoyed remarkable success during the past few years. One reason for this success can be found in the development of computing as a whole. Computers quickly became such powerful processors of data that the sheer quantity of their output was fast outstripping our own human capacity to deal with it. When a machine makes millions of calculations every second it sends back answers that are often as complex as the questions being fed to it. Thus the design of a graphic interface was prompted by necessity, and eventually became a branch of computing in its own right.

A brief history

Digital computers made their first appearance in the 1940s. The IBM Mark I computer was a massive electromechanical device, weighing 5 tons and occupying a whole room. It contained over 3300 relays — mechanical parts that registered 'on' or 'off' states — and over 800 km (500 miles) of wiring. Yet the Mark I could perform only relatively simple arithmetic, such as multiplying two 23-digit numbers, a task that took six seconds to complete.

Vacuum-tube computers, with electronic *flip-flop* (on-or-off) circuits replacing the relays, appeared just after World War II. The ENIAC (Electronic Numerical Integrator And Calculator) was the first of these, built for the US Army in 1946. Since the circuits were now all-electronic, the speed of computation showed a dramatic increase. With machines built in the early 1950s, 10-digit numbers could be multiplied in 1/2000 second. The vacuum-tube machine is now generally acknowledged as the first viable computer; it was marketed for business and scientific applications, despite its limited memory capacity and still — by today's standards — relatively low speed. Such a machine was the UNIVAC I, and it represents the 'first generation' of computers.

The second generation brought computing to the forefront of technology. Transistors replaced vacuum tubes, bringing still greater speed, and, above all, reliability. The size of computers shrank dramatically, since a transistor was only 1/200th the size of a vacuum tube. It also gave off only a fraction of the heat, and transistors could thus be packed together in a very small space. Software advances were made, and with these new techniques the number of potential computer users was greatly expanded.

Towards the end of the second generation, interactive computer graphics made its first appearance. At the Massachusetts Institute of Technology, a brilliant young student was working on his PhD thesis. It proved to be the seminal work in computer graphics, and it did more than any other single piece of research to launch the computer graphics industry.

The student was Ivan Sutherland, who is now one of the partners in the Evans & Sutherland Corporation, many of whose graphics displays were used in producing the illustrations that are shown in this book. Sutherland introduced the concept of using a keyboard and a hand-held *light pen* for selecting, pointing and drawing — in conjunction with an image displayed on a VDU. He built computer images by a method of replicating standard picture components, adding together points to make lines, and lines to make shapes. These, and many other techniques that Sutherland pioneered, are still in use today.

Most significantly, the data structure built by Sutherland on the TX-2 computer was very different from anything that had been done before. It was based on the *topology* of the object being represented, that is, it accurately described the relationships between the various component parts. Prior to this, computer representations of an object had merely been representations of the picture — not of the object itself. To an engineer, for example, the usefulness of the earlier method was extremely limited. With Sutherland's system, which he called Sketchpad, a clear distinction was drawn between the model that was represented in the data structure and the picture that you saw on the screen.

Sketchpad, introduced in 1963, caused great excitement in the universities. With a further touch of brilliance,

Sutherland made a documentary film about his new system, and a print of it was sent to every computer centre in the United States. Being primarily a visual subject, computer graphics was most vividly explained by means of a visual medium. The film showed a number of techniques, many of which have since become familiar to millions of users.

One such technique Sutherland called 'rubberbanding'. He used a light pen to fix a point on the screen and then, by moving the pen, stretched a line from it to another part of the picture area, eventually anchoring it in position. But most exciting of all was the demonstration that the computer could work out which of the lines defined the front surface of an object, while eliminating any other lines that would be temporarily hidden from view. The hidden lines remained in the data structure, stored in the computer memory, and would reappear when the object was rotated on the display.

The limitations of Sketchpad were in the computer rather than the concept. The second-generation machine could not contribute any 'richness' to the image. Only one graphics command existed: the facility to place a dot on the screen at a particular location. Collections of dots would make a line, but that would produce only a skeleton of an image.

▽ Business presentation graphics

Audio visual users have been among the first to take advantage of the unique features offered by computer graphics slide-production systems. The finished slides can be included in synchronized audio visual shows or used simply as 'speaker support' visuals during live presentations. Not only can a great variety of images be produced very quickly, but their quality or 'finish' cannot easily be imitated by a graphic artist using conventional materials.

Shown here is a typical example of a business presentation graphic. It was one of hundreds of images that were made for an internationally-shown audio visual presentation. While only six basic images were made by the designer, many variations on them were also required. For example, animated effects were quickly achieved by zooming in on parts of each image, thus making a whole sequence of slides which gave an illusion of movement. Additionally, the client needed foreign-language versions of the show, and thus many of the slides were duplicated with alternative text being inserted in each case. The chief advantages of computer graphics in this application are therefore speed of production, economy, high impact, and flexibility

Eidographics, London, England

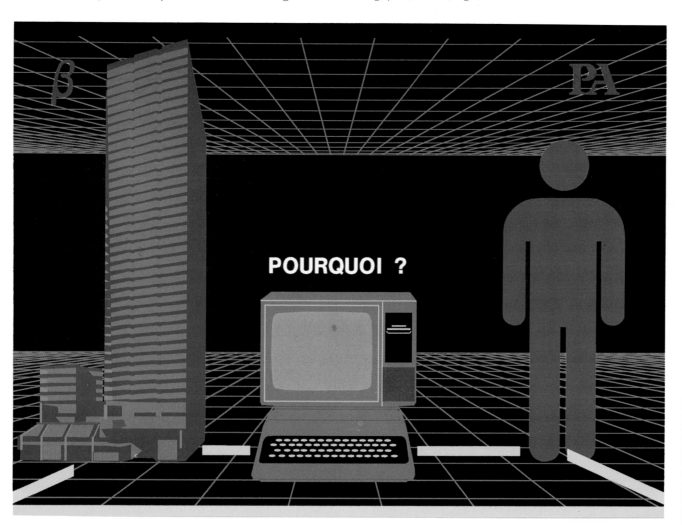

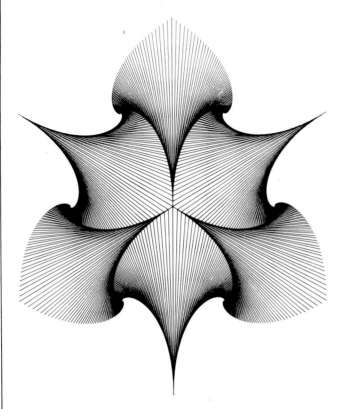

△ Early computer graphics

During the 1960s the computer plotter was perfected, with the result that a whole new industry began to flourish. Computers demonstrated their power as drawing accessories, useful to artists and engineers alike. This plotter-drawn picture, called *Crest*, is reminiscent of Spirograph images, but is far more precise and complex. It was among the entrants in a competition held in 1968 by CalComp, a leading plotter manufacturer of that era and now a fully diversified graphics equipment manufacturer

CalComp (California Computer Products, Inc.), Anaheim, California

In the development of non-interactive graphics, which preceded Sutherland's work, the problem of image richness had prompted the invention of other *peripheral* (auxiliary) *devices*. Foremost among these was the computer plotter. This is a drawing device that connects endpoints of lines by moving a pen from one *coordinate point* (known position) to another. Both coordinate points are held in the computer memory and the plotter obediently performs the task of drawing the image. In this instance an electronic screen for viewing the picture may be completely optional. Here the *display surface* is paper rather than a cathode-ray tube. Highly complex and rich drawings could be generated by using a computer plotter, as the illustration of an early plot, taken from a CalComp competition (above), demonstrates.

Around 1965, in computing technology, solid-state integrated circuits, the forerunners of today's 'chips', began to replace circuitry composed of individual components. Further miniaturization took place with this third generation of machines, and more peripheral devices were introduced. In order to 'talk' to the computer, researchers found that they needed other graphical input devices that would simulate the more conventional techniques of drawing a picture. The *data tablet and stylus* were introduced, eventually becoming a standard means of data entry.

Somewhat like a drawing board in appearance, the data tablet has a sensitive surface and can register any coordinate point when the stylus is pressed on to it. A *screen cursor* – a small cross – indicates the point on the VDU. This development provided a far more accurate method of entering coordinate data than using a light pen directly on the screen. The resolution of the tablet in terms of the number of points it could indicate was far greater than the resolution of the electronic display. Again, the distinction that had been made between the object in the computer's memory and the image of it on the screen enabled devices such as the data tablet to be of real usefulness to a designer.

With the fourth generation of computers, dating from the early 1970s, computer technology moved into the modern era. Computers could now be connected together to form networks. In graphics, this meant that a single host computer could support a number of design *workstations*. Minicomputers, such as the Digital Equipment Corporation's PDP-11 series, became ideal for the new graphics applications. They offered high speed at an economical price, and thus more computer time could be devoted to graphics research within the budget of a university. Microprocessors – each one a computer on a chip – enabled small personal machines to be manufactured at rock-bottom cost. An Apple II, at the end of the 1970s, was more powerful than the 5-ton IBM machine that heralded the Computer Age.

The growth of graphics

The watershed year for computer graphics was 1980. Until then it had remained largely the domain of scientists, mathematicians, engineers and computer-science experts. But in 1980 the market for computer graphics products began to take off. Graphics systems found their way into broadcast television; into animation studios; and into a variety of businesses that previously had little or no acquaintance with the medium. Yet it was still early days for the new technology. One sure indication of this could be seen in the fact that no art school in the world had yet equipped its facilities with a computer graphics system. Two more years were to pass before this finally happened.

The spectacular growth of computer graphics is recorded in some of the statistics given by the industry. For instance, at the end of 1979 IBM launched its 3279 colour terminal. Within nine months it had received more than 10,000 orders for the system, two-thirds of which were destined for first-time users of computer graphics. In the following year, the total value of all the services, systems and hardware associated with computer graphics topped the billion-dollar mark for the first time. When we remember that barely two decades had passed since Ivan Sutherland gave the industry its initial impetus, we can appreciate the social and economic impact of the new imaging technology.

Again, the exponential growth was reflected in figures for conference attendance. The Association for Computing Machinery (ACM) is the official American organization that promotes, and to some extent regulates, the computer industry. When computer graphics first appeared, the ACM established what it called a Special Interest Group on Graphics. This sounded like a small and select body of experts, and it was. In 1976, the group – known by its acronym SIGGRAPH – allowed exhibitors to take part in its annual conference for the first time. Ten corporations displayed their equipment and services. Yet, only four years later, at Seattle, 98 corporations took part in the event, and nearly 7000 visitors attended the exhibition.

Nor did the growth of graphics taper off at this point. In fact, quite the opposite occurred. A breakaway group from SIGGRAPH was formed: called the National Computer Graphics Association (NCGA). It held its own annual conference and exhibition in the United States, and it placed a greater emphasis on the commercial and industrial applications of computer graphics. By 1983, NCGA was attracting over 35,000 visitors from all over the world. Yet SIGGRAPH's annual meeting remained the major academic forum, running no less than 14 simultaneous courses and (incidentally) receiving just as high an attendance as the 'upstart' NCGA. Certainly, the title 'Special Interest Group' had become something of a misnomer. To paraphrase Winston Churchill: 'Some group! Some special interest!'

Research and development

Bringing computer graphics to its launching pad of the 1980s required a substantial investment in research and development. This was underwritten largely by the aerospace, automobile, and defence industries. The bulk of the work was carried out at corporations and universities in the United States and, to a lesser extent, in Britain. Among the corporations who saw the potential at an early stage – at around the time of Sutherland's seminal work – were Boeing, Lockheed and General Motors.

General Motors was the first user of an elaborate graphics system developed by IBM specifically for automobile design. It was called DAC-1 (design augmented by computer). Installed under a cloak of secrecy, the system was eventually made public at the 1964 Fall Joint Computer Conference. The DAC-1 was the first of many purpose-built computer-aided design (CAD) systems that would be used for designing motor cars by the end of the 1960s. The design of cars, planes, and other highly-engineered products provided the necessary stimulus to the development of more versatile

△ **Design evaluation**
CYBERMAN is a three-dimensional wireframe manikin, invented by Chrysler Corporation and used for evaluating layouts of interior components in, for example, the driving compartments of vehicles
Chrysler Corporation, Detroit, Michigan

CAD equipment that could be used by thousands of different manufacturers.

One of the most successful projects was an early system developed by Itek Laboratories for lens design work. The geometric calculations necessary to lens design are so complex that computer-aided design seemed to be the natural route to follow. The Itek researchers were right. Their system was later bought and marketed commercially by Control Data Corporation, again making the new techniques available to a broader range of users.

It was perhaps surprising that the first major research centre for computer graphics – as opposed to the more general field of computer-aided design – was destined to be established at a small university in the middle of the western United States. The University of Utah enjoyed a golden period of intensive academic research, yielding one breakthrough after another as students and teachers worked together on the problems posed by graphic representation with a computer. It was one of those rare occasions when a unique combination of personalities and circumstances produced a remarkable result.

While teaching at Berkeley, in Northern California, Professor David Evans had seen the film made by Ivan Sutherland

on Sketchpad. 'I was excited by it,' he said, 'but I didn't immediately do anything about it.' Shortly afterwards Professor Evans accepted a post at the University of Utah where he had the task of directing the department of computer science. Constrained by the relatively small budget of the university (Utah, for all its beauty, is not a wealthy state), Evans was forced to concentrate the resources of his department on one carefully-chosen area of research. He opted for graphics.

Computer graphics was an unusual and challenging field of research for the students at Utah. It involved working on subjects whose scope extended far beyond the traditional confines of computing. For instance, it included the laws of perspective, the composition of light and the science of colour. Even geometry could now be reinstated into the mainstream of academic research, some 350 years after René Descartes had reduced it to algebra.

In 1972 at Utah, students worked around the clock, discovering how to describe the shapes and appearances of objects to the computer. One of them was Ed Catmull, who now heads the graphics research team at Lucasfilm. Reflecting on his days in Utah, he said: 'There was very little equipment. But *magic* happened at that time. A lot of good ideas just kept rolling forth.' Catmull's own research was

△ ▷ **Space simulations**
Realistic simulations of space vehicles flying past planetary bodies have become familiar to millions of people through television. Conceived originally as public relations films for NASA (National Aeronautics and Space Administration), these simulations by Dr James Blinn are scientifically impeccable. Even the stars are in their correct positions

3

4

1 Voyager 2 at Saturn: closest approach
2 Hugh crater on Mimas, a moon of Saturn
3 Voyager 2 leaves Saturn for Uranus
4 Neptune and Triton, seven hours after Voyager 2 encounter

Jet Propulsion Laboratory, Pasadena, California

directed towards finding ways of generating images of curved surfaces – not simply regular shapes such as spheres and cones, but surfaces that had general shapes to them. He did it by dividing each surface into very small patches, whose relationships to each other could be defined mathematically to the computer. Eventually, this research proved to be of great value in such fields as aerospace, where curved surfaces on wings and bodies are a major part of the design.

Another student of Professor Evans was Dr James Blinn, whose computer simulations of space voyages for the Jet Propulsion Laboratory have been seen by television audiences around the world. Dr Blinn tackled many of the most difficult problems of computer graphics representation. He discovered several ways of making the techniques, known as *surface modelling*, effective for the realistic rendering of three-dimensional objects. Starting with a *wireframe* drawing composed of lines, he added solid blocks of colour – creating surfaces – and then overlaid these surfaces with textures to give them the appearance of reality. All of these effects were created by writing computer programs, and assembling the object piece by piece on the screen. But once the programs had been written, it was relatively simple for a less experienced person to repeat the process and to create a totally different object using the same techniques.

After the success of the work at Utah other institutions began to take an increased interest in computer graphics. One major influence was the establishment of a new and exciting project at the New York Institute of Technology. A founder of the NYIT, Dr Alexander Schure, set in motion an ambitious multi-million dollar research program called 'The Works'. This was also the name of a motion picture that Dr Schure had in mind to produce, whose title came from the original meaning of the word 'robot', derived from the Czech *robota*, '(forced) work'. The film was not to be made with conventional tools such as cameras, lights, and stage sets. It was to be entirely generated by computers. The task for the students was to find a way of doing it.

Naturally many of the most brilliant students of computer graphics were intrigued by the idea, and several ex-Utah graduates moved to the Old Westbury campus of NYIT. The focus of research was now on purely graphical aspects of computer imaging: on graphics as an end in itself. Particular attention was paid to computer painting, computer art, and animation. Conventional techniques of film animation were analyzed, and computer software was written which could simulate 'in-betweening', that is, the drawing of frames that come in between the key frames of an animated sequence. Other researchers, among them Alvy Ray Smith, tackled the problems of computer painting. How to fill bounded areas with colour; how best to describe colour to the computer; how to simulate the effects of watercolour and oil painting – these were the kind of problems that concerned Dr Smith and his colleagues. The new set of problems were characteristic of a new era in graphics research. By focusing on the image itself, and by developing methods of creating sophisticated images, researchers at NYIT attracted the attention of the graphic design world. Television companies, advertisers and film makers began to notice that people were making images with computers. At the annual SIGGRAPH conference, a few tantalizing minutes of *The Works* were shown each year, and, although it is still far short of its intended 90-minute length, work on *The Works* continues.

The main thrust of research at NYIT has become the development of *user-friendly* systems, that is, systems designed so that non-experts can operate them. This is a most important aspect of graphics research. If the full range of techniques is to become available to *all* designers, animators, and illustrators, then user-friendliness needs all the attention it can get. Some of the work at NYIT culminated in the packaging of a computer painting system that was marketed commercially at the beginning of the 1980s. As a consequence, many designers who had previously been unfamiliar with computer graphics techniques were able to experiment with them. The illustration at the beginning of this introduction is an example, made on the Video Palette painting system at Digital Effects, in New York.

However, further advances in hardware, particularly in display technology, need to be made before computer graphics techniques become readily available to designers at a price they can afford. The investment that a graphic designer makes in conventional tools is relatively low compared to the cost of a powerful computer – complete with a high-resolution display, *hardcopy* output to film or paper (as opposed to the evanescent image on a screen), and a versatile package of *software* routines (*programs*, that is, sets of instructions, so named to distinguish them from the '*hardware*' of the actual computer and its peripherals).

Will such a development take place? This is a question that needs to be answered before we examine the existing techniques of computer graphics in greater detail. The illustrations in this book have been produced on systems costing between $1000 and $10 million, with the majority of them having been made on the more expensive hardware. Although computer-generated graphics has finally emerged from the laboratory and is being used by an astonishing range of professions, it is still not at a stage that allows its most sophisticated techniques to be used by everyone. As Derrick Sherwin, a leading British computer animation expert, has said: 'The best has always been high tech. There are no corners to cut, and you cannot build machines to do what has to happen in the human brain: namely, the writing and manipulating of complex computer programs.'

If Mr Sherwin is right, then computer graphics will remain largely the province of the skilled user working with high-powered equipment that is owned by a corporation or an institution. Yet, before the end of the century, there may well be some more startling developments in computer science. After all, facilities equivalent to those of the original IBM Mark I are now available to schoolchildren, who are becoming highly skilled in operating their personal computers. A small personal computer already has a good graphics capability, although it cannot match the speed and resolution that are necessary for top-quality images. Great advances need to be made in the design of the most powerful available 'chips', known as *very large-scale integrated circuits* (VLSI) before the small, cheap, graphics computer can cope with the millions of calculations necessary to the manipulation of realistic imagery. For it is the ability to generate realistic, shaded images, in full colour, and complete with automatically-calculated light sources, that will make computer graphics a powerful rival to photography.

By 1984, computer graphics research had enabled a skilled practitioner to match photographic reality. What photographers call a 'pack shot' – a picture of an article for use in an advertisement – can now be so accurately simulated on a computer that it is almost impossible to distinguish between the two. By the turn of the century, if high-resolution displays, cheap film recorders and ultra-fast personal computers are available, it is probable that computer graphics will begin to replace conventional photographic technology. It will have a fundamental and dramatic impact on our whole approach to making pictures.

Unique characteristics of computer graphics

The techniques of computer imaging are the most flexible and comprehensive of all the imaging techniques at our disposal. All man-made images can be divided into two simple groups: moving and static. And there are only two ways of obtaining them: by recording or by constructing them. Photography, for instance, deals with the recording of static images, while cinematography is concerned with recording moving images. Yet when it comes to constructing a picture, neither photography nor cinematography is very helpful. With these techniques you first have to construct an object and then record a trace of it by taking its picture.

The alternative is to fall back on traditional, manual methods of drawing and painting. With these conventional techniques we can create elaborate and detailed pictures – yet, alas, they are only static. If we want to construct dynamic images in any detail we have to turn to the computer for help. Never before in history have we been able so effectively to construct dynamic images.

To be sure, we have had kinetic art, Chinese puzzles and film animation – all of which are, in a sense, dynamic imagery. But kinetic art is as a rule three-dimensional; Chinese puzzles require manual rearrangement; and film animation is a time-consuming and exacting profession. The only convenient way of constructing a dynamic image is to work with a 'dynamic

environment' that will transform the still image into a moving one. An analogy might be that you can fly a kite only on a windy day. The dynamics of the atmosphere keep it aloft. In a somewhat similar way, the flow of electric current through the circuits of a computer enables us to construct dynamic pictures that can be transformed and controlled as we watch them.

The first unique characteristic of computer graphics, therefore, is that it provides a dynamic environment to the user. The artist can call on routines for automatically transforming a shape that he has constructed manually. Suppose, for instance, that he draws a champagne glass. He plots each point of the familiar saucer shape of the bowl, adding a long stem to it and selecting the appropriate highlights. This picture is then stored in the computer memory. The artist draws another glass: a tall, narrow one such as would be used for serving sherry. Because the

◁ △ **Film making**
The film *Four Seasons of Japan*, made by the Japanese television network, NHK, showed how computer graphics could be used for evoking moods and 'aesthetic emotions'. Art direction was by Tatsuo Shimura; technical direction by Junnosuke Kutuzawa and Kenji Kira

NHK, Tokyo, Japan

computer system provides a dynamic environment, the two objects can be made to *transform* from one to the other. The result is a fluid movement of the glass on the electronic screen. It gradually changes from a champagne shape to a sherry shape, and back again. The image is most startling. Significantly, it is the kind of image that could not be made with any technique other than computer graphics. Neither photography nor film animation could simulate the effect. The complexity of the changing shadows, highlights, and geometries is such that a powerful computer is required to calculate the transformation.

This example with the glasses has actually been done, and a frame from the sequence is illustrated above. As an experimental work it required considerable expertise to write the program. However, it demonstrates the point that a computer graphics system is a most unusual tool, not merely more complex but quite different in type from conventional tools such as a paintbrush or a pair of compasses. Rather, it is a complete environment into which an artist can insert pictorial data. These data can then be transformed by the computer according to a number of selected routines.

A second unique characteristic of computer graphics is the speed at which it enables a designer to work. Much of graphic design – and indeed design for engineering and other applications – requires a combination of images and text. In printing and publishing this requirement is particularly strong. Yet by conventional methods it is extremely difficult to combine lettering with pictorial imagery. Not only are there thousands of typefaces, but these are often needed in dozens of sizes to fit the specific task in hand. Dry transfer lettering has become very popular, but it is surprisingly difficult to obtain a professional result without considerable practice. If one letter is just fractionally out of alignment it will be immediately noticeable.

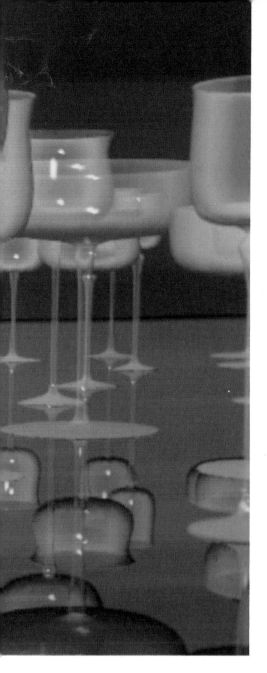

Here again, computing is providing an answer. A piece of text can be considered as a pictorial image. Whereas one technique of computer graphics is to use *alphanumeric* (letter and figure) characters for assembling the image, the reverse can also be true. A letter or any other visual symbol can be given a full graphics treatment. Its shape can be described to the computer, and it can be stored in the memory until it is needed. The artist can instantly recall it, position it, change its size, colour, and shape. In other words, text and pictures need no longer be treated separately, and the result is a significant increase in the speed designs can be produced.

A third unique characteristic of the new imaging technology is its ability to generate charts, graphs and plots that contain a wealth of information. Particularly for the scientist and the businessman, this is an indispensable aid. Once the routines have been written to show the computer the graphical format of the information, an infinite number of

◁ **Dynamic pictures**
Wineglasses, from an animated sequence in which the glasses transform from 'sherry' to 'champagne' shapes, and back again

Michael Collery, Cranston/Csuri Productions, Columbus, Ohio

△ **Calculated halftone images**
Computer images can be made from existing photographs by using a set of characters that display varying proportions of black and white. Any set of symbols having this quality may be used – but here Ken Knowlton has ingeniously created a picture with 24 complete sets of uncut double-nine dominoes. Each picture element was calculated by the computer, and the dominoes then assembled by hand and pasted onto particle-board. The original measures 1650 × 1245 mm (65 × 49 in)

Ken Knowlton, Bell Laboratories, New Jersey

1

2

variable plots can be generated. While it is feasible to make a complex chart by manual methods, constantly referring to lists of figures, by the time it is finished the information can be out of date. Computer graphics enables informative, up-to-the-minute charts, graphs and plots to be made, showing anything from variations in weather patterns or ocean currents to changes in share prices on the stock market.

The fourth characteristic has already been mentioned: the interactive nature of the graphics system. This, indeed, is unique – although it is also found in millions of homes in the form of *video games*. A video game is an interactive device and has a crude graphics display with which a player can interact. The relatively small power of a microprocessor-based video game, however, is devoted to handling all the options of the game itself. It is not really concerned with graphics as a creative medium. For instance, you cannot change a Space Invader into an image of Charlie Chaplin by interacting with the machine. Instead, you have to play by the rules of the game. Yet there are now programs available for personal computers that *do* allow you to draw your own characters. One of them even has a miniature figure of Charlie Chaplin which can be set in motion and 'directed' to perform a number of 'gags' on the electronic screen.

Finally, a fifth characteristic of computer graphics is its ability to render, with visual images, *simulations* of many different processes. Several of the examples quoted in the opening paragraph of this introduction (and all of them are actual applications) are instances of simulations. The architect who is able to take his client on a guided tour of an unbuilt office has created the structure on a computer graphics display. He is then able to use the computer model to simulate a walk through the office, showing the viewer exactly what it will look like when it is eventually constructed. Similarly, the choreographer is using a system that simulates the movements of the human body. When she sets the electronic dancers in motion on the screen she is confident that the constraints built into the system will allow her to create only those movements that are possible for real

dancers to perform. But the chief advantage is that the choreographer can experiment and preview the dance before a rehearsal begins. The more realistic the graphics, the more exactly will she be able to see the pattern of the dance.

Simulations are essential, too, in science and engineering. Graphic simulations can show how a product will perform before expensive manufacturing processes are put into operation. With realistic techniques of computer graphics even the need for a prototype is often circumvented. A manufacturer can test a product with a simulation, examine its working design, and then put it directly into production.

Nor is graphic simulation restricted to a few specialized fields of activity. Whenever an image can replace a real object, for the purposes of interaction, a graphic simulation could conceivably be devised. For instance, in sports, athletes can improve on their performances by a technique known as 'image rehearsal'. In this technique the athlete mentally experiences a ski run or a motor cycle race as if he were living it. Psychologists foresee this as becoming a most important factor in the highly competitive world of sports. Computer graphics, with its other unique characteristic of interactiveness, will allow the athlete to perfect his skills by simulating the environment in which he performs. This has already been done for pilots in flight simulators; for astronauts rehearsing moon landings; and for ships' captains who must manoeuvre oil tankers into busy ports.

The infinite adaptability of computer graphics techniques to thousands of different tasks ensures that the majority of people will eventually be exposed to the medium. While over the next few years much of the equipment may change, the basic principles of generating images by computer are likely to remain the same. Certainly, there have been relatively few changes in the fundamental techniques for the past decade. The most significant event has been the accessibility of cheap processing which has made these techniques more widely available. With this in mind we can move on to considering the variety of systems that are now being used, beginning with a brief review of computers in general.

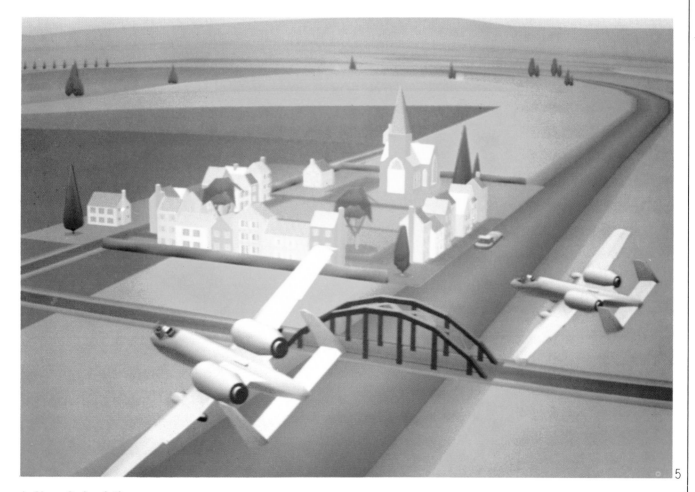

△ Aircraft simulation

Used in pilot training and in many engineering applications, aircraft simulation rivals photography in its realism and far outstrips it in flexibility. Dynamic images of landscapes and of other aircraft must be made to move in real time, in response to the actions of the pilot. The operator is thus given an accurate illusion that he is flying a real aircraft.

The computer not only calculates the handling characteristics of the plane under a variety of conditions but also displays a picture that corresponds to what a pilot might see in reality. The most advanced displays show convincing representations of other aircraft – essential in military training. Although even greater realism is obtainable in other graphics applications, the need for real-time dynamics is a limiting factor in flight simulation. Each frame must be computed in 1/30 second or less

1 General Dynamics F-16 Fighting Falcon aircraft in formation: from the Evans & Sutherland CT5 simulation system
2 US Marine Corps AV-8B Harrier II multi-role combat aircraft, an American version of the VTOL (vertical take-off and landing) aircraft, manufactured by McDonnell Douglas under licence from Hawker Siddeley: modelled on the CT5A, which extends the performance of the CT5
3–5 Fairchild A-10 ground-support aircraft, simulated in tactical training scenarios over western Europe: again, these pictures are taken from the CT5 display used by Rediffusion Simulation in the world's most advanced flight simulation systems

Evans & Sutherland, Salt Lake City, Utah, and Rediffusion Simulation

Computer art *Paul Jablonka, Tucson, Arizona*

PART I:
TECHNIQUES AND HARDWARE

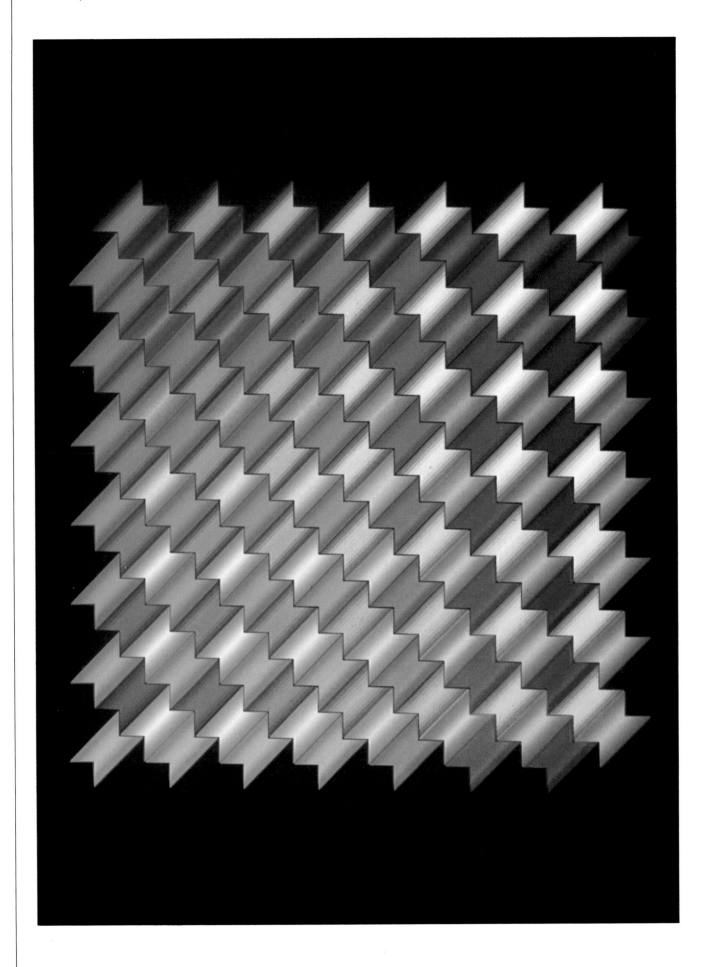

COMPUTER PROCESSING

A computer is a powerful electronic calculating system that makes comparisons between its calculations and remembers the results.

Although that is what a computer *is*, it is not a very good definition of what a computer actually *does*. A computer does nothing until it is given a role to play. The role may be that of a calculator, but can equally well be a role in which the computer manipulates ideas, concepts, languages, or – in the case of computer graphics – images. John von Neumann, who is often referred to as 'the father of modern computing', saw this potential in digital computers as early as the 1940s. All of these more complex tasks have to be reduced, ultimately, to *machine language* – in other words, to the *binary code* that the processing circuits of the computer can understand. However, the first step must be to master the system of binary counting before thinking of encoding it.

Binary counting

The binary system of counting uses a base of two rather than the more familiar base of ten which is used in the decimal system. Consequently, there are only two symbols: 0 and 1. These symbols on their own refer either to zero or to one. A second column has to be added in order to count to two. The symbol for one is shifted to the left, and the other symbol – the zero – is inserted on the right. Each time a unit is added it goes into a right-hand column. If that column already contains a 0, that 0 changes to 1. When all the available columns contain a 1, then another column must be started.

Thus, instead of jumping up in tens, hundreds and thousands as the number of spaces for digits expands, the binary system jumps up in the higher powers of two. This is why so many decimal numbers associated with computing are 4, 8, 16, 32, 64, etc. In the binary system, 4 is written as 100; 8 as 1000; 16 as 10000.

Now it is possible to count towards infinity, or do simple addition, as shown in the table below.

DECIMAL
0, 1
2, 3
4, 5, 6, 7
<u>8</u>, 9, 10, 11, 12, 13, **14** etc.
14 (total of first column)

BINARY
0, 1
10, 11
100, 101, 110, 111
<u>1000</u>, 1001, 1010, 1011, 1100, 1101, **1110** etc.
1110 (total of first column)

Binary coding

The binary system of counting can be used for representing the symbols of languages or those of other systems of counting. But first, the lengths of *bits* (binary digits) must be standardized. A computer bit can signify either a 1 or a 0 in

◁ **Computer art**
This abstract image was made on a Ramtek system with a program written in Fortran 5. Paul Jablonka is here using the computer's vast capacity to manipulate complex geometries, constructing images which it would be impossible to achieve by other methods. Further examples of this artist's work appear on pp 146–7

Paul Jablonka, Tucson, Arizona

the binary system. Counting up to an arbitrary number, one finds that the binary equivalent for decimal 347 is 101011011. This number has nine bits. Another number might have 17 bits, or 21. Clearly, these lengths had to be standardized so that they could be efficiently handled by the processor.

The solution was to fix standard bit widths, called *bytes*. Since bytes are transported around the computer in parallel, they must now be referred to as 'widths' rather than lengths. Typically, a byte has eight bits, although some systems depart from this standard. It is now easy to see what is meant by *encoding*. A 9-bit number such as 347 can be represented as a set of characters (3 – 4 – 7). Using just one-half of a byte, each decimal digit can be interpreted as 0011, 0100 and 0111.

However, this is only half the code. Because a byte consists of eight bits, four of them can be used for representing the character while the other four are used for *classifying* it. They describe what the other half of the byte represents. For example, four bits can specify the decimal number 8, and the other four can say: this is a decimal number. Alternatively, four bits could represent an alphabetic letter – and the second half of the byte could say: this is a class of letter.

In one byte there are 16 classifications of 16 characters: a potential total of 256 bit patterns.

BIT NUMBER	7	6	5	4	3	2	1	0	
BYTE									
	0	0	0	0	0	0	0	0	0
	0	0	0	0	0	0	0	1	1
	0	0	0	0	0	0	1	0	2
	1	0	0	0	0	0	0	1	129
	1	0	0	0	0	0	1	0	130
	1	0	0	0	0	0	1	1	131
	1	1	1	1	1	1	0	1	253
	1	1	1	1	1	1	1	0	254
	1	1	1	1	1	1	1	1	255

△ **Decimal value of several bit patterns**

The ASCII (American Standard Code for Information Interchange) is the most popular coding scheme for representing characters. All the characters on an alphanumeric keyboard are given standard bit patterns, and the remaining patterns are used for coding standard commands for handling keyboard operation (such as 'carriage return', 'backspace', etc.).

The principle of encoding is equally fundamental to graphics. For instance, instead of classifying characters, the binary code can classify colours. If a painting system offers a choice of 256 colours, this number has not been chosen arbitrarily. It is the maximum number obtainable by making 16 classifications of 16 colours, using two halves of the 8-bit byte.

Information theory

The bit is the fundamental unit of information, according to *information theory*. The theory itself is derived from logical principles, and hence computers operate according to rules of *logic*. They answer questions. One bit of information is defined as the answer to one question, expressed in binary form. Thus, at the very lowest level of processing, the answer given by a single bit can be either 'true' or 'false', that is: 1 or 0. Since a single bit has only these two states, more complex information must be represented by a *collection* of bits. All information, however complex, can be represented thus.

Electronics

A computer physically handles the bits and bytes of information by means of electronics. The simplest definition of electronics is this: *the use of electricity to carry information*.

Electricity flows from a source, around a circuit, and back to its source. During its journey it encounters *resistance*. Electricity can do more informational work when all the unnecessary resistance is removed. Circuits are thus made as small as possible, and sometimes they are supercooled to extremely low temperatures, which lowers the resistance even further. Yet whenever electricity is conducted, even when it meets resistance, it moves very rapidly. Free electrons, travelling through a vacuum, attain the speed of light, which is about 299,800 km (186,300 miles) per second. In one nanosecond (a billionth of a second) free electrons meeting no resistance can travel almost 300 mm (11.8 in.). When electricity is used for carrying information, by the simple expedient of switching it on and off, it provides the most rapid means of communication within the known laws of physics.

While some materials conduct electricity very well – copper, for instance, or aluminium – others, such as porcelain, scarcely conduct it at all. Between these two extremes is a class of materials called *semiconductors*. They can allow electricity to pass, or not pass, according to electrical forces acting on them. This is very convenient for the designer of a computer because 'pass' and 'not-pass' can represent the two different states of the binary system. Semiconductors can therefore be made into tiny electronic switches. These are used for channelling pulses of electricity around a circuit, and they can turn each other on and off in rapid succession.

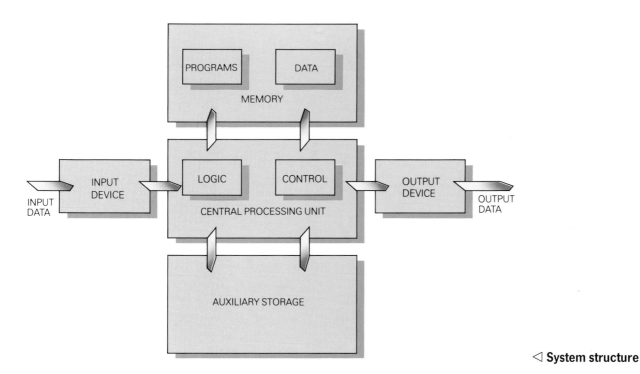

◁ **System structure**

Electronic switches can mimic logical functions. For example, a high voltage can mean 'true' (or 1) and a low voltage can mean 'false' (or 0). A switch with several *inputs* can be fed with several different true or false statements. It compares these statements, makes a decision, and passes on a 'true' or 'false' signal (1 or 0) accordingly.

There are three basic logic gates: AND, OR, and NOT. If an AND gate receives two signals simultaneously it will pass on a 'true' signal when both statements are true. The OR gate passes on a 'true' statement if only one input is true. And the NOT gate simply reverses a statement.

These and similar switches comprise the logic unit of the computer. This is the heart of the machine: the part that does all the processing. However, it is only one part of a much larger system. Computers not only process information; they receive it, send it, control it and memorize it.

Basic computer architecture

In every computer system, there are *five* fundamental components: logic, control, memory, input and output.

The *logic unit* carries out the arithmetical and logical calculations.

The *control unit* regulates the flow of information, preparing the logic unit for its next task and passing on instructions to the memory to deliver or retain the patterns of bits. It contains the internal *clock* that times all the operations.

Memory stores the bytes in memory locations, both before and after processing has taken place. One byte is normally stored in each memory location.

Input ports allow data to enter a component.

Output ports allow data to leave a component.

Computers have always had these five basic components, ever since Charles Babbage conceived his 'analytical engine' in 1883. But in Babbage's time there were no electronics to carry the information from the memory to the processor and back again. It was all done, crudely and mechanically, by a system of wheels and gears. Today, the bits of information can be sent from one part of the machine to another (the main circuit that carries them is called a *bus*) at speeds measured in nanoseconds, and they can be arranged in an infinite variety of patterns that can be stored, retrieved, and altered.

Data and instructions

Units of information, before they are processed, are called *data*. Strictly speaking, the word 'data' refers to the numerical (binary) as opposed to non-numerical information, although it is often used loosely to denote all the facts, symbols, and even images, that can be fed into a computer. (The word is also strictly plural.)

This terminology is important because there is also a distinction to be drawn between a chain of bits that are data to be processed and a chain of bits containing the *program* of *instructions*. A program is a set of instructions sent to the processor to arrange the logic circuit so that it can handle a specific calculation. If the logic circuit of the processor were always the same, the computer would be able to carry out only a single computational task. A programmable computer is a very versatile device, and it allows a programmer to invent new tasks for it. Now, in fact, some of the most advanced computers are quite capable of modifying their own instructions as if these were data.

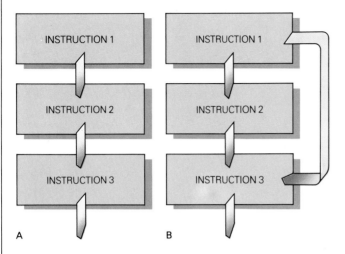

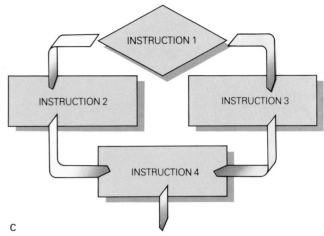

A

B

C

Logical ideas and physical reality

A concept that is fundamental to computing concerns the relationship between logical ideas and physical reality. For example, a user or a programmer of a computer does not have to be unduly concerned about the physical location of the information inside the machine. Indeed, if programmers had to think about all the registers, accumulators, buses, buffers and processors through which the bits of data and instructions must pass, they would never be able to conceptualize any programs. What matters is the logical structure of the computer system. Ultimately, this boils down to how the bits are classified and what they represent.

However, it is helpful to know at least in broad outline how a computer works electronically, as well as knowing how the software is structured. The distinction between data and instructions should be borne in mind, even though it is now no more than a conceptual distinction.

The central processing unit

The *central processing unit* (CPU) consists of an arithmetic and logic processor; a control unit; some memory; and the input and output ports through which data enter and leave. In other words, the CPU is a complete computer in its own right. It may very well be implemented on an integrated microprocessor chip, about 3 mm (⅛ in.) across.

The CPU is itself only the brains of the larger system, and it contains just enough memory in its *registers* to perform the immediate processing task. This tiny collection of integrated components is by no means the whole computer, for this needs additional short-term memory capacity. Yet the expression 'CPU' is often used colloquially to mean the entire unit, packaged in a single metal box.

The CPU responds to, and executes, a fixed number of instructions, which, taken together, comprise an *instruction set*. There may be between 40 and 200 instructions in the set accepted by a microcomputer, and each one of them is represented by a unique number. They are taken from a

△ **Program structures**

A Straight program: a straightforward sequential arrangement

B Loop program: instructions 1 to 3 are repeated as specified

C Branch program: instruction 1 chooses either instruction 2 or 3

program memory and loaded into the CPU under the supervision of the controller.

Instructions act upon data that are brought from the *data memory*. After the data have been rearranged they are sent back to the data memory and another set of data is brought to the microprocessor. But the program instructions are *not* returned to the program memory, since the program is usually in a form that requires no alteration. A subsequent instruction set simply adjusts the switches in the micro-processor to the new arrangement.

The time taken for a complete event sequence, as described, can be as brief as 400 nanoseconds. This is called a *machine cycle*, and it corresponds to four *clock pulses*. A clock signal with a period of 100 nanoseconds is said to have a 10 megahertz (MHz, millions of cycles per second) signal. Fetching the instructions takes one clock pulse; executing them takes three clock pulses.

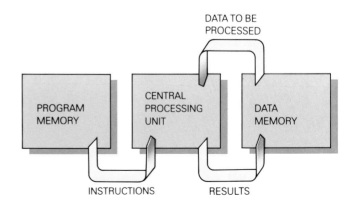

△ **Function of the central processing unit**

As we have noted, the CPU deals with all data and instructions in fixed bit widths. Hundreds of machines work with 8-bit bytes. More powerful computers can handle 16-bit double bytes. Thus, the capacity of the processor is indicated by its bit width, or, as it is also called, its *word size*. In a 16-bit microprocessor, the possible number of permutations jumps up to 65,536, a considerable increase over the 256 combinations of the 8-bit CPU.

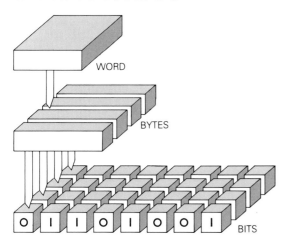

△ **Memory capacity**
A unit of 8 bits (usually, but not universally) = 1 byte. An 8-bit byte can have $2^8 = 256$ different states

A byte is the smallest addressable unit in memory. Larger units of storage, called *words*, are commonly used. A word may consist (typically) of 4 bytes, i.e. 32 bits

Each memory location has an address. Memory capacity is described in units of 1024 (2^{10}) words, i.e. a 'K'. Microcomputers may have 32K or 64K; larger machines have 1000K and upwards

Computer buses
Information is distributed around the CPU and beyond by a *bus*. Computer buses carry at least three types of signal: address, data and control signals. (Here, 'data' means those bits that contain the essential data to be operated on *plus* the program instructions, in 8-bit or 16-bit widths.) Address signals, which may be 'wider' than the data themselves, specify the source and destination of the information. Control signals are embodied in other lines in order to coordinate the operation of the system components.

A *backplane* bus is a link between all the components inside the computer, and it also carries electrical power to them. It is therefore simply a collection of conducting lines through which binary data and electrical power can be transported. The presence of voltage indicates a '1' bit, and the absence of voltage indicates a '0' bit. Components that are slotted into the bus can cause the voltages to change their state, and one line can be triggered to change another. But lines of communication are established by the commonality of the bus. Once this is broken, an *interface* is required to continue the transmission of data over other routes.

Memories
Registers in the CPU are the most transitory of all the different types of memory that are used in computing. In this sense only, a CPU might be said to treat the present moment rather as human consciousness does: by immediately passing on to the next moment. But real memory lasts more than a few nanoseconds, so computers must have places to store information before and after processing.

Data and program memories may be distinguished from each other logically and, as already mentioned, to some extent physically. Both of them may be stored within the same physical device: the *random-access memory*, or RAM.

Data and their addresses are delivered to and from the RAM over the bus. Each cell of the RAM can contain a minute electrical charge. When the charge is present it signifies 1, when absent 0. However, the smallest addressable location is usually an 8-bit word, which may need a 16-bit address. The address has to be this length because a random-access memory can have many thousands of storage locations. A 64K RAM will actually have room for 65,536 characters or bytes. (1K is equal to 1024 spaces.)

The essential feature of the RAM, or main computer memory, is its ability to deliver any single piece of information at the same speed. Whether the CPU wants location number 5, 58, or 65,527, the RAM can produce it in roughly 250 nanoseconds, or even less. Furthermore, the RAM can receive information as well as make it accessible. It is thus a *read/write* memory.

There is another important type of memory, also found in the main computer. This is the *read-only memory*, or ROM. Information can be accessed from it, but cannot be put into it. The purpose of this is to provide sets of routines that are always needed. Putting some of the instructions into a permanent internal memory *dedicates* the machine to performing certain tasks, without the possibility of accidental erasure.

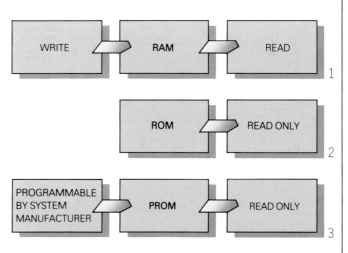

△ **High-speed random access: semiconductor memories**

The ROM can also deliver its contents with great efficiency, needing fewer steps than the instructions from RAM, yet achieving the same result. For example, in a dedicated graphics computer, a ROM might provide the routines for drawing basic shapes, such as circles and squares. If so, it is quite likely to be a special kind of ROM: a *programmable read-only memory*, or PROM. This can be programmed by manufacturers of special-purpose systems, rather than by the manufacturer of the memory-chip itself. PROM instructions are called *firmware*, since they can be programmed on to a chip yet cannot be loaded by the user like software such as a program on a disk.

At this point it is worth while explaining the difference between 'hard' and 'soft', terms much used in the field of computers. 'Hard' means fixed or permanent; 'soft' means changeable or replaceable. For example a tape recorder would count as 'hardware' and the tapes for it, whether prerecorded or blank for one's own recording, as 'software'. Thus computers themselves are hardware and programs for them software.

External memories

While internal memories are fast and convenient, they have a strictly limited storage capacity which is not nearly sufficient for most applications – least of all graphics. Many kinds of more capacious external memory have therefore been tried, of which the most popular and reliable are *disks.*

Both *floppy disks* and *hard disks* retain the data and instructions by using electromagnetism. They are both descended from the earlier technology of *drum storage*, which, in improved form, is still in use today. *Magnetic tape*, in either reel-to-reel or cassette systems, is a fourth and highly popular type of long-term storage medium.

External memory, of which disks, drums and tapes are examples, can be either *on-line* or *off-line* to the computer. If they are on-line, their data and instructions are available for access by the CPU, albeit at a speed of delivery that falls far short of the speed of the internal RAM.

The method of access from magnetic tape is predominantly sequential, since a specific memory location has to be found by winding through the tape from one end to the other. This is called *serial access.* By contrast, a RAM offers any part of its contents in the same short span of time, and this alternative and efficient facility is known as *parallel access.*

Disks fall somewhere in between these two extremes. They offer random access, but without the speed of the internal RAM. It is this random access capability that has made the disks such essential adjuncts to computer systems. 'Floppies' are housed inside stiff cardboard envelopes. They come in various sizes – conventionally measured in inches – of which 8, 5¼, and 3 in. diameters are the most popular;

and in four kinds: single or double sided, and single or double density. Floppies rotate at the speed of one revolution per second, with the read/write head actually touching the smooth surface of the magnetic coating on the disk.

Hard disks may rotate at 50,000 revolutions a minute, so the read/write head cannot be allowed to touch the surface. In fact, so sensitive is this surface that a tiny speck of dust or a puff of cigarette smoke can seriously interfere with its recorded data. For this reason, the *Winchester* disk was developed.

A Winchester has a rigid disk permanently sealed inside a clean, airtight space. It is widely used in graphics applications; it can store as many as 100 million characters of information within an area equal to an 8-in. floppy. The Winchester gives faster access than a floppy disk because of its greater rotation speed. Its disadvantage is that, being air-sealed, it cannot be swapped as can a floppy or a removable rigid disk. Yet Winchesters are relatively inexpensive, and come in four sizes: 14, 8, 5¼, and sub-4-in. categories.

All systems of external storage are far cheaper than internal RAM, if capacity is also taken into consideration, and they can therefore be used more liberally. They can contain the bulk of the *data base* – a collection of data that relates to a specific application. A portion of the data base is loaded into the main computer memory when it is needed. This is why auxiliary storage must be on-line to the computer. One can usefully regard the data base as being like a library of reference books, or a collection of files, but with the difference that all the data are more fluidly arranged, and, in big systems, supervised by a *data base management system.*

Buffer memories

Back inside the computer, there may be yet another type of memory: a *buffer memory.* This type has become very important in graphics applications. Indeed, without it computer graphics would not be possible.

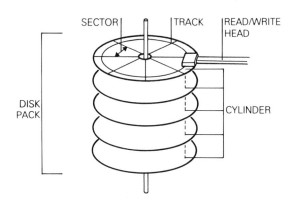

△ **Lower-speed random access: Winchester disk**
In an exchangeable disk pack there is a read/write head for each surface. The same track on successive surfaces of a disk pack can be read simultaneously and constitutes a cylinder. The *sector* is the smallest addressable unit, and will contain (typically) 1024 bytes

MEMORY	High-speed random access	Lower-speed random access	Serial access
ACCESS TIME	Fast (millionths of seconds)	Slower (hundredths of seconds)	Very slow (seconds or minutes)
COST PER BYTE	High	Lower	Very low
CAPACITY	Low (thousands or millions of bytes)	Higher (tens of millions of bytes)	Unlimited (billions of bytes)

△ **Comparison of computer memory types**

The buffer memory is a temporary *storage register* that transfers data at high speed to internal storage from the physical input devices, and also transfers data at a lower speed from internal storage to the output devices. A third important function of the buffer memory is to accept data in one form – either serial or parallel – and change it into the other: it can perform this task while changing the speed at which the data are passed on. It is aptly named because it acts as a buffer between parts of the system that work at different speed and in different modes.

Since any graphics display is showing data in parallel form (all the elements of a picture are displayed at once) the buffer memory has become a subject of intense interest.

The extended system

Computer systems accept data and instructions as *input*. They use the instructions to perform operations on the data, and then they return the results as *output*. Inputs and outputs are the connections with the outside world.

The extended computer system can include several *peripheral* input and output devices: printers, plotters, keyboards, data tablets, displays, etc. In fact an entire graphics computer may be considered peripheral, dependent on a *host computer* for most of its processing.

The modularity, or organization, of the extended system echoes the modularity of the miniaturized logic/memory/control components of the host computer. And logic/memory/control are themselves duplicated at the periphery of the extended system. A printer or a display will certainly have a microprocessor to look after its specialized functions.

Here some problems may arise. The electronic and electromechanical input devices, output devices, and external memories have to communicate with the core of the whole system. There is no universal standardization, so computer peripherals cannot be added without the correct interface.

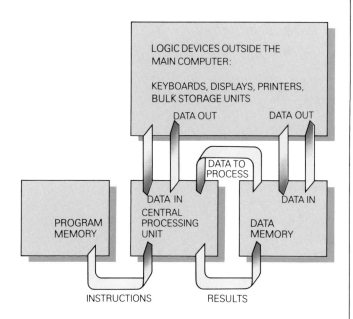

△ **Organization of the extended system**

Routes of communication between components are called *information paths*. They can make direct connections between the internal memory and the physical input/output devices, as well as between these devices and the CPU.

External devices are treated by the computer as if they were memories, even though they may be, for example, a stylus and data tablet. By *direct memory access* (DMA) data can be written into the main computer memory from any source, providing that the appropriate interfacing is in place.

As one would expect, with thousands of manufacturers developing better components and systems, interfacing has become a very complex issue. Consistent attempts are made to standardize parts of the system, within defined boundaries. For example, buses within the CPU are largely standardized, so that microprocessor chips can be produced cheaply in vast quantities. But standardization decreases as you move away from the centre, mainly because by the time a single standard is approved someone has discovered a new way of achieving higher performance.

As peripheral devices become more intelligent, this may change. Computer hardware could conceivably become as interchangeable as, say, stereo system components (cassette decks, turntables, etc.). The SCSI (*Small Computer Systems Interface*) is an example of a move in this direction. It is a peripheral bus, much like the backplane buses described above, but implemented on a *ribbon cable*, a flat plastic ribbon inside which wires run side by side, so that any wire can be reached at any point. With such a standard being generally observed, computer users could plug in dozens of compatible peripherals to the cable, without worrying whether these additional pieces of hardware will be able to 'talk' to each other and to the host computer's memory.

Languages and programming

Computer programming is partly an art and partly a science. There are many possible ways of writing a computer program, all of which may perform the same task, but by different routes. Some programs will do it efficiently, requiring the computer to make only a minimum number of calculations. Others, less well designed, will force the machine to make many more calculations, with a corresponding increase in the time taken to do them. Of necessity, many graphics programs place a heavy burden on the computer, and some of the most elegantly-structured graphics software requires greater computing resources than even a modern and moderately expensive machine can provide.

A person who programs a computer carries out two major tasks: he puts a problem into a mathematical form that the computer can solve, and he translates this basic scheme into a *language* that the computer can understand.

Computer languages have been designed to make programming both more efficient and less arduous. Since computers work only in machine code at the processing level, they require all data and instructions to be translated into machine code before they will carry out a task.

It is our grammar that gives language a structure. Words perform different functions as nouns, verbs and prepositions, while sentences have a subject/predicate structure. In a similar way, computer languages have been given structures, although the vocabulary of words is necessarily more limited, and the grammar is more rigidly logical.

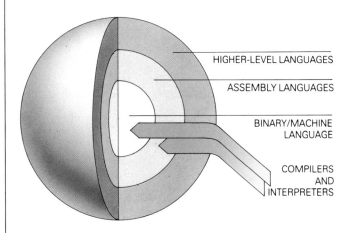

HIGHER-LEVEL LANGUAGES

ASSEMBLY LANGUAGES

BINARY/MACHINE LANGUAGE

COMPILERS AND INTERPRETERS

△ System software

The final language of all computers is *binary* or *machine* language. Other programming languages must be translated or compiled into binary code before entering the processor.

The task of translation is carried out by special internal programs which are called compilers and interpreters. A *compiler* takes a source program as input and compiles an object program in machine or assembly language. An *interpreter* translates the instructions of a source program, line by line, and executes them immediately. The sequencing and processing of programs is controlled by an *operating* system. These three are collectively called the *system software*

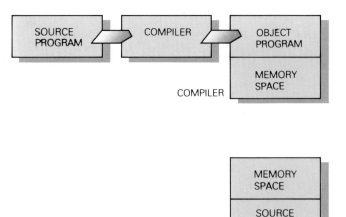

SOURCE PROGRAM → COMPILER → OBJECT PROGRAM

MEMORY SPACE

COMPILER

MEMORY SPACE

SOURCE PROGRAM

INTERPRETER

INTERPRETER

△ Distinction between compiler and interpreter

Synthetic languages such as FORTRAN, ALGOL, COBOL and BASIC can be used for writing instructions for a great variety of machines. These 'higher-level' languages are transferable from one machine to another, thanks to a degree of standardization in the computer industry. There are also 'lower-level' *assembly languages* which tend not to be transferable, and which use mnemonics to describe operations rather than English words. Assembly languages are more difficult to use, and most computer programming is carried out in one or other of the high-level languages.

The purpose of a computer language is therefore twofold: it describes the problem that the operator wishes to solve, and it translates the operations into a form that the computer can understand.

In practice, the translation is carried out by special devices called *compilers* and *interpreters*. These are internal programs that accept input from a particular programming language and turn them into machine code. They perform this task automatically, and the programmer is now far less concerned with machine coding than in previous years.

There is a subtle difference between compilers and interpreters. A compiler reads the *source program* that has been written by the programmer, and turns it into an *object program* that resides in the computer memory. By contrast, an interpreter sits in the memory alongside the source program and makes translations into object code as they are needed.

There is one other category of program that must be mentioned: the *operating system*. This performs all the housekeeping tasks associated with processing. It controls and reports on sequencing, compiling/interpreting, loading and execution of programs, and deals with the input and output of programs to and from the computer. Different machines must have a common operating system (such as CP/M in micros) if they are to run interchangeable programs.

The purpose of a computer program is to set parameters, or pathways for the computer to follow, so that it will be able to make deductions, draw conclusions, or suggest alternatives when data are fed into it. Once a computer has been given such an *application program* for performing a particular set of tasks, it is relatively simple for a non-skilled operator to insert data and have them processed by the machine. However, if the operator wants to change fundamentally the way in which data are manipulated, he has to learn how to program for himself. This has been particularly true in graphics applications, where much of the work has been new and experimental.

Microprogramming

Even simple tasks, such as the multiplication of numbers, are reduced to straightforward *addition* by the computer. In order to multiply, say, 63 by 28, the machine will actually add together 28 sets of 63. Hence the processing that is taking place inside the machine is almost infinitely repetitive, although of course there are many formalized short cuts it may take. In order to reduce the time of performing repetitive tasks, *subroutines* can be built into the computer in the form of miniature programs. These are then always available, and the computer can subtract, multiply and divide numbers by referring to them. An index register counts the number of times that the subroutine cycles through its set of instruction steps.

The same principle is used in *microprogramming*. A microprogram is a computer program stored on a microchip: a ROM or PROM. It can contain a special set of instructions that would normally be part of the main computer software, and it therefore allows the programmer to dedicate the machine to a specific application. Thus, a single line of program code can now call upon a complex number of subroutines in order to complete a repetitive task.

The ability to manufacture special-purpose microprograms has taken great strides in the 1980s. Although it is still more expensive than writing software in the conventional way, it has great potential for graphics users. Graphics applications are very varied, making the scope for standardizing the hardware strictly limited. CAD systems, for example, cannot be packaged as simply as calculators, in which most people require basic functions such as multiplication, square roots and logarithms. Computer graphics and CAD demand a wider range of programs than other computer tasks such as word processing or accounting. As a consequence, the program itself must carry most of the instructions, including many sets of subroutines. These place a heavy burden on the main computer memory. With microprogramming, the efficiency of graphics software can be greatly enhanced.

Hardware, software and the user

The basic components and functions of a computer as a general-purpose machine have been briefly explained in the preceding pages. Individual pieces of equipment, such as the CPU and the physical input and output devices, are collectively known as the *hardware* of the whole computer system. Programs that come with the system, including the compiler, or the interpreter, and the operating system, are collectively called the *system software*. Programs that are written to enable users to perform their tasks are called the *application software*.

Three important points are now worth noting. First, there is no rigid division between those computer tasks that can be performed by hardware and those that can be carried out by software. A computer system can be either hardware-intensive or software-intensive, depending on how it has been designed. When a graphics capability is added, it may take the form of additional software or of supplementary hardware. If the hardware solution is chosen, new sets of instructions might be provided either as additional circuit boards which can be slotted directly into the machine, or alternatively as an integral part of a whole entirely new *standalone* computer.

A second point is that computer systems are now being designed more for the *end user* than for the programmer. While computer programming is still very much a central role in the industry, the new generations of equipment allow users to set the parameters of many different tasks that they wish to have performed. This increased flexibility of computing is very evident in graphics applications, where interactive operation has become standard. For example, a graphic designer has a huge range of choices available to him when he sits down to operate a painting system. Finding his way around all the facilities of the system requires something of the logical skills of a programmer – and this aspect of computer operation is becoming more prominent as the industry grows.

Finally, it should be acknowledged that the computer is not, strictly speaking, a 'machine'. It is an electronic system that can simulate logical operations. But even though it works logically, it is by no means entirely mechanistic. A system is a complex collection of parts which interact among themselves under the guidance of a central controller. The human body, for example, is actually a collection of systems: a super-system, regulated by the central control of the brain. Even though computers are nowhere near as complex as the human brain and body, they are unique among machines in their ability to solve problems. They are infinitely adaptable. When they allow for maximum interaction with a human operator – as they do when computer graphics has been added to them – they provide a powerful extension to the operator's own abilities.

GRAPHICS

SYSTEMS

The development of computer graphics has been closely associated with advances in electronic display technology. In 1950, MIT's Whirlwind I computer became the first system to have a computer-driven display. It could generate simple pictures, and for this it used a *cathode-ray tube* (CRT) similar to those found in ordinary home television sets. But the slow speed of early computers made them unsuited to interactive operation. The electronic display was therefore used simply as an output device rather than as a two-way interface between the human operator and the computer.

However, the CRT was already proven as a most convenient means of carrying pictorial information. It was developed and improved over the years until many different types were available. As a result, the CRT dictated the development of computer graphics techniques. The approach taken by a graphics programmer was largely determined by the type of CRT being used.

There are two main categories of graphics display, both based on the CRT: the *vector* and *raster* display systems.

Vector displays

Vector displays (sometimes called *calligraphic* or *line-drawing* displays) use an electron beam in the CRT to connect *endpoint coordinates* by drawing lines between them.

◁ **Workstation**

This typical example is a powerful engineering workstation from the HP9000 family. Unlike a terminal, it has a large internal memory and input device(s) for interactive communication. Output devices too are often located here

Series 500, Hewlett-Packard, Wokingham, Berkshire, England

▷ **Vector system for aircraft design**

Cambridge Interactive Systems, Cambridge, England

For example, the coordinates of a triangle can be found by drawing the shape on a grid of horizontal and vertical lines. Each angle can be given an 'x' coordinate and a 'y' coordinate, corresponding to the horizontal and vertical indicators of their locations. These coordinates are entered into the computer and the machine arranges them as a *display list*. This is a sequential list of instructions, stored in a *refresh buffer* memory. In order to create a picture on the screen, the computer converts these digital commands into a scale of voltages that displaces a narrow beam of electrons in the CRT. The beam then 'writes' the triangle on the phosphor coating of the screen, starting with the first set of x,y coordinates and moving down the display list until the entire shape has been written.

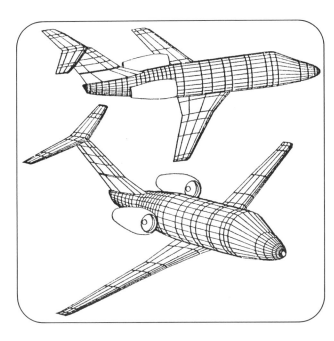

PHOSPHOR COATING

METALLIC COATING AT
HIGH POSITIVE **VOLTAGE**

ELECTRON BEAM

DEFLECTING SYSTEM

FOCUSING SYSTEM

CATHODE

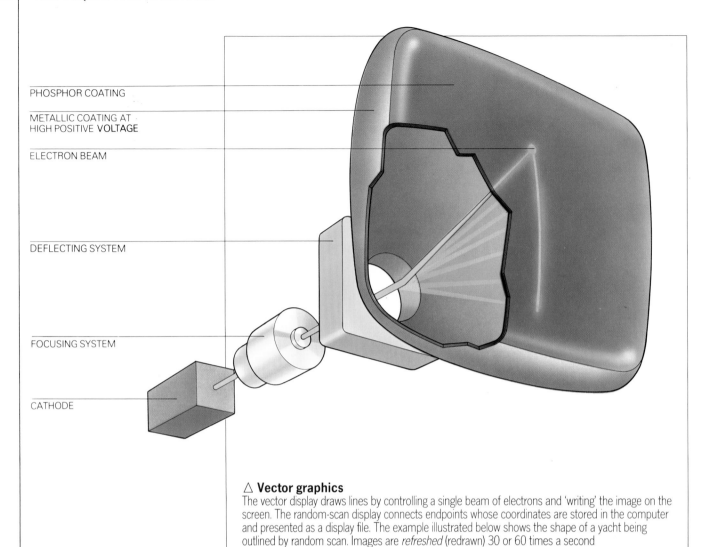

△ **Vector graphics**
The vector display draws lines by controlling a single beam of electrons and 'writing' the image on the screen. The random-scan display connects endpoints whose coordinates are stored in the computer and presented as a display file. The example illustrated below shows the shape of a yacht being outlined by random scan. Images are *refreshed* (redrawn) 30 or 60 times a second

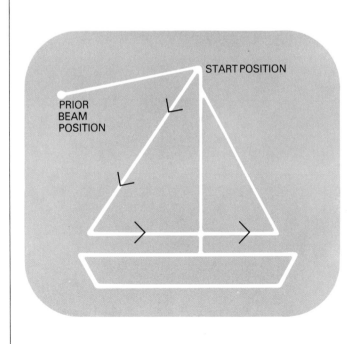

START POSITION

PRIOR
BEAM
POSITION

Light is emitted when an electron beam strikes a phosphor. This *phosphorescence* can last for only a fraction of a second, the exact duration depending upon the characteristics of the particular phosphor coating on the screen. Consequently, the image must be rewritten, many times a second, to create a steady and flicker-free image. This is called the *refresh cycle*, and it takes place at least 30 times a second. At the end of each cycle, the *display processor* jumps to the top of the display list and repeats the instructions. The result is a triangle — or a much more complex shape — defined on the CRT screen as a network of finely-drawn lines. It is not uncommon in a quality vector display for 150,000 short vectors to be traced every 1/60 second, with longer lines being written at a rate of 25 mm (1 in.) per microsecond.

The vector display is in fact a descendant of the familiar oscilloscope tube which 'draws' waveforms, such as that of a hospital patient's heartbeat. Both devices draw a line by actually tracing the electron beam along that line.

▷ Display processing unit

This special-purpose computer decodes display instructions and data, and contains *counters* and *registers*. Its x and y registers are loaded with coordinate values of vector endpoints. Analog voltage equivalents are sent to a deflection system in the display, and lines are drawn on the screen

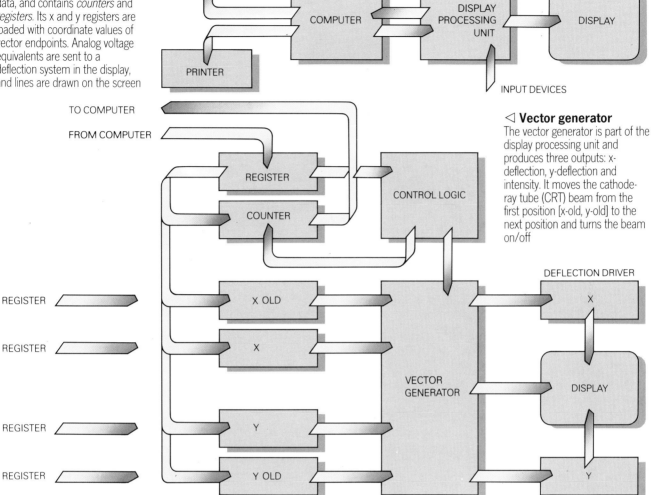

◁ Vector generator

The vector generator is part of the display processing unit and produces three outputs: x-deflection, y-deflection and intensity. It moves the cathode-ray tube (CRT) beam from the first position [x-old, y-old] to the next position and turns the beam on/off

Raster displays

A raster display, on the other hand, is quite different. It uses the CRT in much the same way as a home television set does, by displaying a raster (parallel array) of horizontal lines into which picture information is inserted. Instead of the vector technique of drawing a shape directly by moving from one coordinate to another, the electron beam now draws a regular pattern of lines, starting at the top of the screen and working its way down to the bottom. As the beam draws one horizontal line, it illuminates tiny dots of phosphor on the screen. A group of these dots makes up a single *pixel* (picture element), the smallest accessible unit of a raster display. In a colour television monitor, the pixel contains red, green and blue dots.* These phosphors are stimulated by three electron guns in the CRT. Thus, for computing purposes, a raster is a matrix of pixels, each one of which can be switched to an appropriate colour and intensity value.

Raster monitors differ from home television sets in two basic ways. First, they are somewhat simpler, not having all the circuitry for decoding a broadcast television signal. Second, many of them are now far superior in picture definition. Instead of displaying the 525 lines of American (NTSC) or the 625 lines of European (PAL) television systems, the computer graphics raster monitor may have over 1000 lines, each of which can be divided up into as many individual pixels. A typical raster display of 1280 × 1024 pixels contains well over a million points with which to represent the image on the screen.

In order to show the same triangle that was so easily drawn by the electron gun in the vector system, the raster display has to be instructed to switch on all the pixels

* Red, green and blue are the three *additive primary colours* – that is, they can be added together to make any other colour including white, composed of all three. Additive mixing works only when the colours come from a luminous object such as a dot on a CRT screen. Ink on paper absorbs white light and reflects only part of it back; in fact it subtracts colour. Therefore colours have to be mixed differently, using inks of the three *subtractive primary colours* – cyan, magenta and yellow – plus black to give shading. Examining any colour illustration in the book will demonstrate this.

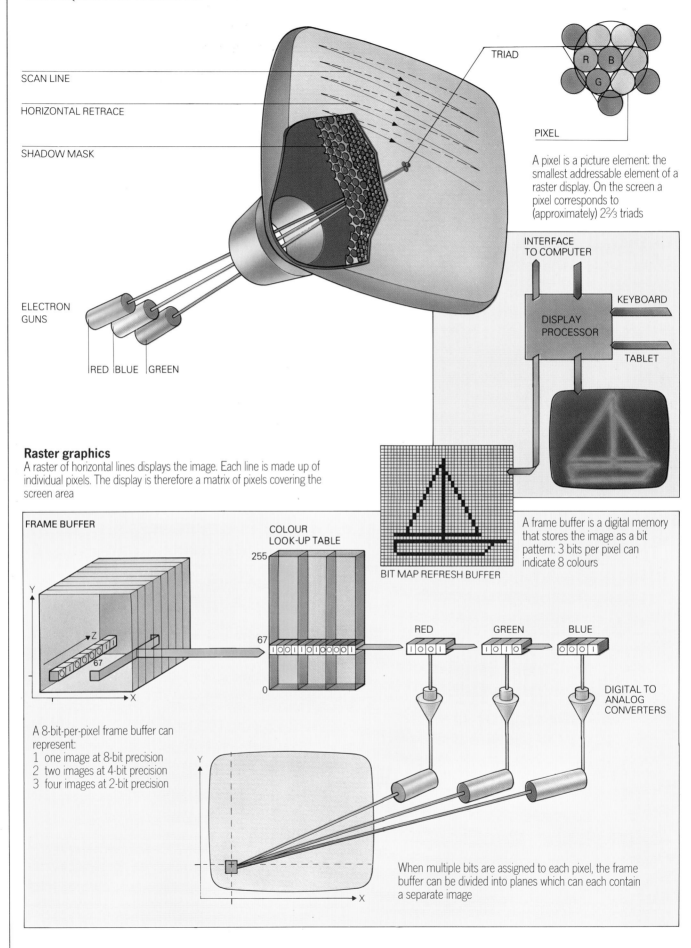

SCAN LINE

HORIZONTAL RETRACE

SHADOW MASK

TRIAD

PIXEL

A pixel is a picture element: the smallest addressable element of a raster display. On the screen a pixel corresponds to (approximately) 2⅔ triads

ELECTRON GUNS

RED BLUE GREEN

INTERFACE TO COMPUTER

KEYBOARD

DISPLAY PROCESSOR

TABLET

Raster graphics

A raster of horizontal lines displays the image. Each line is made up of individual pixels. The display is therefore a matrix of pixels covering the screen area

BIT MAP REFRESH BUFFER

A frame buffer is a digital memory that stores the image as a bit pattern: 3 bits per pixel can indicate 8 colours

FRAME BUFFER

COLOUR LOOK-UP TABLE

255

67

RED

GREEN

BLUE

DIGITAL TO ANALOG CONVERTERS

A 8-bit-per-pixel frame buffer can represent:
1 one image at 8-bit precision
2 two images at 4-bit precision
3 four images at 2-bit precision

When multiple bits are assigned to each pixel, the frame buffer can be divided into planes which can each contain a separate image

between the three coordinate points. If they lie along a horizontal line the result is a smooth line on the screen, but somewhat thicker than that drawn by the vector display. However, if the illuminated pixels form a diagonal, they will appear to be more like a 'staircase' than a smooth line. From a distance, or with your eyes half-closed, you could imagine that they represent a straight line, but not if you can see the screen clearly. In the early days of raster graphics, the 'staircase effect' was a major vexation to users. To eliminate it, engineers have increased the *resolution* of raster screens – that is, the number of pixels – but even now the definition is still inferior to that of vector displays. Standard vector resolution is 4096 × 4096 points – with no staircases, since diagonal lines are drawn with one clean stroke of the electron gun. There are, therefore, some serious disadvantages to raster displays. However, there are compensating advantages which have made them increasingly popular.

Vector versus raster

Computer graphics applications began with *x,y plotters* rather than with electronic displays. These machines trace out the pattern of lines, connecting coordinate points by moving a pen across a sheet of paper in obedience to the computer's instructions. When electronic line-drawing displays were developed, they were immediately useful. The processing power needed to calculate the coordinate locations was quite modest, while the lines were also sharp and well defined. The vector display could be updated rapidly, allowing the *real-time* animation of moving shapes – that is, at the operator's own speed. For the first time, an operator could interact with the machine, controlling the shapes by means of input devices such as light pens, joysticks and digitizing tablets. Vector displays were thus immediately put to use in computer-aided design: in the production of engineering and architectural plans, where outlines defining the edges of objects had traditionally been used.

However, a separate technology was being developed in which picture information was being *enhanced* – rather than constructed – by the computer. This is known as *image processing*, and it deals with images based on rectangular arrays of picture elements. In image processing, picture information is obtained directly from the external world: by scanning the human body, as in computer-aided tomography; or the environment, as in remote sensing devices such as infra-red night scopes; or the heavens, as with radio telescopes. The data obtained by scanning are converted to digital signals which can be stored in a computer memory prior to processing. Parts of the picture – corresponding to areas of the original object having, for instance, different reflectance characteristics – may be given synthetically-generated colours by adding a colour description to the digital information. Several bytes of data may be needed to store

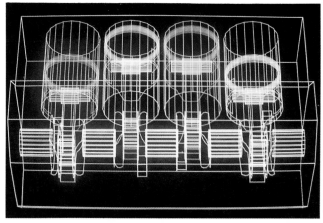

△ **Vector and raster compared**
1 Vector displays use an electron beam to connect endpoint coordinates by drawing lines between them, as shown in this three-dimensional line drawing of a four-cylinder engine design
2 Raster displays use solid blocks of colour, comprised of pixels, to display the image. In high-quality images, individual pixels are too small to be detected unless part of the image is enlarged

1 *Evans & Sutherland, Salt Lake City, Utah*
2 *Electronic Arts, London, England*

the whole description of each pixel comprising the display. Image processing prompted the development of high-definition raster displays capable of keeping all this information up to date. Eventually, they began to challenge vector systems in speed and quality, despite the enormous amount of processing power they demanded.

Manipulating thousands – indeed millions – of pixels requires much larger computer memories and much more powerful processors than are needed when dealing with endpoints. But whereas vector systems remained monochrome for many years, raster technology dealt with colour almost from the start. A raster display represents an image with blocks of colour rather than with lines. It is a 'painterly', area-covering medium rather than a line-drawing medium, and thus has a different range of applications. Surfaces of

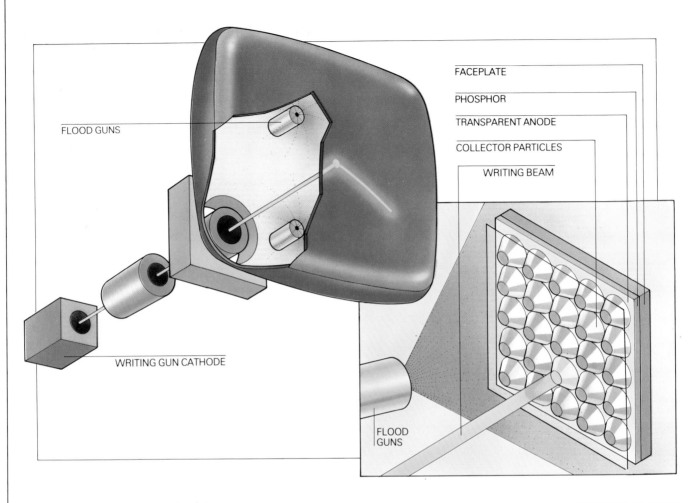

FLOOD GUNS

WRITING GUN CATHODE

FACEPLATE

PHOSPHOR

TRANSPARENT ANODE

COLLECTOR PARTICLES

WRITING BEAM

FLOOD GUNS

△ Direct-view storage tube (DVST)
This stroke-writing device stores the image as a pattern of electrical charges behind the inside surface of the screen. A flood of electrons transfers the positive charge to the phosphor-coated screen. DVSTs have very high resolution and do not require refresh buffers to sustain the image

objects are more easily represented than in vector graphics – as are all the component elements of a graph or a chart in which colour is an essential ingredient.

In recent years, the raster technology of image processing has been 'married' to the vector technology of image generation. Whereas 'computer graphics' originally referred to line-drawing systems, it now includes the whole gamut of techniques supporting the raster display. To some extent, the two techniques are interchangeable, and a picture generated on one system can be converted for display on the other. However, it is the type of electronic display that determines the 'look' of the image – and the reader will be able to distinguish between the two kinds from among the illustrations in this book.

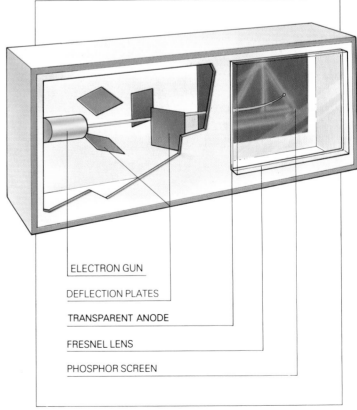

ELECTRON GUN

DEFLECTION PLATES

TRANSPARENT ANODE

FRESNEL LENS

PHOSPHOR SCREEN

▷ Flat-screen CRT
Still at the experimental stage in the graphics field, this type of display deflects the beam sharply to one side. It will have obvious space-saving and energy-saving advantages

Other display systems

It would be wrong to give the impression that vector and raster are the only types of display currently being used in computer graphics. However, the fact is that nearly all graphics displays are based on variations of the CRT. As mentioned earlier, the ancestor of the vector 'tube' was the oscilloscope, a simple monochrome CRT. What the oscilloscope lacked was a means of storing picture information, and the subsequent development of low-cost vector systems was hampered by the need to keep refreshing the image. As a result, storage-tube CRTs filled the gap until such time as powerful, inexpensive processors became a reality. They are still widely used, and their basic technology is worth noting.

The *direct-view storage tube* (DVST) contains a storage grid, mounted behind the phosphorescent screen. As in other vector systems, an electron gun writes the image by connecting the endpoints of vectors. However, it now writes onto a storage grid, while a second gun emits a flood of electrons directed at the entire picture area. These 'flood' electrons are attracted by the pattern of positive charges on the storage grid and they transmit the image to the phosphor-coated screen. The cost of the more elaborate tube is more than offset by savings in the associated electronics, since the displayed information is now held by the very last link in the chain: that is, by the display device itself. When the image on the screen needs to be altered, the whole picture is erased by increasing the positive voltage on the grid, causing the flood electrons to wipe the picture from the display surface. There is, therefore, a tradeoff between speed and cost. The DVST operator needs patience, but he is rewarded by having a display that is not only flicker-free, but also has very high resolution and an extremely high capacity to contain picture data. As an approximate measure of DVST capacity, a 635-mm (25-in.) screen may contain the equivalent of 15,000 typewriter-sized characters – considerably more than any other type of display.

Development of CRTs continues at a great pace, so enormous is the market for them. Every effort is being made to reduce their bulk and their energy consumption, and to improve their resolution and colour definition. The first flat screens, though still small, crude and monochrome, are already in production for televisions, and their arrival in graphic displays is only a matter of time. At the same time, other methods of displaying dynamic images are being investigated. These fall into two groups: those already being used in one form or another by industry; and those that are still purely experimental. These so-called 'flat-panel displays' are adequately described in two books: *'Flat-Panel Displays'* by Lawrence E. Tannas Jr (Van Nostrand Reinhold Company, 1981) and 'Electronic Displays' by Sol Sherr (John Wiley and Sons, Inc., 1979). None of the alternative display systems has yet reached the quality of the CRT. The two which at present

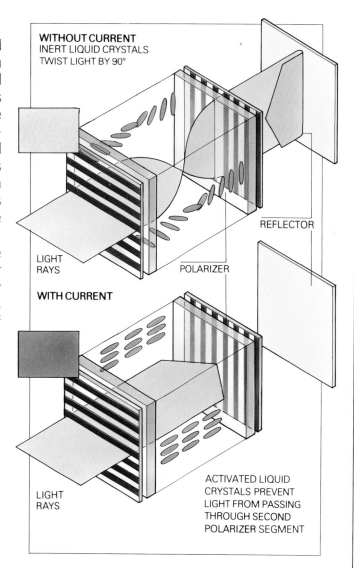

WITHOUT CURRENT
INERT LIQUID CRYSTALS
TWIST LIGHT BY 90°

REFLECTOR

LIGHT RAYS

POLARIZER

WITH CURRENT

LIGHT RAYS

ACTIVATED LIQUID CRYSTALS PREVENT LIGHT FROM PASSING THROUGH SECOND POLARIZER SEGMENT

△ Liquid-crystal display (LCD)
Within a specific temperature range, some organic molecules form crystals that flow like liquids. In LCDs the crystals are sandwiched between insulated conductive-pattern layers and align themselves in one of two directions, depending on the presence or absence of electric current

appear to be the most promising are the liquid-crystal and the plasma-panel displays.

The *liquid-crystal display* (LCD) is among a group of technologies called 'non-emitter' displays, which modulate external sources of light rather than generating light themselves. Liquid crystal material is a layer of organic molecules, having the property of arranging themselves into rod-shaped crystals at certain temperatures. Under the stimulus of an electric field, the rods can be made to align in different directions: either perpendicular or horizontal to the viewer. A reflective coating behind the liquid crystals provides the light 'source', while the crystals themselves allow light either to pass or not pass. Obtaining colour is a major problem, but LCDs are already familiar in watches and pocket calculators. However, more elaborate, experimental

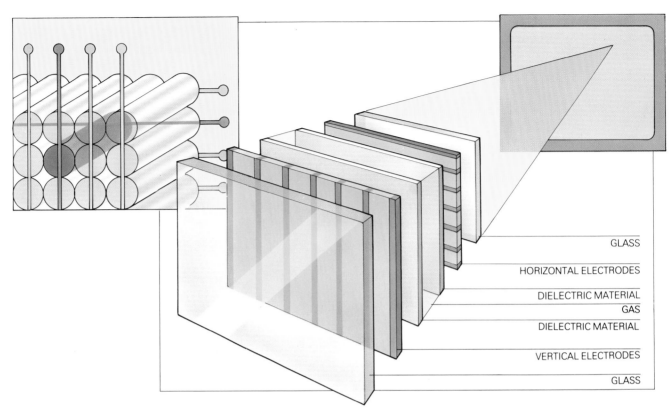

GLASS
HORIZONTAL ELECTRODES
DIELECTRIC MATERIAL
GAS
DIELECTRIC MATERIAL
VERTICAL ELECTRODES
GLASS

△ **Plasma panel displays**
This non-CRT type of display uses neon gas to produce localized glows at thousands of points, connected by horizontal and vertical conductors. An alternative design of plasma panel (top) uses thousands of individual neon 'bulbs' to produce the image

displays have been built, and these contain around 200,000 individually-addressable points in arrays measuring up to 500 mm (20 in.) across.

The *plasma panel* is an array of tiny neon bulbs, each of which can be switched on or off. Rather than being separate units, the bulbs are part of a panel composed of three layers of glass. The rear layer contains rows of horizontal conductors that connect the bulbs in one direction, while the front layer makes all the vertical connections. When the differential in voltages between a horizontal and a vertical conductor is sufficiently high, the neon cell at that location in the grid will fire. A single neon cell can be switched on and off in 20 microseconds. Already plasma panels more than 1 metre (39 in.) square have been constructed, containing several million cells.

Both the liquid-crystal display and the plasma panel are akin to CRT raster systems in that they consist of arrays of dots. If a new, flat, and inexpensive display system were to be developed it would be unlikely to affect the theory and practice of computer graphics, and would simply provide another vehicle for showing the images. You would unplug your raster monitor, plug in your plasma panel, and continue to generate images just as before. Nonetheless, the rest of this discussion of graphics hardware assumes that CRT-

based vector and raster systems will continue for several years as the industry standards.

Graphics computers
While the electronic display device is an important part of a computer graphics system, several other pieces of hardware are necessary. These fall into four categories, each of which can be subdivided further. They are the *host computer*, the *display processor*, and the *input* and *output devices*.

What a computer is and does has already been explained. There remain three categories, the most complex of which is the display processor. This, too, is a computer: its job is to organize the source data processed by the host computer and to prepare a picture for display on the screen.

Suppose, for instance, you have constructed a computer model of a chair, in three dimensions, and you want to see a picture of this chair displayed on the screen. The host computer has all the coordinates of the chair stored in its memory, but these are details about the object as a whole, and they do not specify a particular view of it. You specify the view by calling up a particular image of it from one *point of view*. The host computer receives this instruction and calculates a number of viewing transformations to produce an appropriate set of image data representing, say, a front view of the chair. In doing this, the computer is made to behave like a synthetic camera, photographing the object in its memory from a particular point of view.

However, the image cannot yet be seen, since the data still have to be rearranged, yet again, in order to produce an image on the display device – a vector or raster screen. The image data must be mapped into the *display memory*, where they become associated with graphic *primitives* – lines, shapes, dots, etc., that will be used to draw the image.

In vector systems, a *refresh buffer memory* holds a display list of plotting commands, while in raster systems a *bit map* contains a map of all the points that are to be displayed on the screen. Simple on/off states for each pixel can be represented by the bit map as a matrix of ones and zeroes. But when the data are more complex, with a variety of colours and intensities to represent, the bit map consists of several layers – or *memory planes* – so that many bits can define the state of each pixel.

The final step is the conversion of all the digital data into the millions of voltage fluctuations that drive the display device: the vector or raster CRT. This is done by a *picture generator*. Vectors are drawn, or pixels are switched to their appropriate intensity levels, and the image of the chair appears on the screen.

There is one fault in this simple explanation of how a graphics system works. Over the years, computers at the top end of the range have become bigger and faster, while those at the lower end have begun to handle more complex tasks – even graphics applications. So there is a whole spectrum of computers, from mainframes, to minicomputers, to microcomputers; and what is more, they can all be linked together. As the display processors have become more powerful, so the range of tasks they perform has grown larger. In other words, the display processor has begun to poach on the territory of the host computer, relieving it of the tiresome business of all those transformation routines.

This evolution in the development of graphics processors is called by some experts 'distributing the intelligence'. Two other experts, T. H. Myer and Ivan Sutherland, have called it the 'wheel of reincarnation' – a much more evocative and ironic phrase. It perfectly describes what has happened. The display processing units have become packed with 'intelligence' – with the ability to make calculations – until they hold so much data which they can manipulate so effectively that, to all intents and purposes, they are CPUs in their own right. Then, once they have usurped the status of 'host computer', they require display processors themselves! The evolution is somewhat analogous to empire building in businesses – where the boss gives his work to a deputy, who hires an assistant, who takes on a secretary, who passes the routine work to the typing pool. However, the boss still makes all the big decisions, based, presumably, on the reports that have been typed by the lowliest employees.

It should be apparent why this evolution of the graphics system has occurred. An interactive computer graphics system is an *event-driven* machine. When that image of the chair finally appears on the screen, nothing else happens until the operator does something. The operator completes the loop. He makes a move, such as entering a new piece of data. Perhaps, for instance, he adds another leg to the chair – in which case, this would be a vital alteration that the host computer would want to know about. Such a move would change the actual description of the object in the application data base, and any subsequent views of the chair would then show that it had five legs instead of four. However, perhaps the operator merely wants to get a closer look at the image. This is the kind of user operation that could be answered without the host computer lifting a finger to help. If the image of the chair has been off-loaded into the display processor, an enlargement of it can easily be offered to the viewer.

Because the graphics system is event-driven, and these events are initiated by the operator, heavy demands are made upon it. The user wants to be able to rotate the chair in real time, as well as see an enlargement of it. He wants to make temporary alterations without affecting the master description of the object in the data base. Given half a chance, the computer graphics user will tie up the corporation's 10-million-dollar mainframe while he plays around with his 'chair' – or some other relatively simple object, such as an aircraft fuselage – and still he begs for more processing capacity, more realistic images, and more definition. By devolving much of the work to the display processor, computer designers have freed the host computer from the clutches of the graphics user.

If there is any remaining doubt about the amount of processing needed in graphics applications, merely consider the simple arithmetic of it. Suppose the picture is a modest raster image of 1000×1000 picture elements. Each one of these pixels might be switched to 10 levels of intensity, that is: 10 degrees of brightness – and each one might assume any of 10 different combinations of red, blue and green, the three additive primary colours. If you wanted to see an image in which most of the pixels were used, and which could move in real time, you would have to use a computer that could consistently perform at least 100 million calculations every 1/30 second, even if the software were 100 per cent efficient.

Software is nowhere near as efficient as this. So such a 'brute-force' approach is usually abandoned in favour of splitting up the processing tasks among several processors working in series. Sometimes software may be abandoned altogether, with the processing instructions becoming fixed and permanent in the hardware of the system. Display processors lend themselves to these so-called 'hardware solutions,' since a computer graphics system may be dedicated to performing a limited range of tasks. The future, however, lies in *parallel processing*, in which the flexibility of the system is retained while increasing its speed by making many calculations simultaneously.

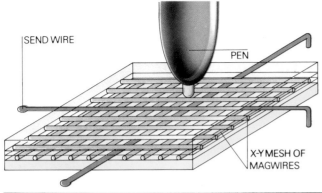

SEND WIRE

PEN

X-Y MESH OF MAGWIRES

◁ **Stylus makes contact with data tablet**

▽ **Self portrait**
Despite the title, this image could not have been made without a human artist's labour. It is a Dicomed D38 Design Station, created on the same machine

Eidographics, London, England

Input devices

Since computer graphics is an interactive medium, great attention has been paid to the tools that are used at the man/machine interface. These are the physical interaction devices, and they can be divided into logical classes according to their individual function.

There are five basic logical classes of input device: *locators* (to indicate position); *pick devices* (to select an item from among those displayed); *valuators* (to input a variable scale of values); *keyboards* (to input characters); and *buttons* (to make a selection from choices given to the operator).

The idea of a human being interacting with a computer-driven graphics display was inherent in the very first step taken by Ivan Sutherland with Sketchpad in 1963. Sutherland showed how an operator of a graphics system could construct computer models by drawing directly on to the screen. Since then, the technology of 'talking' to the computer has been refined to a point where even voice recognition is beginning to play a significant role. Most interaction, though, is still achieved by 'touch' devices – and these are used both for inputting and for controlling the graphics primitives: the lines, dots and shapes that comprise the picture.

Part of the fascination of computer graphics stems from the variety of physical input devices. Whereas word processing needs only a keyboard to put characters into the computer, graphics requires tools whose handling more closely imitates traditional drawing and measuring devices.

Here is a partial list of the most widely used physical inputs:

stylus	keyboard
hand cursor	light pen
data tablet	joystick and tracker ball
function switches	touch-sensitive screen
control dials	'mouse'

The *stylus* looks and feels like an artist's pencil, but it will not make any marks on paper. It has a pressure-sensitive switch at its tip which closes when pressed down on the data tablet. This action picks up an electrical signal from the data tablet which indicates the exact position of the stylus upon its two-dimensional surface. At the same time a cursor is made to appear on the display screen, indicating the same location. Instead of looking at the point of the stylus, the operator watches the screen cursor. In practice it has been found that

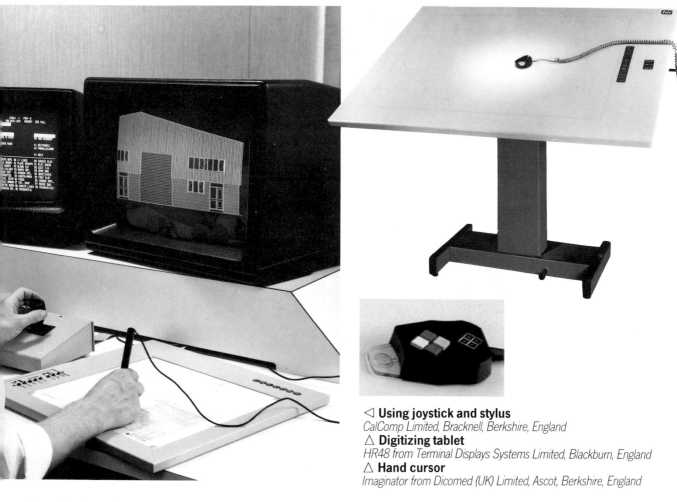

◁ **Using joystick and stylus**
CalComp Limited, Bracknell, Berkshire, England
△ **Digitizing tablet**
HR48 from Terminal Displays Systems Limited, Blackburn, England
△ **Hand cursor**
Imaginator from Dicomed (UK) Limited, Ascot, Berkshire, England

this redirecting of attention is not in the least distracting or difficult to master. After only a few minutes, an artist can become accustomed to this new method of working.

The *hand cursor* is used for entering precise coordinate data derived from existing materials: plans, drawings, photographs, etc. Like the stylus, it works in conjunction with a data tablet, and has fine cross-hairs to indicate its exact location to the user. Included on most hand cursors are a number of function switches that can give various instructions to the computer, such as 'select this item', or 'delete this item'. The hand cursor is, therefore, a miniature control panel as well as a locator device. In scientific applications it is frequently used with a back-lit tablet for entering digital information from large-format transparencies.

The *data tablet* itself contains the coordinate grid that enables the stylus or hand cursor to indicate position. Over the years, data tablets have been made to work on a variety of different principles. Sonic tablets, for instance, measured the stylus position by means of strip microphones, mounted along two adjacent edges. The microphones picked up sound waves from the tip of the stylus, which emitted a small electrical spark. More accurate (and quiet!) is the tablet that has a grid of wires embedded in its surface. The coordinates

of a point are then picked up by the stylus as variations in voltage. Yet another method is to use special material for the surface of the tablet through which electrical pulses can travel at right angles to each other. These pulses are emitted at regular intervals, so again the stylus position can always be calculated.

Function switches simply provide a quick and convenient way of entering commands that are frequently used. Examples of function switches are the automatic dialling buttons on some modern telephones. Just as a telephone number that you call frequently can be associated with a single button, so can the function switches in a computer graphics system be programmed to issue sequences of complex instructions.

Control dials ('knobs' rather than buttons) introduce to the growing arsenal of input devices an *analog* capability – that is, they register a continuously variable quantity, rather than one which changes in digital steps. They are basically potentiometers (devices resembling volume controls) and their variable voltages are converted into digital data (*digitized*). Any number of functions can be assigned to them, for example controlling a screen cursor position, rotating a three-dimensional image or implementing a variable zoom.

▽ **Light pen**

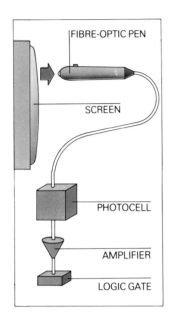

FIBRE-OPTIC PEN

SCREEN

PHOTOCELL

AMPLIFIER

LOGIC GATE

The *keyboard* is familiar as an integral part of most computer systems. Keyboards for graphics applications are usually based on the standard alphanumeric (letter-and-figure) arrangement, although one corporation does offer a choice of 18 different 'standard' keyboards – which rather destroys the meaning of the word 'standard'. Most graphics systems require keyboards since program instructions are not always entered under the guidance of a *menu* – a list of choices from which the user can select an option simply by operating the stylus and tablet, thereby controlling the position of a screen cursor. Inserting alphanumeric commands, using strings of characters, is still a universal graphics technique.

Less familiar is the *chord keyboard* – a small device that can be played like a piano. It resembles a set of function switches, except that the number of buttons is reduced to, say, five 'keys'. From these five keys, 31 different instructions may be generated by pressing various combinations.

The *light pen* has become a less popular device since the introduction of the stylus and tablet. Light pens detect light on the screen by means of a photocell located either in the pen itself or at the end of a fibre-optic pipe. They are more useful as positioning devices on line-drawing displays than as mere pointing devices in raster systems. For positioning images they require the use of a 'tracking program' which, after the pen has picked up the image, allows movement of the pen to pull the image across the screen.

The *joystick* and the *tracker ball* are used for 'scrolling' or 'panning' the screen image. In scrolling, the image moves up and down; in panning, to the left or right. A joystick is also

△ **Drawing on screen**
This unusual workstation fits comfortably into an office environment. Intended for combined text/graphics applications, the Qubix system allows users to assemble technical documents, giving complete control over positioning of text, diagrams and illustrations. The screen itself is fully adjustable. Interaction takes place by drawing directly on its surface rather than on a separate drawing tablet

Qubix Graphic Systems, Inc., Saratoga, California

△ **Mouse**
M3/100, Penny & Giles Potentiometers Ltd, Christchurch, Dorset, England
△ **Tracker ball**
TB15/360, Penny & Giles Potentiometers Ltd, Christchurch, Dorset, England

convenient for 'tumbling an object in space' or in steering a cursor around the screen.

A *touch-sensitive screen*, on some systems, can replace the need for a screen indicator. It is positioned in front of the normal phosphor screen, and, being transparent, enables the user to point to a location on it. Surprisingly, they can be quite accurate. There are both low- and high-resolution touch screens, having 10, 50 or even 500 *resolvable points* (positions) vertically and horizontally. Again, like data tablets, they work on several different principles, including both light and sound detection.

The '*mouse*' is another hand-held device, somewhat similar in shape and size to a hand cursor. However, it can keep track of its own position when slid around on any flat surface, and does not require a data tablet to supply coordinate data. Underneath the device are two small wheels or sets of wheels set at right angles to each other. Each wheel is connected to a 'shaft encoder' which produces a pulse for each revolution of the wheel. By means of these incremental pulses the computer can determine the mouse's position as long as it remains in contact with the surface.

So far the list has covered 11 interaction devices, and it could be extended even further. For instance, computer scientists have investigated various ways of inputting three-dimensional coordinates from actual objects rather than from flat plans. Such devices still have a limited range of applications, unlike the twelfth, and final, input device to be mentioned here.

This is the *video camera*. It must be included because the use of scanned input is becoming increasingly important, particularly in television and the graphic arts. Entering pictures by scanning the data into the system has long been a technique of image processing. However, it has been of limited use in image generation because the objects or images that are scanned do not have precise mathematical descriptions associated with them, unless the input system is equipped with some form of pattern-recognition capability.

When data are entered via tablets and cursors, the coordinates are pinpointed by the operator manually. But the coordinates in a continuous-tone photograph or video image have to be determined by the user — and in any case a coordinate is no more than an abstract notion. Yet some scanning systems can now recognize lines, angles and edges, and the use of such devices will gradually be extended.

In the graphic arts, the ability to 'grab' a frame from a video sequence, and then to digitize and manipulate the frozen image, is often a desirable function. For instance, a graphic designer working in television might want to alter a still frame by removing the detail of the background and substituting a plain colour on which lettering could be placed. He would view the video recording, select the appropriate frame, and enter it into the computer memory. Once in digital form, the picture can be enlarged until individual pixels are displayed. Then the designer can work precisely on the image, removing details or adding colours until he gets the desired result.

A video camera, therefore, is an input device, although it is not an interactive tool like the others. It puts in a relatively low-resolution image rather than a *description* of an image. And it is on mathematical descriptions of images and objects that computer graphics is essentially founded.

Resolution

Resolution is an important consideration, particularly as regards output devices. It relates very closely not only to the quality of images seen by the operator on the display, but also to the quality of images in the computer memory, and consequently again to the quality of the final hardcopy output.

Ideally, resolution should be a simple measurement of the whole computer graphics system, in terms of the fineness of

detail it can deliver. In the related field of photography the resolution of a photograph is determined by many factors: by the optical system of the camera, by the film speed, exposure level, development time, resolving power of the enlarger lens, and printing methods and materials. The resolution of the print at the end of the process depends on the weakest link in the chain, just as the sound quality of a stereo system is restricted by the fidelity of the loudspeakers, or whatever is the least efficient component. Computer graphics systems are comparable. They have many components influencing the definition of an image, and often confusing the user because digital resolution appears — somewhat misleadingly — to be easily quantifiable, unlike the irregular grain of a photograph.

In computer graphics, resolution is associated with three factors: the picture data base description, the device memory and the display surface. The use of pixel arrays in raster systems can be the basis for examining resolution, a pixel array being normally expressed as $A \times B$ — where A is the number of horizontal pixels, and B the number of vertical pixels. To these, another quality, C, may be added: the number of bits per pixel that have been allocated in the system. Thus, in the picture data base description, the word 'resolution' could refer to $A \times B \times C$ — in other words, to how much data is used in defining the image. Here, it would be a measurement of picture complexity, with C being the bit depth of the picture. C would also indicate how many colours and intensities could be displayed at any one time.

In the device memory — the second area where resolution is important — colour resolution is traded off against spatial resolution. For instance, 512×512 ($\times 256$ colours) requires the same number of bits as 1024×1024 ($\times 4$ colours). The number of colours frequently has to be restricted when moving to a higher degree of spatial resolution. Unfortunately, the power of the random access memory (RAM) to process data does not necessarily equal the amount of data available to it. If data are compressed by special encoding techniques in order to pack more data into the RAM, a misleading impression can be given of RAM capacity — so the manufacturer's specifications of the RAM need not be taken as a measure of picture complexity.

The resolution of the electronic raster display — one among many possible display surfaces — is an approximation of the picture data base resolution. A quoted 512×512 pixel array will actually appear on most monitors as 482 visible scan lines. Just as there is a 'safe area' in a television picture, in which all the picture information can be guaranteed to reach the viewer after being transmitted, so there is in computer graphics. Quite a few pixels are lost in the process.

When people talk about low, medium and high resolution in raster displays, what they are usually referring to excludes the bit depth, and is simply $A \times B$ — the measurement of the pixel array. It is generally accepted that 'low' resolution is 512 × 512 (or below); 'medium' is 1024 × 1024; 'high' is 2048 × 2048 (or above). Despite this, an apparently high-definition picture can be obtained on a medium-resolution screen, for the following reasons.

In one sense, resolution is not an objective measurement at all. It involves the eye's ability to distinguish between different points. In fact, the origin of the scientific use of the term 'resolution' was in astronomy, where it was a measurement of a telescope's power to show an observer that the two stars in a double star were separate points rather than a single point of light. Much depended, then as now, on the astronomer's eyesight. All kinds of astronomical phenomena were observed by hopeful star-gazers – such as canals on Mars – which do not exist in reality. The astronomer Cassini's name has gone down in history because he noticed that there was a division between the 'two outer bright rings of Saturn'. Of course, we now know, thanks to image processing, that Saturn has innumerable rings and many divisions between them – enough, probably, to bear the names of everyone in the image processing department at JPL (Jet Propulsion Laboratory) where the images were deciphered. It is all a question of our ability to detect the differences in the images available to us.

Psychologists use a threshold measurement of the eye's ability to perceive variations, which they call a 'psycho-physical measurement', in recognition of the fact that it cannot be totally objective. The unit is the 'jnd' – the just-noticeable difference. Oddly enough, it bears little relation to the quality of the image being perceived. People have different powers of perception, depending on their age, eyesight and cognitive ability. A skilled observer under favourable conditions (for example the painter Monet on a clear day) can distinguish over one million colours of varying hue, saturation and brightness. With over 130 million light-sensitive receptors in the human eye, of which around seven million are near the centre of the visual field, we are superbly equipped to resolve the differences in light and shade around us. These figures put the use of the term 'high resolution' in computer graphics into another perspective.

There is, however, much that can be done to enhance the computer graphics image. Ironically, this is achieved by blurring the edges where one block of colour meets another. So called *anti-aliasing* techniques give the effect of sharpening the image by switching pixels to intermediate intensities along either side of otherwise jagged diagonal lines. More processing is needed when these software routines are employed, so one is enhancing the display resolution at the expense of available memory. This is an example of the extent of the problems associated with resolution.

Among input devices resolution varies considerably. The light pen has a relatively large field of vision, whereas digitizers can distinguish between points in the range of 4–40 units per mm (100–1000 units per in.). Among output devices resolution again varies according to the precision of the particular electromechanical device that is used. In general, plotters and printers far exceed electronic displays in their ability to delineate display detail. Likewise, photographic devices in which the image is scanned one line at a time exceed the resolving power of camera systems that record images directly off a CRT screen. In fact the only way to get a good-quality image is to employ a display device that has the capacity to exceed the resolution of the data being produced by the computer.

Resolution means different things to different people. A printer of high-quality art reproductions requires a higher resolution than the businessman who wants a printout of a weekly sales performance graph. Computers, with their enormous memory capacities, can often exceed the ability of a display device to present an image quickly and conveniently. If the user demands high resolution he must be prepared both to pay for it and to wait for it.

Output devices

Graphics experts use another term that many people find confusing at first. They refer to a 'display surface' in much the same way as printers refer to a 'substrate'. Why cannot the printer say 'paper', like everybody else? Of course you can print on other materials besides paper, and the printer is playing safe by using a more general expression. In the same way computer graphics experts talk about a display surface, meaning not only electronic screens – as one might expect – but also the paper that is written on by plotters and the film that is scanned by film recorders. The display surface is whatever receives the image when the computer turns it out.

Vector and raster displays certainly come in the category of output devices. However, these devices, excellent though they are for displaying dynamic images, do not put them into a form that could be viewed without the aid of the display device itself. Similarly, electronic storage on video disks and video recorders requires a considerable amount of hardware. It was to be expected that the boom in electronics would stimulate the demand for more conventional printed materials on which the images could be placed. In order to put them there, more electronics are needed initially – but once installed, these output devices will turn out quite considerable quantities of plots, prints and photographs.

They can be listed under seven headings:

Pen plotter	Non-impact printer/plotter
Electrostatic printer/plotter	Photographic recorder (for stills)
Laser printer	Film recorder (for stills and movies)
Impact printer/plotter	

◁ **Ink-jet plot**
This illustration has been reproduced directly from the paper output of a desktop ink-jet plotter. The original image, an oriental rug pattern, was designed by the Van Heugten Company, Holland

Advanced Color Technology, Chelmsford, Massachusetts

△ ▽ **Pen plotters**

1 *Zeta 8, Nicolet Instruments Limited, Warwick, England*
2 *107X Series, CalComp Limited, Bracknell, Berkshire, England*

In this list the first thing to notice is the prevalence of printers and plotters. The difference between the two is comparable to that between the two main types of computer graphics display, vector and raster. The vector system delivers a *random scan*, connecting endpoints by drawing vectors; the raster system divides the picture into horizontal lines, delivering the image by means of a *raster scan*. Likewise, the pen plotter, moving its pen in any direction across the paper, is a random-scan device, while the computer graphics printer, with its print head moving repeatedly across the paper in horizontal lines, depositing a series of dots along each line, is a raster scan device. Both types of output can often be taken directly from the display processor, regardless of whether the user possesses both vector and raster displays.

A *pen plotter* draws lines with a writing instrument which may be a wet-ink pen, a ballpoint pen, a scribe tip for coated material, or some kind of cutter for the strippable film that is used by graphic artists to create areas of flat, even colour. The pen is lifted off the paper (or other substrate) at moments when it is not writing. Pen plotters range from quite small (30 cm/12-in. diagonal pen stroke) to enormous (7 m/ 24-ft pen stroke). Some machines can interchange pens automatically. All work with great precision. There are three

basic types: flatbed, drum and beltbed. The difference lies in how the pen or pens and substrate material are handled.

On a *flatbed* plotter the paper is held in a flat, horizontal plane, while a pen carriage moves in both x and y directions. It can move in both directions at once, producing diagonal lines, circles or ellipses. Curved lines are actually composed of tiny, straight segments – but so small that they are obscured by the thickness of the line. Direct current (DC) motors drive the pen carriage, one motor controlling each axis, and these receive a series of pulses from the computer telling them how far to move with each stroke.

In a *drum* plotter one axis is handled by moving the paper backwards and forwards over a drum, while the pen carriage simply moves in a horizontal line and raises and lowers the pen as required. It may take only 10,000ths of a second to raise the pen, and 1/100 second to lower it on to the paper. Many systems contain a rack of pens from which the carriage chooses an appropriate colour, rapidly snatching it from the rack and then replacing it after use.

The *beltbed* plotter is a development of the drum plotter, having a wide continuous belt instead of a drum for holding the paper. Most of the plotting surface is vertical, allowing the operator to view what is being drawn; but the pen carriage itself is mounted at the top of the machine, moving to and fro along the narrow horizontal strip where the belt loops over the top rollers.

Through the processes of the 'wheel of reincarnation' and 'distributed intelligence', discussed above, plotters are becoming very intelligent. Most of them contain built-in microcomputers to interpret computer data and turn them into vectors, circles and characters; in fact the plotter has its personal display processor. The same microcomputer can handle some of the plotter's own business, such as controlling the acceleration of the pen carriage by predicting the length of the vector about to be drawn. This is a technique that has greatly enhanced plotter output speed. Pen accelerations now reach a rocket-like 4g. A good-quality plotter can draw diagonal lines at a rate of 1.06 m (42 in.) per second, to an accuracy of 0.25 mm (1/100 in.).

The *electrostatic printer* is a raster output device. It works by depositing patterns of negative charges on paper surfaces which are then coated with positively-charged toner (coloured powder). Particles of toner cling to those parts of the paper that have been charged, and the image is sealed by applying heat. Unlike the familiar Xerox system of reproduction where the charge is placed on a drum and then transferred to the paper with one rotation, electrostatic raster printers scan and print directly on to the paper one line at a time. The paper – which may be 1.8 m (6 ft) wide – crawls through the system at speeds of up to 75 mm (3 in.) per second.

Despite the apparently slow paper speed, electrostatic printers are actually faster than pen plotters. The comparison is that between the tortoise and the hare in the fable: one crawls along at a steady speed, while the other dashes backwards and forwards showing off its incredible powers of acceleration. In fact, electrostatic machines can be 10 to 20 times faster, although it is true that their images have lower contrast as a result of some of the toner adhering to uncharged parts of the paper. With the techniques of *scan conversion* – where vectors are translated into a raster

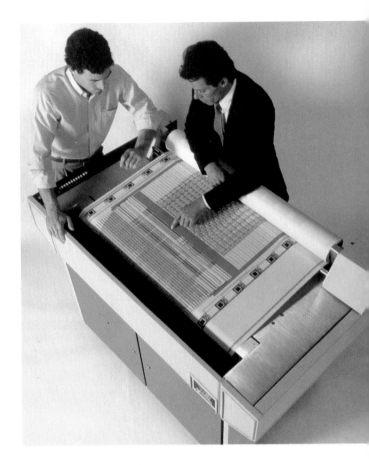

pattern – the electrostatic printer can be properly classified as a plotter, receiving vector output that has been converted into data that the printing devices can understand.

The *laser printer* is a development of an alternative electrostatic process in which light from an internal CRT is transformed into a charge on the paper by means of a photoconductive plate which transforms light into electricity. The plate transfers the whole image at once. However, in the laser printer, the CRT is replaced by a laser beam which scans across a rotating selenium drum, laying down a negative charge as before. In fact the device is like a Xerox with a laser instead of an ordinary lamp. The strength of the charge is varied by controlling the intensity of the beam. In both methods, a range of colours can be obtained by applying toner particles in six hues: cyan, magenta, yellow, red, green and blue. Black is added for shade, and white is obtained from the paper.

High-volume laser printing of computer graphics is now possible, though still very expensive and likely to remain so. Laser machines made by Xerox can print around 200 copies an hour in full colour. With black and white the speed increases to 7000 charts or graphs per hour; high enough, one would think, to satisfy the most demanding business executive. Inevitably the use of such a machine is limited to large corporations, and even then it has to be placed in a centralized facility.

◁ **Electrostatic colour plotter**
ECP42 Colour Plotter, Versatec, Newbury, Berkshire, England

△ **Flatbed drafting machine**
GT5000, Kongsberg System Technology, Maidenhead, Berkshire, England

▷ **Photographic recorder**
Palette, Polaroid (UK) Limited, St Albans, Hertfordshire, England

The *impact* or *line printer* is somewhat like a sophisticated typewriter, using ink ribbons and hammers to print the images. Some printers use dot matrices to print rows of individual dots at resolutions of up to 100 points per 25 mm (1 in.). Character (daisywheel) printers have much lower resolution, with effects of light and shade being achieved by overprinting the characters – or by using symbols that contain different proportions of ink to space. Most impact printers are relatively inexpensive, and quite practical for home use as part of a personal computer graphics system.

The *non-impact* or *ink-jet printer* is a relatively new technology, gradually being perfected after immense research and development. Rather than 'imprinting' the image on paper, it sprays it on – each microscopic droplet of ink being directed to a predetermined point on the page. Just as a cathode ray tube 'sprays' a beam of electrons on to a static phosphor surface, the ink-jet printer sprays a controlled stream of ink on to moving paper. In the same way as the CRT's electron beam is deflected by fluctuations in voltage, so the ink-jet printer's droplets of ink are electrically deflected to their proper positions on the page. The flow of ink is broken up into the smallest possible drops, and each one is given an electrical charge before it passes between the electromagnetic deflection plates.

The mechanical and chemical problems associated with ink-jet printers have not been easy to overcome. Special inks had to be developed so that they would not only flow through the incredibly fine jets without clogging them, but also dry quickly enough to allow the overprinting of different colours. Once the problems had been solved ink-jet printers lent themselves to printing on unusually delicate materials. For instance, one team of ink-jet scientists amused themselves by spraying the logo of their establishment on to live butterflies, then releasing them unharmed into the surrounding countryside.

The *photographic recorder*, sometimes called a 'computer graphics camera', brings the techniques of conventional photography into the realm of computing. They have been specially designed to replace the 'homemade camera systems' that people (even graphics experts) still use for snapping the images directly off the monitor. Unfortunately for the amateur photographer, a video screen is curved, and this tends to reduce the overall image sharpness. Lack of definition in the corners is, however, only one of the problems. The monitor produces colours by an additive process, displaying separate red, green and blue dots, and these phosphor colours are not very compatible with the three corresponding layers of photographic colour film. Ideally, the characteristics of the emulsion have to be matched to those of the display; this is done in professional photographic recorders by using a system of red, green and blue filters through which the light passes before it reaches

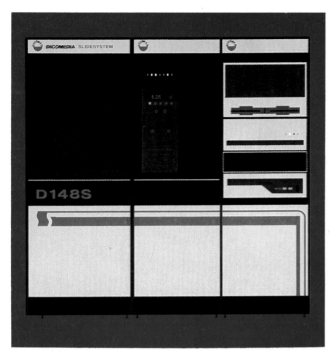

△ **Film recorder**
This image was created on a Dicomed D38 Design Station and outputted to 35mm transparency in 4000-line resolution

Eidographics Limited, London, England

the emulsion. A finely-adjusted internal CRT supplies the image source in this type of camera system.

The two most important features of photographic recorders are that they eliminate the lines of the raster, and extend the contrast range of the image. All electronically-displayed pictures lack contrast because the deepest black can be obtained only by an absence of light emission from the phosphor, and in practice it is impossible completely to stop light from being emitted from any part of the screen. But using a computer graphics camera system, with the right settings for exposure, contrast and brightness, you can get a better picture than that displayed on the monitor.

The hardcopies produced by photographic recorders match many of the photographic formats which have found general acceptance over the years: 35 mm, 4 × 5 in., and 8 × 10 in. (for transparencies used by overhead projectors). To change the format you change the back of the camera, which carries the film holder. An instant developing process such as that used by the Polaroid cameras allows the operator of a computer graphics system to obtain an instant photographic print of an image whenever it is needed.

A *film recorder* that can cope with the large amounts of data in the creation of images for movie projection is much more elaborate and expensive than a still photographic recorder. A graphic film recorder uses a black-and-white, single-line, raster-scan CRT. This is a most unusual and specialized version of the cathode-ray tube. Light is trans-

mitted through rotating colour filters, each wedge of colour coinciding with each scan. A film transport mechanism is instructed to move the film forward very slowly in coordination with the scanning speed. In this way the image is gradually constructed as the computer first analyses the picture into its particular component colours and intensities, and then reassembles it.

Computer graphic images with the highest resolution, suitable for 'art-quality' reproduction or large-screen projection, can be made on film recorders. All the standard film sizes can be handled: 16, 35, 70 and 105 mm. At the time of writing there are only four manufacturers of film recorders, although there might well be a million people, and numerous corporations, who would like to use this equipment if only it were more affordable.

The list of hardware grows longer by the day. Quite apart from all the central computing, display processing, and electronic displays, only twelve categories of input devices and seven categories of output devices have been mentioned here. The images you see reproduced in this book have been made using, between them, all of these devices. If you were to go shopping for an example of each input and output device, selecting just one from each category, you would be spending between one and ten million dollars.

Clearly, the medium of computer graphics is orientated towards corporate and institutional users, rather than to the individual with a limited budget.

Making the model
All the hardware of 'graphics peripherals' is only a vehicle for the heart of the graphics process: the *model*. This is really the most important concept in computer graphics, and it will be useful to pose some simple questions in order to find out more about it.

The first one to ask is: *what* is a model? That is by no means easy to answer. In computer graphics, when people refer to a model they usually mean the *geometric model* that is constructed by the user of a graphics system. But this can represent many different types of structure. It may relate to something that has, or is intended to have, objective existence, such as a molecule or an engineering structure. Equally, it could represent a purely conceptual structure. Into this category fall the organizational and quantitive models that have long been a focus of computer applications. An organizational model is a manmade classification of interrelating parts, such as a bureaucratic organization, or a library classification scheme. Quantitative models, on the other hand, are attempts at fitting the results of measurements to theoretical structures, and they deal with data in such subjects as economics, finance, statistics and physics. Both kinds of model can be given a geometric interpretation, bringing them within the scope of computer graphics.

A model, therefore, is a description of a structure that supposedly exists elsewhere – 'supposedly' because the physical models used in science are recognized to be only approximations to what actually exists or takes place. They are neither true nor false, but simply have such qualities as 'good' or 'bad', 'useful' or 'useless' associated with them. However, computer graphics enables the scientist and engineer to construct dynamic models to a high degree of precision – and, moreover, allows them to view the model, examine it and improve upon it. As James Foley and Andries van Dam say in *Fundamentals of Interactive Computer Graphics* (Addison-Wesley Publishing Company, Reading, Massachusetts, 1982), their monumental textbook for the graphics programmer: 'Computer graphics is the creation, storage and manipulation of models of objects and their pictures via computer.'

Another question is: *when* does a model exist? That is, is there always a model? Computer graphics can, after all, be an end in itself. There is a difference between creating an image – for purely decorative, artistic or informational purposes – and constructing a model. For instance, in a computer painting system there is no facility for creating a model, as such. In this case the image *is* the model. It may be remembered and stored inside the computer, but it is only a description of itself and bears no relationship to any external structure.

The question of *where* the model exists can be an awkward one to answer. The short answer is: in the application data base. As graphics systems have evolved like a multi-headed hydra, sprouting brains at every possible opportunity, increasingly often the description of the geometric model is offloaded from the host computer – where one might reasonably expect it to dwell – and now resides in a more local memory, closer to the user. But it makes little difference: the model still exists in an application data base, where it occupies what is called *'world coordinate space'*.

World coordinate space is a netherworld in which a geometric object exists as a set of mathematical descriptions. It has no shape, only numbers. The numbers define the relationships of the component parts of the structure – that is, they specify how the parts are connected together. Furthermore, the coordinates of world coordinate space are dimensionless. They can be given two dimensions, or three or more, according to whether the user needs a flat picture, an image of a solid structure, or even an image of something that could not exist in the real world. Objects existing in world coordinate space occupy fixed or absolute positions, although relative coordinates may also be used for those parts of the object that will move in relationship to the rest of the model. In order to view the geometric model, what is called a *window* must be opened up on to world coordinate space. The window is defined by a mathematical procedure in the

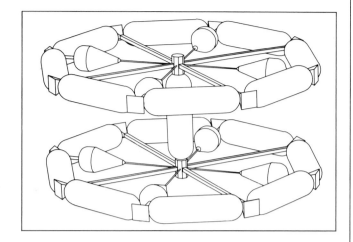

△ Geometric modelling
This hypothetical space manufacturing facility was developed using the ROMULUS solid geometric modelling program on the PS 300 computer graphics system. The station was ingeniously designed to make use of empty external tanks from the Space Shuttle, which are currently simply jettisoned back to Earth. Measuring 85 m (280 ft) in diameter, the manufacturing facility would be capable of providing a zero gravity environment at the hub of the station, and a 0.2 Earth gravity environment in the peripheral tanks

Evans & Sutherland, Salt Lake City, Utah, and McDonnell Douglas Corporation

application program, which 'clips' the world coordinates from a selected point of view – that is, it cuts down the information to what is necessary to produce the view from that window.

The next question is: *how* is a geometric model constructed? An entire book could be devoted to explaining this subject – and, indeed, many have been. The data structure of a geometric model is created by a user interacting with a graphics display. The user sends instructions down the 'input pipeline' of the system, and awaits the images that are sent back by the computer through the 'output pipeline'. A graphics display is thus *the link between the user and the model*.

Being an event-driven process, an interactive graphics system has what is called a 'current position'; this is rather like the state of play in a game such as chess. At any given time it is either the operator's turn, or the computer's turn, to make a move. To create a geometric model, the operator can build a structure by entering coordinate positions of the structure's component parts. A 'wireframe' model composed of lines can be built one line at a time, a solid object one shape at a time. Software instructions handling these data are always at the current position (if not for very long), and in creating the geometric model this can be thought of as an imaginary stylus writing in world coordinate space.

Constructing a model is made easier by the use of graphical input devices, such as digitizers and tablets. Before these and the software that accompanies them were

CARTESIAN COORDINATES · Y

Y · **RIGHT-HANDED COORDINATES**

Y · **LEFT-HANDED COORDINATES**

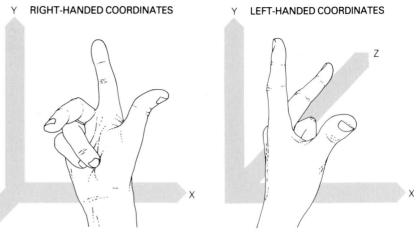

X

ORIGIN

Z

△ Two dimensions
In the conventional coordinate system the value of x increases left to right, and, likewise, y increases from bottom to top

△ ▷ Three dimensions
Depth dimension is expressed by z coordinates. In viewing operations, programmers change conventional right-handed coordinates into left-handed coordinates, so that the z-axis increases infinitely into the monitor screen

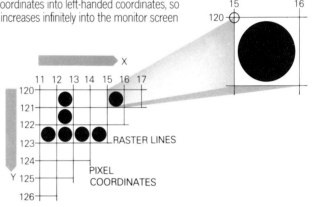

RASTER LINES

PIXEL COORDINATES

△ Raster scanning
The TV raster scan begins in the top left corner of the screen, y coordinates being automatically reversed by the computer. Raster coordinates are identified by hypothetical lines between the physical raster lines and pixel columns. Pixels are identified by their preceding coordinate lines

developed, the graphical elements – called *primitives* – had to be entered as numerical descriptions via the keyboard. Experienced programmers still like to use a keyboard, but purely graphical input methods are now much more widely used. The computer now does the routine work of attaching numerical tags to the input primitives – the lines and shapes – and uses its 'knowledge' of geometry to combine the primitives into complex object descriptions.

Graphical input techniques allow the user to take some short cuts in creating a geometric model. One of these techniques is called the *extrusion* method. Normally, all coordinate information has to be entered in two dimensions, even when a three-dimensional model is being constructed. The operator works with one plane at a time: for instance, the x,y or the y,z plane. With the extrusion method he can now extend a line into a plane, and the plane into a solid, simply by moving the stylus across the tablet.

A cylinder can be extruded from a circle, or a solid box from a rectangle. The extruded dimension is made to relate correctly to the original primitive, and the distance travelled in this dimension can be as long or short as the operator chooses, and in any direction. In representing regular but complex shapes such as mechanical parts or architectural elevations the extrusion technique is very convenient.

Geometric models that have complex curved surfaces can be constructed out of 'patches'. Modelled in this way, by the techniques of *free-form sculpted surfaces*, the shell of an automobile, for instance, will look rather like a patchwork quilt when it is displayed on the screen. The mathematics of this technique are very complex; they are based on the fact that even curved surfaces can be reduced to numerical descriptions. Every point on the surface of a patch is a mathematical function of the boundary curves defining the patch. Fortunately, the designer does not have to build the model by

drawing one patch at a time. Most CAD systems will now fit appropriate curves to a series of points, in much the same way as a flexible drawing curve was once used.

Another short cut to building the model is to take advantage of the computational power of the machine in being able to subtract one complex shape from another. This is something that can be done only by computer, since so many calculations are involved. To take a simple example: an ashtray could be designed by starting with a cube, subtracting a hemispherical shape from it to form the hollowed bowl of the object, and then subtracting semicylindrical portions at each corner to create indentations for holding cigarettes. The entire model could then be subtracted from another cube to provide an exact design for a mould that could be used in manufacturing the ashtray.

Thus a geometric model is constructed by defining its geometry and topology in numbers, the work of translating the geometry of shapes and surfaces into numbers now being done automatically by the machine.

Finally, one might ask: *why* go to all the trouble of making computer models? One answer is that once a model has been built, it is possible to extract certain types of information from it that could not otherwise be obtained. Computer programs can traverse the model, extracting such information as the quantity of components of a particular shape, or the number of joins in a structure. A typical question that an architect might pose might be: supposing we extended the building by a certain distance, how many more steel beams will be needed in construction? The computer takes the data from the geometric model, and calculates the quantity for the new alternative.

A second answer is that geometric models can be aids to visual understanding. They help the engineer or the scientist to perceive relationships in a structure that were not apparent before the model was built.

Thirdly, a model may be the basis of a design – that is, it can be used as the master geometrical description of an object that will eventually be constructed out of physical materials. In this case, the physical measurements of the object will also be stored in the computer.

A fourth reason for making models lies in their predictive capacity. A model of a process, rather than of an object, is called a *simulation*, and it helps us discover what will happen in reality under a similar set of conditions. For instance, from the first astronomical models of the solar system, rotating mechanical orreries of the early eighteenth century, accurate predictions of solar and lunar eclipses were made. The accuracy of the predictions is a good guide to the validity of the model.

Fifthly, a model is a vehicle for trying out new ideas. It can be modified within the range of its basic structure, and this

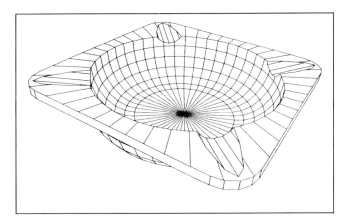

△ **Solids**
This ashtray looks like a simple wireframe with hidden lines removed but in fact it demonstrates a frequently used solid modelling technique. By subtracting one solid shape from another, the computer can calculate complex three-dimensional objects, and give precise details of their volumes. A manufacturing mould could easily be designed – by subtracting the shape from a larger cube

Cambridge Interactive Systems, Cambridge, England

helps the scientist to determine what further data need to be collected in order to increase the subtlety of the model. This might be termed the 'influential' role of the model, because it influences the direction which scientific investigation follows.

Finally, making models leads to making better models. Scientific attention is now focused so intently on model making that one might suspect scientists of finding it a more absorbing activity than examining reality itself. A model is a pattern of information that links together data too complex and numerous to be considered in a serial, deductive manner. In general, scientific models do not have to be geometric, but when they are given a geometric interpretation by a computer graphics system they become more 'real' and convincing as a result.

So models may be made for any of six reasons. The purposes of model making might be listed – in no particular order of importance – as information, visualization, construction, prediction, direction and education.

In the average industrial application of computer graphics, approximately 80 per cent of the application program deals with geometric modelling, while the remaining 20 per cent is concerned with 'taking pictures of the model'.

Taking pictures of the model

When we photograph an object in real life, we often walk around it – or rearrange it – in order to find the best angle; we frame the object in the camera's viewfinder; we adjust the settings for focus, aperture and shutter speed; then we press the button, and allow light to strike the emulsion of the film.

Similarly, the viewing operation of the synthetic camera in a graphics system is a four-stage process. First the application program transforms the data structure of the geometric model (or of one part of it) into a list of demands that are sent to a graphics 'package' of routines. This opens up a window on to world coordinate space. The viewing processor then clips the resulting primitives (elements comprising the outlines) to the limits of the edges of the window, and maps the visible portion into its own *viewport*. Thirdly, a display code generator takes the data and turns them into device coordinates that can be understood by the display processor. Finally, the DPU (display processing unit) transforms the output into lines on a vector screen – or, in raster graphics, converts them into the scan pattern of the raster, and refreshes them from the frame buffer.

It sounds complicated, and it is. But what is happening is that the data describing the model are being changed into increasingly device-dependent descriptions. The world coordinates of the model are first transformed into '*normalized* device coordinates' in order to 'take a picture' of the object – then these are transformed into *physical* device coordinates for creating the display. At the same time, turning the object into an image involves the laws of perspective. A three-

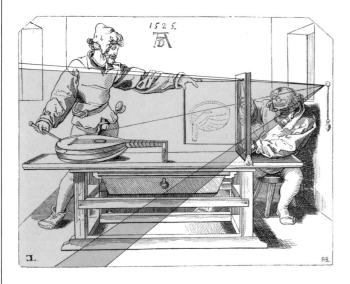

△ **Pyramid of vision**
A perspective view of a lute is being generated dot by dot, using a simple device consisting of a 'window' and a thread. The viewpoint is the nail in the wall to which the thread is fixed. The thread is stretched to a point on the lute, and the man on the right holds his finger to the point where the thread passes through the window. Then the thread is released and the hinged drawing board is swung into the window so that the point can be marked. The wooden window corresponds to the 'window' chosen by the modern computer operator, and the real lute to the form encoded in the computer. Just as the lute can be turned on the table to give a different view, so the computer data can be 'turned' to produce a different screen image

Albrecht Dürer, 'Treatise on Measurement', 1525

dimensional description of a geometric model must be changed into a two-dimensional description for display on a flat screen.

Perspective calculations, carried out by the computer, transform points from the *object coordinate system* to the *eye coordinate system*. This is the basis of the viewing operation. The model exists in its own space, quite independent of anyone looking at it. If we want to see what it looks like – in three (implied) dimensions – we have to assume that the flat display surface has 'depth'. The eye sees a *pyramid of vision* when it looks at the three-dimensional world through a square frame, and a portion of this pyramid must be represented by the display. Thus when the primitives are clipped against the edges of the frame they are also clipped against two imaginary depth planes that can also be adjusted by the operator. The front (or 'hither') plane, and the back (or 'yon') plane separate a finite three-dimensional wedge of the model called the *view volume*. For display purposes, as in an ordinary photograph, everything falling outside the view volume is ignored.

There is, of course, one big difference between a photograph taken of reality and one taken by the synthetic camera of the graphics system. The view volume in computer graphics is completely transparent, so that even lines and surfaces that would normally be hidden (by other lines and surfaces) are clearly visible – unless they are concealed by

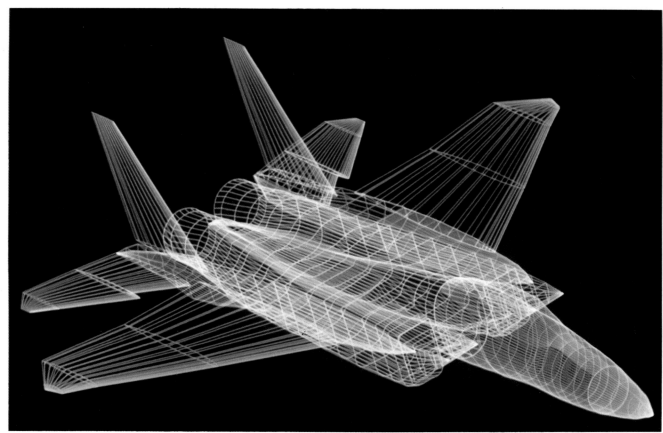

techniques called *hidden-line* and *hidden-surface algorithms* (an algorithm is a step-by-step mathematical procedure).

Several software solutions can be applied to the task of removing the parts of the image that would not be seen in reality. Computationally, this is a sorting problem in which all the shapes are compared to each other before the computer decides which one is nearest to the viewer. These routines can work in 'image space' or in 'object space', depending on the degree of accuracy required. In general, object-space algorithms are more precise. This is because image-space algorithms rely on sampling techniques, dealing only with the portion of the object that appears in the image, while object-space algorithms consider the entire object.

Obtaining a dynamic image of the model – one that can be rotated and tumbled in the view volume – is quite straightforward once you have built a viewing system for looking at static images. You just need to take a sequence of static views. However, real-time dynamics require at least 10 pictures per second, and this puts a heavy strain on the system. The transformations that create the different views of the object can occur – as before – in object or image space, or even in between, in the viewing transformation itself. In general, programmers prefer to work in image space where they are dealing with primitives that have already been reduced by clipping.

The end result of all these millions of calculations is a display of an image of the model – one in which hidden surfaces remain hidden, changing as necessary when the phantom object is rotated on the screen. The image can take the form of any type of geometric projection: perspective projections are only one option among many. By turning the pyramid of vision into a 'cube of vision', the system designer can provide for parallel projections of the object, including all the oblique and orthographic representations that a drafts-man might otherwise laboriously achieve by other means.

Towards realism

The 'snapshots' taken of the geometric model by the synthetic camera are 'realistic' only in the sense that they look realistically geometric. If the programmer wants them to look like the real objects in the real world, he has to devise ways of simulating what happens when light falls on surfaces. Not since the Renaissance has so much attention been given to examining the nuances of representation; but now graphics experts have a wealth of scientific information to help them. In the main it has been put to good use. Knowledge of the composition of light and its behaviour when it strikes an object has enabled programmers to model the process mathematically, yielding realistic images of which examples are included in this book.

When we see light falling on a surface, we are witnessing three possible events: the absorption of the light by the

◁ **Aircraft design**
The use of computer modelling has enabled very complex aerodynamic designs to be achieved, many of which could not be calculated without graphics displays. This can clearly be seen in the designs of the latest generation of military aircraft
1 McDonnell Douglas F-15 air superiority fighter, displayed in coloured vectors indicating the aircraft's main sub-assemblies
2 McDonnell Douglas/Northrop F-18 Hornet shipboard fighter: three-dimensional line drawing of a fuel tank, used for fuel volume calculations and system routing. The small indentations allow for clearance of structural frames; larger indentations for routing systems such as controls, hydraulics and electrics

Evans & Sutherland, Salt Lake City, Utah, and McDonnell Douglas Corporation

1

object, as on a black surface; the reflection of the light, as from all visible objects; or the transmission of light through the surface, as in translucent materials – glass, water, etc. To model these effects, the programmer not only describes the reflectance characteristics of the surface but also specifies the composition and direction of the light source. Since parts of the object will usually be at different angles to the light source, their orientation must also be taken into account. Mathematical descriptions of how objects reflect light are called *shading models*, and they treat reflected light as consisting of ambient, diffuse and specular components.

Ambient light is the presence of illumination from all directions. *Diffuse* light comes from a specific source, but scatters in all directions. *Specular* light, again from a specific source, bounces off the object mainly in one direction; it may, to some extent, be 'diffused' by a rough surface.

The most successful shading models consider the surface

△ ▷ **Shaded modelling**
Shading and reflectance models, created on a VAX11/780 and displayed on a custom-built 640 × 484 × 32 bit frame buffer
1 *Vases on Pedestals*
2 *Building*

Michael Collery, Cranston/Csuri Production, Columbus, Ohio

of an object as consisting of thousands of facets, a technique that lends itself to systems in which surfaces themselves are described to the computer in a similar way. A complication that has to be overcome is that colours change when the direction of the light, or the orientation of the object towards the light, is changed. You can see this clearly by, say, tilting the front cover of this book towards the light until you can see the reflection of the light source in the shiny surface.

When the programmer works out how to put areas in shade, or cast shadows, into his realistic simulation he discovers a very convenient fact: if the illumination is from a

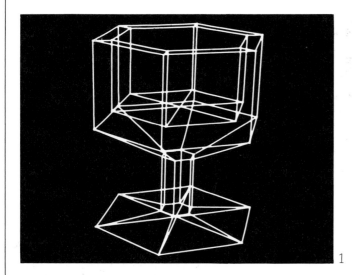
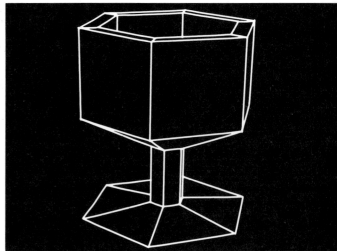

1

point source of light, a shadow algorithm can be exactly the same as a hidden-surface algorithm. Just as hidden surfaces are determined by finding out which of them can be seen from a single point of view, so all those surfaces that cannot be seen from the 'point of view' of the light source will be in shade. An alternative method is to trace the rays in reverse, from the viewer 'through' each pixel to the first surface, and thence (eventually) to the light source. The second method allows refraction through translucent objects as well as reflection to be modelled.

These methods of creating realistic scenes are both exciting and effective. In fact they are exciting because they *are* so effective. However, it would be wrong to overestimate the degree of realism that can be attained by all the techniques of *image synthesis*, of which those described above are examples. Whereas some experts see no limit to the representational powers of the computer, others are more cautious: they point out that the rich appearance of reality is unlikely ever to be reduced to a set of mathematical formulae. Even though the computer can match the resolution of photographic emulsions, shading models come nowhere near to approximating the subtle interplay of light under most normal circumstances. One expert who was among the first to study realistic simulation – Bo Gehring – has said: 'I don't think the visual vocabulary of computer graphics even approaches what you can do with live action photography. Sometimes, when I see a great movie, I look at the lighting and realize that the computer couldn't do it in a thousand years!'

The reader must examine some of the realistic computer images in this book, and judge accordingly. Bear in mind that many of the pictures were produced on very powerful equipment, and that some of them needed immense expense of both human and computer time. Remember, too, that there is an element of 'illusioneering' in making realistic pictures. I am not suggesting that graphics experts enjoy

'faking it' in the best Hollywood tradition – but some of the representational techniques for enhancing the images are really little more than superficial embellishments. One such technique is called *texture mapping*.

The purpose of texture mapping is to provide the modelled surfaces with characteristic textures while not having to define every individual irregularity. A surface texture can be taken from a photograph and then 'mapped' onto the computer-generated image. In this way, a pattern of bricks can be superimposed on a model of a house, or a wallpaper pattern can be mapped on to interior walls. Perspective is retained in the textures, allowing them to be wrapped around curved surfaces. It is a technique that heightens realism, and it has some obvious applications in architecture and design. Yet it also raises the question: is it an appropriate way of using the power of the computer? When the programmer *adds* texture to his picture, is he not really dodging the more complex problem of generating surface characteristics? Texture mapping is an interim solution to the problem of turning fundamentally geometric pictures into echoes of reality. If computer processing capacity continues to be expanded at its current rate, other – and more elegant – solutions may one day be developed.

The same might be said of all the anti-aliasing techniques that are designed to reduce unwanted distortions in the image. Many of these effects creep into the picture because programmers frequently use routines that only sample the data – rather than dealing with the entire quantity of data. Consequently, very small objects can easily be lost, and errors accumulate until the omissions become very noticeable. The well-known aliasing problem of jagged diagonal lines on raster displays is only one type of aliasing effect. Like the others, it is caused by insufficient definition – in this case, picture definition. Temporal aliasing effects such as we notice in films – wheels spinning backwards, or the unpleasant jerkiness when a static scene is shown in a rapid panning

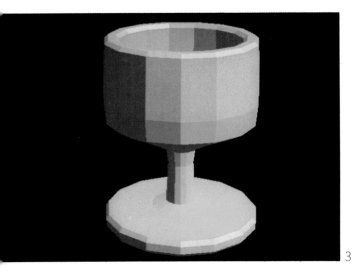

shot – are the result of insufficient *temporal* definition. Using a greater number of frames per second would eliminate them. It is a question of increasing the definition, and therefore of raising the processing and memory capacity of the computer by several orders of magnitude.

Colour

One major omission so far is a detailed discussion of colour, and of the problems posed by colour for the graphics programmer and system designer. In its efforts to measure, analyse and describe colour mathematically, science has been unable to produce a totally objective theory with which everybody can agree. Nor will it ever do so, for ultimately colour cannot be completely reduced to mathematical formulation. It is impossible to divorce a proper consideration of colour from our perception of it. Manufacturers sometimes claim that their graphics systems can 'manipulate 16 million colours'; but such claims are really meaningless. Computer systems do *not* handle 16 million colours. They merely have the capacity to tag the continuous variation of colour with 16 million numbers – which is a very different matter. The implication that computers are somehow better at distinguishing between the hues and shades of colour than the human eye can be very misleading.

Raster graphics is pre-eminently a domain of colour. All the mathematical calculations performed by the computer eventually have to determine the shade of each individual pixel on the display. Yet our eyes perceive colours as relationships, and not at all as separate entities. The human visual system automatically corrects colour perception, even when heavily-tinted glasses are worn by the viewer. Another factor is that in the real world light is reflected from a variety of surfaces, whereas in computer graphics displays it is emitted by a single surface. This is partially overcome by using a range of other display surfaces, including paper and photographic film, yet it remains a major limitation.

◁ △ **Five steps in the creation of a realistic object**
1 The basic surfaces are outlined and displayed as a wireframe model which can be rotated on the display for viewing
2 Hidden-surface removal: surfaces normally hidden from view are automatically removed by applying special algorithms. For clarity, the versions of the goblet in steps 1 and 2 show a six-sided object, not the more detailed description used later
3 Colour has been applied to each surface, and its intensity calculated on the assumption that a light source illuminates the object. This is called *computing the shading model.* When objects are modelled, as here, by using plane-faced polyhedra, the intensity of light on individual faces remains constant. A shading value is associated with each face, taking into account its orientation towards the light source. Whenever the hidden-surface algorithm finds the face visible, the appropriate intensity value is interpreted by the display
4 The application of smooth-shading algorithms: here the faces of the object are greatly multiplied until the whole shape becomes a collection of microscopic facets. Calculations ensure that each facet appears to reflect both diffuse and specular light
5 The final realism comes with the application of a surface texture. Rough surfaces are simulated by changing the orientation of sampled facets

Dr James F Blinn, Jet Propulsion Laboratory, Pasadena, California

Digital scene simulation *Cityscape*, an early work *Digital Productions, Los Angeles, California*

PART 2:
CURRENT
APPLICATIONS

GRAPHIC

DESIGN

The graphic designer today works in a variety of media, producing designs not only for the printed page but also for films, video and television. Media that require the additional dimension of movement are considered later in the book. This section is concerned with the application of computer graphics in graphic design; the following one considers illustration for the print media alone.

The word 'graphic' comes from the Greek γραφειν, meaning 'to write'. That would seem to imply only the use of an instrument for making lines, marks and characters on a two-dimensional surface; yet the activity of graphic design also includes the handling of images made by photography. In turn, photography has enabled practically any image-making process to be used in graphic design. It can reproduce paintings done in oils, tempera or watercolour just as easily as it records diagrams and line drawings which are closer in spirit to the modern principles of graphics. Photography has been a synthesizing medium, allowing any image to be reduced to a 'lowest common denominator' for the purposes of reproduction. Once images shared this common form, they could be cropped (trimmed), sized, adjusted for colour and contrast, and then placed in a graphic arrangement on the page.

What photography achieved in extending the range of images that could be manipulated by the graphic designer, computer graphics has taken one stage further. Just as photography reduced every symbol and image to the common vehicle of *film emulsion*, computer graphics reduces all two-dimensional imagery to *numbers*: to the binary digits of computer processing. This has profound implications for the graphic designer.

A photograph must be considered as a single graphic element. While it can be easily enlarged or reduced in size, it does not freely permit a graphic designer to change individual parts of it. Although a skilled photographer working with an elaborate rostrum camera can construct very complex images, the final product is still a piece of film emulsion, or a photographic print, and this is what the graphic designer must use when a pre-assembled picture is to be an integral part of the design. In addition, whether he is creating an advertising poster, or a book, or the page of a magazine, he will normally have to add *text* to the illustrations. The manipulation of text is a primary function of graphic design.

Traditionally, text and images have been treated separately. A typesetter produces the text, acting on the instructions of the designer. Artists and photographers supply the images, all of which can be made into photographic prints for layout on the page. By means of process photography, text and pictures are then combined into a single plate from which the printer can reproduce the finished work. It is a long and intricate process involving many stages of production.

Computer graphics dramatically changes and simplifies the whole procedure. The new technology not only helps the designer to create sophisticated graphic layouts but, more significantly, it removes several later stages of production. Previously a designer had relatively little involvement with the specialist work of the pre-press companies who prepare the plates for the printer. Once the layout of the page and the elements to be slotted into it had been completed, the work was passed to a pre-press house for assembly. To 'design'

◁ **Mathematical art**
Kerry Jones here takes an ancient device, the mandala, and creates complex patterns using mathematical routines that are executed by the computer. (See p 148 for another example of Kerry Jones's work.)

Kerry Jones, Huntsville, Alabama

1

meant to create a plan, to arrange the component images, shapes and text into a meaningful pattern. Other people, further down the production line of printing and publishing, would fit the components together.

Today powerful computer graphics systems are being installed by the pre-press companies. This move represents a fundamental change in the way printed material is designed and produced. For the new systems have the capability to accomplish the whole process of design, pagination (page composition) and layout in one swift operation. As in so many computer graphics applications, the use of computers in graphic design has initiated changes in working practices, and in the very structure of how work is organized.

The reason why·computer graphics has the potential to provoke such fundamental changes is that it is an even more powerful synthesizing medium than photography. When pictorial information is held in digital form it can be manipulated very efficiently. A photograph, a watercolour sketch, a diagram, page numbers, symbols and text can all be reduced to digital form. Any component, or group of components, can be exchanged. The entire design, fully assembled, can be communicated electronically to a printing press anywhere in the world. Even the task of designing can itself be enhanced by routines that automatically observe 'good design principles'. Clearly, this technology is worthy of close attention by every graphic designer.

Development of graphic arts technology

In order to understand the current capabilities and limitations of graphic arts technology, one must look at its historical development. The most important factor has been the growth of full-colour printing during this century. When colour pictures are printed with inks on paper, it is necessary to make four colour *separations*. These contain dot patterns representing the yellow, magenta, cyan and black components of the picture, the size of the dots representing the intensity of the colour – cyan, magenta or yellow – and the depth of grey. Such dot images are called 'halftones'. At one time colour separations could only be done photographically, using a process camera and photographing through a perforated 'contact screen' to produce the halftone dots. The four images were retouched by hand, dot by dot, thereby consuming vast quantities of photographic materials.

In 1937 a young Scotsman, Alexander Murray, working for the Eastman Kodak Company in the United States, invented the *colour scanner*. This was a device for making colour separations automatically by electronic means. In Murray's device a photographic transparency could be mounted on a revolving, transparent drum, while a scanning head picked up light from within the drum. The light was converted into electronic signals as the drum moved slowly past the scanning head. With the addition of filters it was possible to separate the four basic colour components, and by reversing

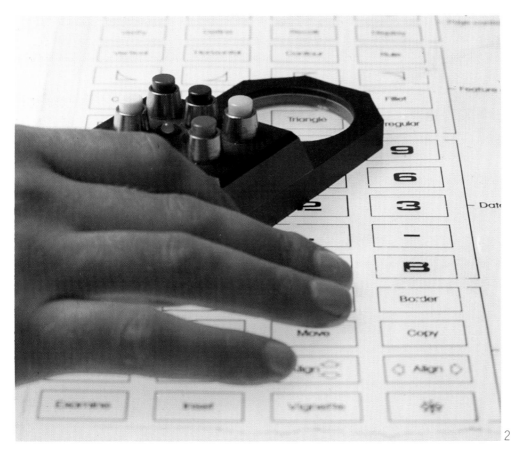

◁ **Pagination**
With the help of computer graphics techniques, page make-up and composition can be automated to a very great extent
1 Magnascan 570 Page Composition System
2 Hand cursor of the Magnascan

Crosfield Electronics, London and Peterborough, England
2

the process ('writing' instead of 'reading') make four images exactly in register with each other. The output medium, then as today, was film. This resulting film was used in the offset lithography process to make full-colour reproductions.

Today colour scanners can produce three types of output film: continuous tone, contact-screen halftone, and electronic-dot-generated halftone. All the early scanners were of the first type, and they still required the use of a process camera to make the screened halftones necessary for offset lithography. Continuous-tone scanners, the least expensive kind, are still needed today for producing positives for the traditional gravure process, an alternative method of colour printing. Contact-screen scanners are more widely used, producing halftone separations without the need for further processing. The third category, electronic-dot generation, is often referred to as 'laser scanning', although not all of them necessarily have a laser light, and those that do use it only for exposing and not for analysing.

The sophisticated electronic-dot scanners produce microdots even smaller than those of the highest-resolution separation screen. Light is fed to the film by a row of fibre-optic cables, six of which are needed to make one microdot. It may take two or three revolutions of the scanner to build up a single halftone dot with 12 rows of microdots. To obtain the dot pattern, a reproduction (pre-press) company now buys a computer tape containing the appropriate information

on screen characteristics rather than buying the screen itself.

At this point it should be clear why computer graphics has become important in graphic arts reproduction. Once a picture has been analysed by a scanner, the digital information can be manipulated *before* the output film is exposed. Now in a few pre-press houses – and the number is growing – it is being used for retouching and for pagination.

Electronic *retouching* is especially spectacular. The image can be greatly magnified on an electronic display until the individual pixels are visible. The slightest scratch or blemish can then be removed from the photograph (now stored in digital form) simply by changing pixels to a different colour or intensity. Even major retouching is easy, and it is quite possible to change the hairstyle of a fashion model, or remove the smile from the face of a politician.

Pagination systems allow the layout artist to assemble a page by displaying a basic layout 'grid' into which he can slot both text and pictures. High-resolution monitors display the retouched images, and the computer allows the designer to crop and mask (remove unwanted portions of) the images before inserting them into the grid. A task that once took all day can now be performed in one or two hours.

The logical development of these systems need not stop at this point. The graphic designer who originates the structure for the layout artist could himself formulate the design on a computer graphics system. Since the workload is so dramatically reduced, the roles of art director, graphic designer, finished artist, typesetter and layout artist may all become intermingled. In the not-too-distant future, only one skilled person, working with a computer graphics system, will be needed for producing an astonishing range of printed material. This raises the question: for whom will the graphic designer work? For an advertising agency, for a publisher or packager of books and magazines, or for the pre-press house itself? Much will depend on which of these organizations installs the equipment, and on whether, in the rough and tumble of business, the workload can be rationalized to take full advantage of the technology's potential.

The state of the art

Computer graphics systems can turn the entire pre-press operation of editing, typesetting, colour separation and retouching, right through to page make-up and plate preparation (lithography) or cylinder engraving (gravure), into virtually a filmless, paperless process. These systems already exist, and they are manufactured by such companies as Crosfield Electronics, Scitex, and Hell GmbH.

At present the operation of an advanced and well-integrated system works like this. A graphic designer will have planned the basic format for, say, a new magazine. All the stories will have been written and typeset, the text being supplied by the typesetter in the form of digital tapes. These are usually delivered to the pre-press house by physical means, though in practice they could be sent through telephone lines. Colour illustrations by artists will have been photographed and delivered to the same address, together with material that has been originated by photography. All the illustrative material is then colour scanned, with the result that this, too, is in digital form. Both pictures and text are now held as a complex pattern of bits on magnetic tape. In other words, digital information has become the lowest common denominator of all the various component parts of the magazine.

Sitting at a graphics workstation – one of several that may be connected to the computer – the layout artist can begin to piece the magazine together. The designer will be peering over his shoulder. One of the standard grid patterns will have been chosen for the magazine and this can now be displayed on the VDU. Beginning with page one, the layout artist can start to place blocks of text and illustrations within the grid. He calls up the text for the first few pages, loading it from the long-term storage medium of tape into the main (short-term) computer memory. A choice of illustrations is also accessed in a similar way. By switching to a 'cut and paste' mode, the artist can arrange text, advertisements, photographs, diagrams and illustrations within the displayed grid.

The images can now be cropped and masked. This is done by placing the image of a boundary rectangle around the picture being treated. The size of the rectangle can be adjusted precisely by using the digitizing tablet and stylus. The screen cursor indicates the position of the stylus which, when pressed on the tablet, creates the rectangle by specifying opposite diagonal corners. Grid constraints – software routines that adjust the size of the rectangle by very small fractions – may be built into the system.

Since each picture is being displayed and examined in full colour, a variety of shapes and sizes can be tried. The pictures can be placed side-by-side on the VDU, so that the artist can visualize the effect of juxtaposing many different images. In sharp contrast to the traditional methods of pagination, many options can be tried and they can be immediately reviewed on the VDU. It is therefore much easier to create a balanced design. Intended effects are achieved much more quickly, and unexpected effects may yield a better solution than the one intended.

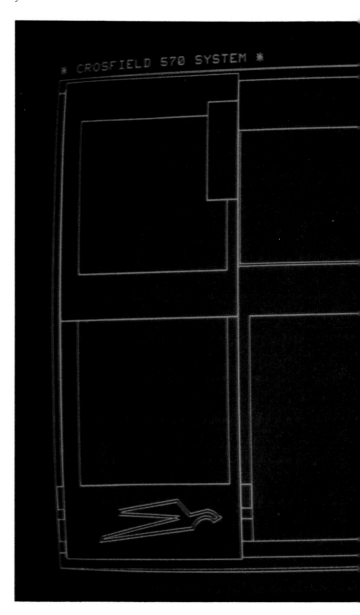

When text is added the page begins to look like a finished product. Even at this late stage, new headlines may be written on the keyboard and inserted into the composition. The original text can still be altered. Not a single component of the magazine is fixed or immutable. Last-minute advertisements can easily be accommodated, provided that they, too, are converted into digital form.

The completed page is now recorded on magnetic tape or disk, where it can remain until the rest of the magazine is fully prepared. The selected and cropped illustrations can still be recalled for retouching. Designers and editors may examine the magazine in its electronic form to give approval or suggest revisions.

The final step is taken when each page is converted from digital to physical output by using the scanning process in its 'writing' mode. (It is interesting to note that the original Greek derivation of 'graphic' has now come into its own.) By this process, lithographic plates or gravure cylinders are prepared directly from the digital data. In a technique called *lasergravure* the copper cylinders for this alternative colour printing technology can be etched by a digitally-controlled laser beam.

In the current state of the art the picture that the artist manipulates on the screen is not necessarily composed of exactly the same set of data as the original colour-scanned picture held on the computer tape. Colour scanning is an extremely high resolution process, making the highest-quality colour reproductions. While the displayed images are among the best that can be seen in all computer graphics applications – more like 35 mm slides than normal television pictures – they do not contain all the original information: they have been assembled by sampling the data. A second stage of processing is usually needed to decode the artist's instructions and produce a master tape from which the edited images can be written on film.

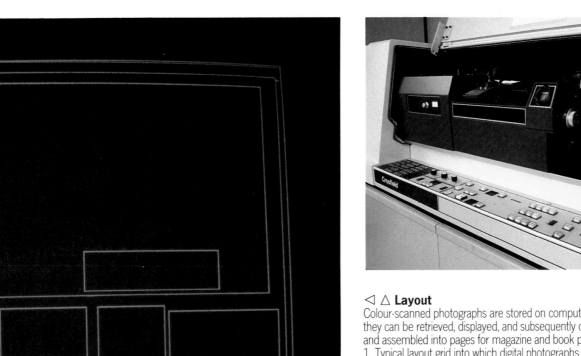

◁ △ **Layout**
Colour-scanned photographs are stored on computer disks, from which they can be retrieved, displayed, and subsequently cropped, masked and assembled into pages for magazine and book publication
1 Typical layout grid into which digital photographs are inserted
2 Colour scanners can analyse any colour picture into its component colours. The digital data can then be used as the basis for computer graphics manipulation: in retouching and in page composition

Crosfield Electronics, London and Peterborough, England

ILLUSTRATION

Not all illustrators are attracted to computer graphics at its current stage of development. Many illustrators produce work that is simply too detailed for the computer to resolve. However, illustration is one of the component elements of graphic design, and individual artists with their own styles and special skills are frequently called upon by designers in the preparation of printed material. The graphics system, with its powerful range of techniques, should certainly be among the tools that the illustrator can command.

Three approaches

There are three types of equipment that the illustrator can use for producing work with computer graphics. Broadly, these fall under three headings: analog *video colorizers*, digital *painting systems* and *digitizing systems*.

If the illustrator is fortunate, he may get access to a machine that will perform the functions of all three. Yet each of these systems represents a different approach to computer graphics, in an ascending order of complexity, and all three have been packaged separately by manufacturers. Only the first two will be described here in detail, since digitizing systems have extensive model-making facilities that are needed more by the engineer than the illustrator.

◁ ▽ **Illustration 1**
For the illustrator, computer graphics provides the tools *and* the 'canvas'. High-resolution systems, like the Genigraphics 100 series, offer extensive facilities, producing true print-quality hardcopy
1 *Eagle*, Dan Wilson
2 *Fifer* (after Manet), Christine Baker

Genigraphics, Liverpool, New York

GENIGRAPHICS

2

Video colorizers

In the section on 'Techniques and Hardware' (see p 49) the video camera was listed as a potential input device for computer graphics. The convenience of scanned input as opposed to coordinate point-by-point input will be immediately apparent. The artist can have a complete image to work with right from the start, rather than having to build it one point at a time. This is the principle of the video colorizer. A black-and-white or colour video picture is scanned into the graphics computer and then manipulated by the operator.

A typical system, such as that developed by Toucan, of San Francisco, consists of a black-and-white video camera mounted on a rostrum; a set of high-intensity lights to illuminate the artwork that is placed under the camera; a display monitor; a computer with analog (continuously-variable) controls; and a photographic camera.

To use the system, the operator prepares some simple black-and-white artwork; or he may work on an existing picture that needs enhancement. This may be an image not in pure black and white but containing intermediate tones of

▽ ▷ Illustration 2
1 *Oriental Woman*, Dan Wilson
2 *Sail*, Mark Baker. The silhouette of the boat has been digitized from a drawing and then automatically matted to the background and other elements added

Genigraphics, Liverpool, New York

1

ILLUSTRATION | 75

GENIGRAPHICS

GENIGRAPHICS

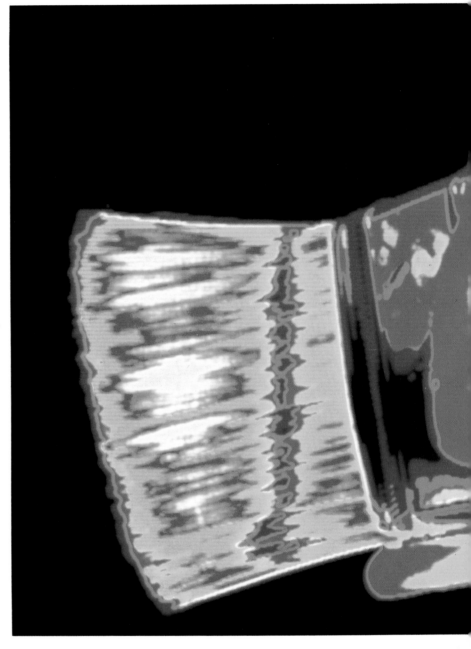

△ ▷ **Analog computer graphics**
Existing artwork, such as black-and-white
drawings or photographs, can be coloured and
enhanced by using an analog system. The
image is fed into the computer by a video
camera and displayed on a screen. Colours
are then superimposed on areas of different
intensity. By twisting the dials on the computer
the artist can mix and adjust each colour
before making a photograph of the result

1 *Metacolor, San Francisco, California*
2 *Gary Brandenburg, Groupmedia, Chicago,
Illinois*

grey. It will have been made by conventional means, using
brushes, pens and inks. It can depict pictorial imagery or
lettering, both of which should be bold and simple to get a
good result. The image is then placed under the camera on
the rostrum and displayed on the monitor.

The operator now has a strictly limited range of controls
for changing the contrast ratio of the image; for colouring the
image; and for distorting it in various directions, for example
widening or compressing it. These controls are continuously-
variable dials, and they do not offer the same degree of
manipulation as is normally associated with a full digital
computer graphics system. However, they enable the
operator to feed colour into the images, creating 'solarizing'
and 'posterizing' effects (both are dramatic colour effects)

which are much more difficult to obtain with colour
photography. The operator can also instantly vary the
contrast range in a way which would be difficult to achieve by
photographic means. By twisting the colour and the contrast
dials the operator creates a constantly changing image which
can be fixed simply by leaving the dials in one position. Then
the picture can be recorded photographically.

A video colorizer may offer other facilities, such as pattern
generation. Although it cannot generate the precisely-
calculated mathematical patterns of a digital computer, it can
make an infinite variety of random patterns, some of which
may be useful to the illustrator. These are created by
introducing controlled interference to the video signal,
resulting in patterns that have a distinctly 'electronic' look.

ILLUSTRATION | 77

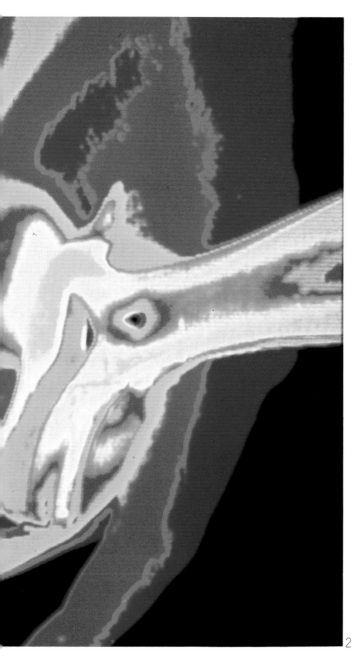

2

Video colorizers can make many interesting effects at great speed, turning simple black-and-white artwork into attractive full-colour images. They can imitate some of the effects of slit-scan photography, making 'zooms' and 'whorls' when the artwork is moved. Yet they do not allow for the sophisticated construction of images by drawing and sketching. In this respect their techniques are more closely allied to those of a special effects photographer than an illustrator.

Digital painting systems

A computer painting system that will be truly useful in helping the illustrator create static pictures has yet to be built, though this is being worked on, especially by the manufacturers of the pagination systems already described. At the beginning of 1984 there were around 30 painting systems available, costing between $7000 and $250,000. Nearly all of these had excellent facilities, and each one had been designed and packaged specifically for use by artists. What they lacked was good resolution.

The term 'high resolution' implies at least 2000 lines, with 4000 lines being both desirable and possible in a computer graphics system. This quality of image is achieved by scanning the output in a film recorder when the hardcopy picture is obtained. It is not the resolution of the VDU.

Most digital painting systems are designed around the video standard, 525 lines in the USA and 625 lines in Europe. Their chief function is the creation of graphics for broadcast television or for industrial video networks. For example, the Flair system which is manufactured by Logica in Great Britain was originally developed by the BBC. The resolution of the vast majority of painting systems does not exceed the requirements of television.

In terms of resolution, therefore, the painting system has some limitations for the illustrator. This is an important factor because all painting systems are raster graphic devices, using blocks of solid colour instead of connecting the endpoints of vectors. The illustrator must work with a 'pointillist' technique similar to that of painters such as Seurat. Yet the artist could compensate for the relatively poor definition of the image by making his paintings very large. By contrast, a computer painting system displays its images on a VDU measuring approximately 480 mm (19 in.) between diagonal corners. Its sketching tablet is usually no more than 300 mm (12 in.) square; the largest are about 460 mm (18 in.) square. Although the image may be enlarged photographically at the output stage, it will have been conceived and executed on a relatively small scale.

These are grave limitations, but it can be argued that the benefits outweigh them. The imaging techniques which have already been developed comprise a long and impressive list. Never before has the illustrator had such an array of techniques to call upon. When these methods of drawing and painting become available with very high resolution displays and inexpensive output devices, every illustrator will want to have a computer painting system.

The hardware of a typical painting system consists of a workstation, with either one or two VDUs, a tablet and stylus, and a graphics computer. The computer itself may be either microprocessor-based with an optional link to a larger machine, or it will have a minicomputer such as a DEC LSI 11/23 to carry out the processing. Two floppy disk drives come with the package, one for the software instructions, another for containing the image output information.

Painting systems are menu-driven, meaning that they offer choices to the operator, such as displaying a palette of colours or a selection of 'brushes'. The menu may be

displayed in one (or more) of three different places: on the VDU screen that the operator uses for creating the picture, on a separate monitor or on the tablet. A tablet menu is more restricted than an electronically-displayed menu, since it cannot be changed. However, basic functions, such as drawing or filling a bounded area with colour, are more conveniently and quickly accessed by tapping the stylus on 'DRAW' and 'FILL' on the tablet than by locating them on the screen.

A screen cursor indicates the position of the stylus (which is sometimes called a drawing *wand*) as it is moved across the tablet's surface. To select a routine from the menu of choices the artist presses the stylus in the appropriate location and the machine switches to the chosen mode. When the menu is very extensive, as it is on the Video Graphics system made by Aurora Imaging Systems, having the menu on a separate monitor is a distinct advantage. The

ILLUSTRATION | 79

3

4

◁ △ **Video input enhancement**

These striking images were produced with a Quantel Digital Paint Box, a videographics painting system for professional designers. In each instance a black-and-white original was input via a video camera

1 *Tribute to Michelangelo*: the original image of Giuliano de Medici (left) was 'reflected' to yield the mirror image and then colour was added to the hair, baton and garments, after which a final photographic print was made

2 *Star*: the black-and-white original photograph of the film actress Valerie French was reflected to make a symmetrical pattern and then hand coloured, using a stylus and digitizing tablet

3, 4 *Horses*: a fragment of Greek sculpture from the Parthenon frieze is decorated with graffiti-like strokes of electronic colour

Vivianne Scott, CAL Videographics, London, England

◁ △ **Graphic design 1**
A relatively small proportion of pure graphic design is currently being created with the help of computers. Gary Brandenburg has had the opportunity of working daily with high-quality equipment

Gary Brandenburg, Groupmedia, Chicago, Illinois

ILLUSTRATION 81

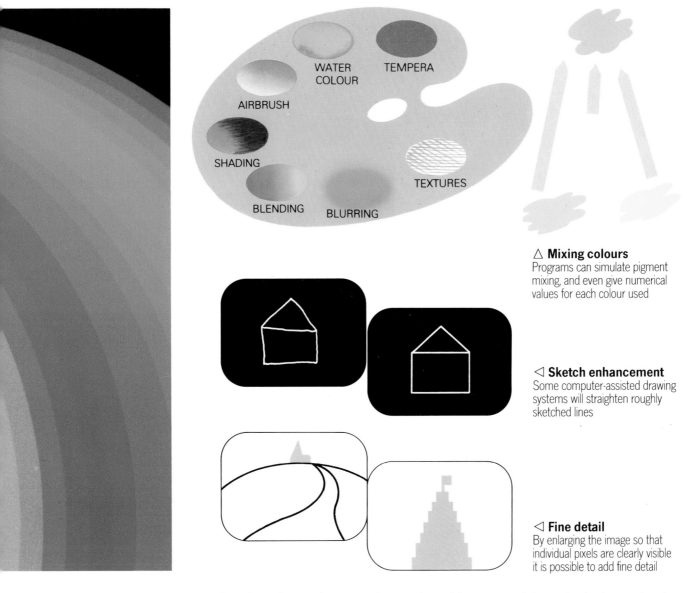

△ Mixing colours
Programs can simulate pigment mixing, and even give numerical values for each colour used

◁ Sketch enhancement
Some computer-assisted drawing systems will straighten roughly sketched lines

◁ Fine detail
By enlarging the image so that individual pixels are clearly visible it is possible to add fine detail

colour palette and the wide choice of routines do not then interfere with the painting area.

Painting systems vary in the number of colours that they can display at any one time. A palette must be chosen, usually from an immense range of potential colours. But the number that can be conveniently displayed at once may vary between 8 and 256.

True colour mixing is available on some systems, although it may be achieved in different ways. In the Digital Paint Box, manufactured by Quantel, colour mixing is enhanced by the use of a pressure-sensitive stylus. When the artist increases pressure on the stylus, the intensity of the colour is also increased. Thus a completely new palette can be created by picking a colour, drawing a line in one direction while increasing the pressure, then choosing another colour and drawing another line on top in the opposite direction, again increasing the pressure. The resulting gradation may contain some colours that have never been displayed before. The

artist can then pick any one of these shades by moving the screen cursor to the appropriate section of the line.

The method of colour selection just described is not universally available. Systems without a pressure-sensitive device can only duplicate a colour that has been assigned to them. In other words, you can only choose one of the 256 colours displayed and increase its saturation (intensity) by incremental amounts. However, it may still be possible to pick a colour that has already been used in the picture, even though the palette from which it was originally selected is no longer being displayed.

For freehand sketching, the painting system offers a wide choice of 'brush sizes'. But the actual constitution of a 'brush' is a subtle matter. The stylus itself is the only physical instrument that the artist uses. It remains the same size and shape no matter what routines are called into play. Yet flexible computer software can allow the stylus to assume the functions of a wide variety of brushes. They can have

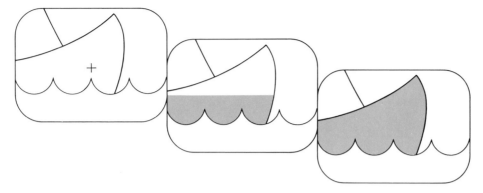

◁ **Seeding colour**
Any area that is completely
bounded by lines can be 'seeded'
with colour. Colour-fill then takes
place automatically, as pixels
adjacent to the seed switch to the
same shade

△ **Brush selection**
Each painting system has a standard set of brushes from which the
artist can select one of appropriate size and shape. This is then
allocated a colour, and sketching can begin

△ **Brush creation**
If none of the standard brushes is suitable, a custom-made version can
be created by the artist and placed in a temporary memory. The new
shape can be accessed like a standard brush

◁ **Pixel close-up**
Painting with a brush: the pixel-
pattern of the brush (left) leaves a
characteristic trail on the display
(right)

different 'shapes' and 'sizes'. One basic requirement is a
choice of circular brushes which will lay down a trail of pixels
on the screen that will remain an equal width throughout the
brushstroke. A standard circular brush can be as small as one
pixel in diameter, or as large as 300 pixels. Eight or ten sizes
might be offered in the menu.

Not all brushes are circular. Artists have always used other
shapes: flat, oval or triangular in cross-section. These too can
be simulated by the computer, and again a choice of other
shapes is provided as standard. A flat brush, when drawn
across the screen, will produce an 'italic' effect, leaving a
broad trail of colour in, say, a vertical direction and a narrow
trail in a horizontal direction. Likewise, other brushes will leave
their own characteristic pattern when a brushstroke is made.

Already, some 20 or 30 individual brushes have been
mentioned, taking their range of sizes into account. But the
choice is not limited to this number. Most painting systems
actually have an *infinite* number of brushes, because they
enable the artist to design his own shape and store it in a
temporary menu. The standard menu may have a few vacant
spaces where such brush symbols can be displayed.

The facility of having an infinite number of brushes might
seem to be unnecessary until it is appreciated that a
brushstroke does not have to be continuous. It can be
intermittent. When an artist draws a continuous line from
point A to point B, the computer can turn the brushstroke on
and off, leaving a pattern that contains the shape of the
brush. There is thus tremendous scope for making repetitive
patterns of all kinds. You simply design a brush, store it in
memory, and use it in the intermittent mode when needed.

One application of intermittent brushstrokes might be in
designing a graphic for a newspaper or a news broadcast. If
you wanted to superimpose the flightpath of an aircraft on a
map of the world you could create an aircraft symbol and
then quickly draw a chain of them across the map. The
interval between each image can be controlled. Individual
symbols can be made to overlap, or there can be a wide gap
between them, as desired. This is just one of the many
techniques that the painting system can provide.

The artistic quality of a computer image made by freehand
sketching is entirely the product of the artist's own skills. The
computer merely gives him the widest possible choice of
tools: an immense number of colours and an infinite variety
of brushes. He is further helped by having automatic 'fill'
algorithms (routines) that allow closed outlines to be filled
with any chosen colour. The methods by which the
programmer has devised the 'fill' routines will vary, but they all
achieve a similar result. The artist simply moves the screen
cursor to a point within the area that he wants to fill with

▷ **Graphic design 2**
Like Gary Brandenburg, Mike Newman has not only created graphic designs
on the highest-quality equipment, but also helped engineers develop
computer systems that can easily be used by other artists

Mike Newman, Dicomed Corporation, Minneapolis, Minnesota

ILLUSTRATION | 83

colour. Then he presses the stylus on the tablet, and all the pixels in that area will change to the correct shade. Some programmers have used the colour-fill technique entertainingly in a moving picture sequence by drawing in a paint pot 'pouring' the colour into the area from above. This is a natural extension of the idea because filling normally takes place from the point at which the cursor is located, the new colour working its way down the area line by line to the bottom, then topping up until the whole outline is filled.

Colour need not be inserted in this way. It can also be painted onto the screen by using a wide 'brush'. Any unwanted overlap at the edges of the area can be easily removed by selecting the background colour, and repainting. Alternatively, colour can be 'sprayed' onto the screen, somewhat like the operation of an airbrush. In this 'airbrush' mode, only a few pixels are switched to the new colour, but their numbers increase until the area immediately surrounding the cursor position is saturated – while a short distance away the pixels are less densely packed. This is a good simulation of an airbrush, but it does not permit the corresponding airbrush technique of masking portions of the area. Without doubt, this will receive more programming attention in the future.

For making outline drawings the artist is aided by many standard routines. Straight lines, perfectly-drawn circles, ellipses, and regular polygons are all within the repertoire of every painting system. The widths of the connecting lines, and their colour, can be determined before they are drawn. Even the order in which they are drawn can be memorized by the computer.

Memory capacity is a governing factor in a painting system, as it is in any graphics computer. It determines what techniques can be made available to the user. With a number of *memory planes* several more facilities can be added. For example, different parts of the image can be placed in separate planes, yielding a foreground, a middle ground, and a background. Because they are described separately to the computer, they can be manipulated independently. If the artist has drawn a complex building in the background, and an equally detailed figure in front of it, he will be reluctant to make any changes to either image. Changing one component will affect the other. Yet with the technique of using memory planes the artist can *scale* the background independently of the foreground. The house can be made bigger, or the foreground figure can be made smaller, without having to redraw either image.

This ability to 'edit' the picture is a completely new concept for the illustrator. With traditional tools – pens, pencils, tracing paper and erasers – the mechanics of assembling an image are very time consuming. With a painting system, the illustrator can quickly move, overlay or scale the image without any hesitation.

A standard technique for *moving* individual components is the 'cut-and-paste' one like that used in pagination systems. Although it requires a powerful processor it is also available on some painting systems. The ability to *overlay* one image on another needs a number of memory planes if subsequent editing is demanded. *Scaling* is widely available, and may be achieved by several methods, including tapping the stylus repeatedly on the tablet, causing small, progressive increases or decreases in the size of the image.

Regular patterns can be made by *reflecting* the picture, creating a mirror image on the other half of the screen. This facility is available on Logica's Flair and on the Dicomed graphics computer. The artist has only to draw one half of a butterfly, or of any image that has an exactly symmetrical shape. Once any item has been drawn in this fashion, and filled with colours, it can be reduced, enlarged, moved around the frame or inserted into the memory. There is really no limit to the creative possibilities of the medium, and an experienced artist can take many short cuts.

ILLUSTRATION | 85

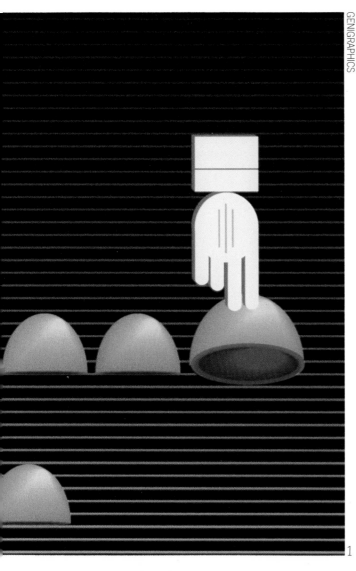

GENIGRAPHICS

1

GENIGRAPHICS

3

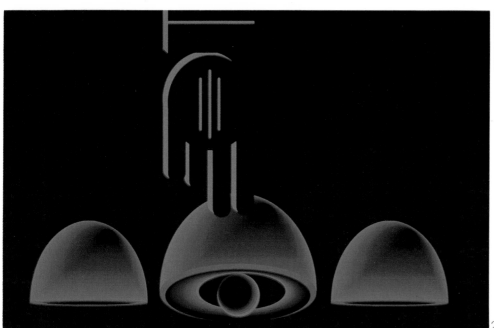

GENIGRAPHICS

2

◁ △ **Graphic design 3**
Using a sophisticated graphics computer, an artist can produce high-quality graphics far more quickly than with conventional tools. Once digitized into the system, a motif can be enlarged or moved within the frame, and backgrounds can be added or subtracted at will. All three pictures were generated on Genigraphics 100 series computers
1,2 *Untitled graphics*, Tom Gilhooly. 1 is a 3-part multiple exposure of a digitized design. 2 is an example of how alternative versions can be created – in this case by adjusting the colour, eliminating the background and printing with a single exposure
3 *Glass*, Mark Baker. This was created in only 35 minutes

Genigraphics, Liverpool, New York

▽ ▷ **Graphic design 4**
When graphic design problems need strongly geometric solutions the computer can help to provide them
1 DEI/*BME Magazine*, cover, 1982
2 DEI/Alan Green, *Madison Avenue Handbook*, 1982

Digital Effects, Inc., New York, New York

1

ILLUSTRATION | 87

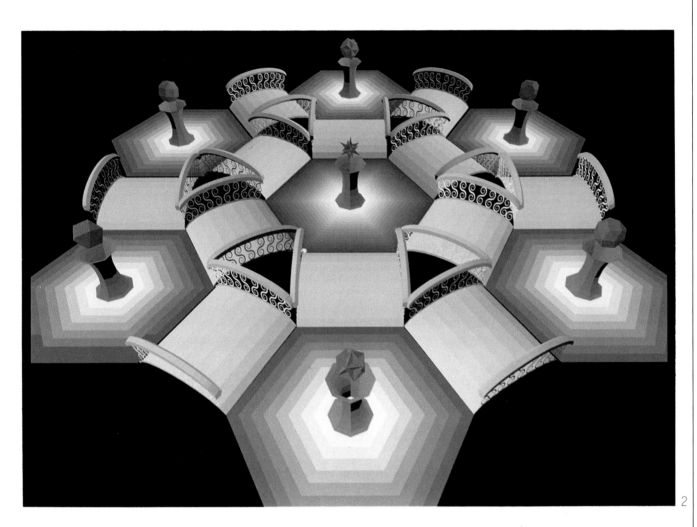

2

There is not space here to describe all the functions of a sophisticated system, but one further facility is worth mentioning. A selection of *founts* (typefaces) is a standard feature of most painting systems. Despite the limitations imposed by screen resolution, the facility to add lettering is a big advantage. When higher resolution is. obtainable, this added facility will help the illustrator as much as it currently aids the television graphics designer. At present, however, we are less inclined to accept printed lettering with uneven edges than impressionistic illustrations. Good software anti-aliasing techniques to eliminate 'staircase' edges help to minimize these problems and a variety of others which derive basically from poor resolution.

Development of painting systems

Computer painting is now a facility offered on small personal computers. Many of the basic techniques described above can be achieved with an Apple II or III, a TRS-80, or an IBM Personal Computer. Picture resolution, speed, colour depth, and the range of available techniques all make demands on the central processing capacity of the computer. For this reason, only the dedicated painting computer can yet offer a sufficient standard of all-round excellence that can attract the interest of the illustrator. The history of these special-purpose machines is worth a brief mention.

A central figure in this field has been Dr Richard Shoup, the founder of Aurora Imaging Systems in San Francisco. When he was at Carnegie Mellon University, Dr Shoup became interested in the video analog computers being developed by Leo Harrison. These machines were similar in their capabilities to the simple video colorizers already described. They were conceived as being new tools specifically for artists.

When Dr Shoup became a resident scientist at Xerox's Palo Alto Research Laboratories he set about designing a *digital* computer system that would carry the techniques even further. This was to become a nine-year project, and it yielded a system, 'Superpaint', which was operational by 1973. An important breakthrough was Dr Shoup's design of one of the first frame buffers ever to be built. These devices were to prove essential, not only in computer painting, but in all graphics applications.

Working with Dr Shoup at Xerox was Alvy Ray Smith, who later moved to the New York Institute of Technology where he helped to develop another system, called IMAGES. Research at MIT, and at Bell Laboratories under Ken

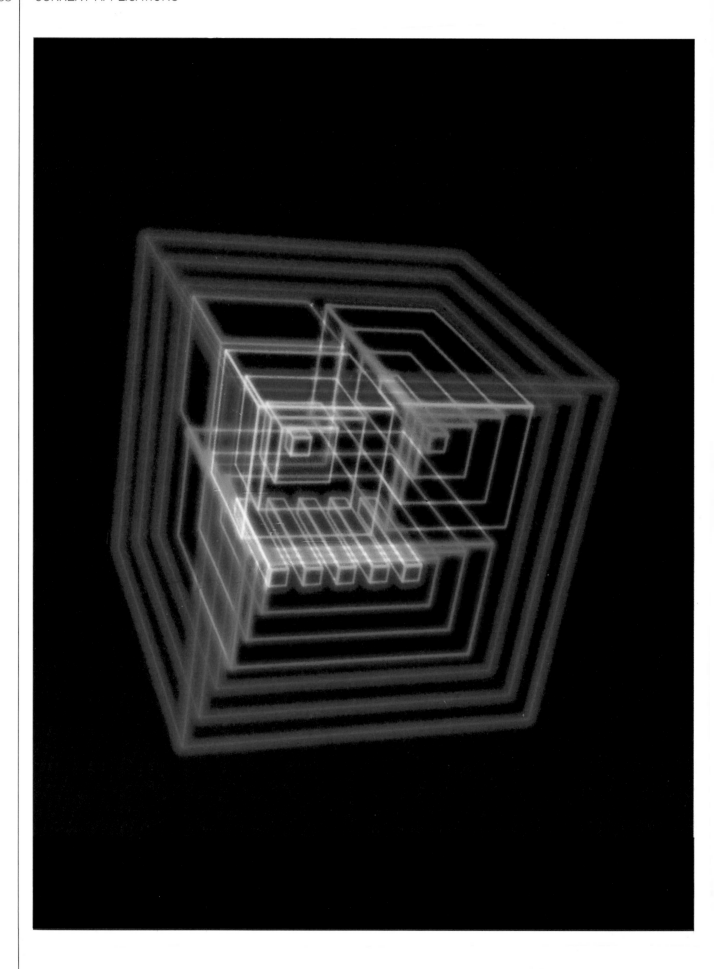

ILLUSTRATION   89

Knowlton, had led to alternative painting systems. By the late 1970s the techniques were far enough advanced to allow packaging by commercial manufacturers. A system called AVA was produced by Ampex, installed at CBS, and marketed in the United States and Europe with modest success. In price and performance AVA was rapidly overtaken by other systems from MCI/Quantel, Logica, Ramtek-Xiphias and Via Video. Meanwhile, Dr Shoup had formed his own specialist company, Aurora, and continued to expand the range of digital painting techniques available to the artist.

Digitizing systems

The future development of computer painting will introduce some of the scientific and engineering graphics capabilities to the artist. These are currently found in the more sophisticated *digitizing systems* rather than in painting systems. The difference between them lies in the structure of the software. In a digitizing system each component of the image is identified by the computer, and arranged with the other components in a hierarchy of relationships. Rather than creating an image, the operator creates a geometric model that describes the object he has in mind. For display purposes, the graphics system 'takes pictures' of the model and thus produces the two-dimensional images on the VDU.

In computer painting there is no geometric model. When the artist draws a picture of a house he is making only an image. It may well be a three-dimensional image, but it will be constructed for the two-dimensional page. The relationship of one component to another is not noted by the computer so relationships cannot be arranged in any particular order.

Provision of more powerful software can make this facility available to the illustrator. Would it be helpful? The illustrator is often concerned with drawing three-dimensional images, although he is not necessarily interested in their representational value. In engineering the images are descriptions of the object, whereas in illustration they are the final product. Yet the facility of constructing a three-dimensional model, in which the relationships of lines and shapes are defined mathematically, could certainly be an attractive option for technical illustrators. The problem lies in the difficulty of writing the software so that the system could be used by artists with very little extra training.

With digitizing systems, the hierarchy of relationships is normally defined for each specific application. For example, an architect uses 'building blocks' different from those used by an automobile engineer. The architect is concerned with rooms, windows, doors, piping, etc., while the engineer is manipulating struts, beams, and sheets of metal. Both sets of

◁ Graphic design 5
DEI/Alex Berry, *STSC Annual Report*, 1981
Digital Effects, Inc., New York, New York

building blocks are represented symbolically by lines and shapes, but the symbol system is different in each case. Since the illustrator's attention can be focused on *any* aspect of the external world, facilities for describing the structure of an object rather than rendering its appearance are by no means easy to provide.

The extent to which the illustrator is concerned with the structure of an object is queried by Susanne Langer in her book *Philosophy in a New Key* (Harvard University Press, Cambridge, Massachusetts, 1942): 'What property must a picture have in order to represent its object? Must it really share the visual appearance of the object? Certainly not to any high degree.' Dr Langer went on to observe that illustrators had considerable latitude in depicting likenesses on paper. 'The reason for this latitude is that the picture is essentially a symbol, not a duplicate, of what it represents.'

An object's structure, as well as an abstracted rendering of its appearance, may be symbolic of the object. For example, a matchstick man is instantly recognizable as a human figure because its lines remind us of the basic structure of the body. The purpose of illustration is not complete realism, and there need be no one-to-one relationship between image and object as there is in engineering. A higher informational content can often be achieved by careful selection of the visual data as, for instance, in wildlife illustrations where the individual markings of birds and animals are subtly accentuated by the artist. The selection of geometric structural data can equally produce effective symbolic representation in certain types of pictures. Its manipulation, however, demands mechanical assistance.

Digitizing systems are used for entering coordinate data concerning the structure of an object, and they presuppose that such data already exist or can be obtained. Illustrators obtain their own data from observation rather than from measurement. Yet, like the engineer, they often need to draw the many classes of shapes that already have mathematical definitions and can therefore be calculated by the computer. Currently, the illustrator would have to learn how to operate a CAD system to have these techniques at his disposal. Eventually many will be packaged for use by artists, and one more barrier between art and science will be broken.

Systems for the illustrator

Of the three types of system examined in this section, painting systems at present offer the most appropriate range of techniques for the illustrator. They are costly and they could benefit from higher resolution, but they have excellent facilities for freehand painting and sketching. The more complex geometries obtained by digitizing spatial data in systems made for engineers require techniques which will gradually become available to the general user for illustrative work, and these should fill some of the current gaps.

TELEVISION AND FILM

Synthetic images generated for film and television require the additional dimension of movement. Considered solely as an extra dimension, movement is not much more difficult for a computer to calculate than any of the three spatial dimensions. The component parts of a displayed image can be moved around the screen by the operator of a graphics system. Now, instead of memorizing just one complete frame, the system must be able to memorize several frames and display them in rapid succession.

The speed at which an object moves across the screen is controlled by specifying its displacement from one position to the next. For example, if you want to show a sailing ship travelling along the horizon in front of a sinking moon, both the ship and moon would be moved by tiny increments. Many frames would be needed to show the smooth motion of both objects. But a shooting star added to the scene would be moved by large displacements of its position, and hence would need only a few frames to create the illusion.

Both film and television reproduce movement by relying on the phenomenon of 'persistence of vision' in our perception. This occurs when we see a progressive sequence of at least nine images every second. Below nine, the illusion of movement disappears and we see separate still images. Film moves at 24 frames per second, television at 25 or 30 cycles per second, both of them creating a near perfect illusion with barely a hint of flicker. Even when film or television cameras record the *analog*, that is continuous, movements of actors they translate them into *discrete* (separate) images, conveying an illusion of continuous movement only when played back to the viewer.

These visual media are therefore already organized on principles that digital computers can handle. To create movement with the computer you simply have to make lots of still images, and program the computer to calculate the relative displacements of objects from one frame to the next. The whole task becomes one of measurement and calculation. It is an ideal application for interactive computer graphics: *you* supply the measurements and the computer supplies the calculations.

This description of *computer animation* is deceptively simple. An operator will quickly discover that his own task of telling the computer exactly how to displace images is really very difficult. After all, how do objects move in real life? Pure Newtonian motion may be observed in outer space, where planets spin on their axes and travel in vast orbits around the sun. But down on Earth motion is infinitely varied. Cats move with cat-like movements; fish swim with fish-like movements; and when human beings move they display their individual personalities. If an animator wants to create a convincing illusion on the screen he must first analyse, then recreate, this world of movement in all its facets.

Broadly speaking, there are three kinds of animation: film and television graphics, cartoon animation and realistic simulations. Each of these may be created by using the techniques of computer graphics.

Film and television graphics are *not* concerned, unlike the other two categories, with the 'world of movement in all its facets'. Here movement is used in a highly abstract way, primarily for the purposes of communicating information. For example, rainclouds can be made to move across the screen

◁ **Television graphics 1**
Television has become a showcase for certain types of computer-generated animation. This is a 1983 station-identification logo. Frequently used programme introductions and station symbols command the substantial budgets necessary for top-quality computer graphics

Rede Globo, Rio de Janeiro, Brazil

in a weather forecast, or concentric circles can radiate from the epicentre of an earthquake on an animated map. Film and television graphics add the dimension of movement to the illustrator's art. But the representations of movement, like those of the images themselves, are purely symbolic.

Cartoon animation, at its best, can be much more sophisticated. It represents the characteristic *ways* in which individual figures and objects move. Cartooning achieves this largely by exaggeration. A bouncing tennis ball will be shown to flatten on impact to a saucer shape and then elongate to a sausage shape when it springs up into the air. Double-decker buses will lean backwards when they screech to a halt. The representations of facial expressions and body movements of figures will capture all the expressive qualities by magnifying them. It follows, therefore, that full character animation, in the tradition of Walt Disney, is one of the most exacting art forms ever devised.

Realistic simulation eschews exaggeration in favour of realism. Whereas the cartoon animator relies on *outline* drawings to delineate movement, the simulator works with full three-dimensional images. He renders a scene in continuous depth rather than in planar depth. One or more light sources are specified, and corresponding shadows are calculated for the entire scene. Camera movements are calculated with the same precision as that given to moving the objects around their three-dimensional environment.

◁ ▽ **Television graphics 2**
The introduction to Rede Globo's
evening news programme
Rede Globo, Rio de Janeiro, Brazil

With the many hybrid techniques that have been developed for making film and television animation, there is considerable overlapping between these three categories. When computer graphics is used, a further distinction must be made between *real-time* and *frame-by-frame* animation. In the spectrum from simple graphics to complex simulation there is a corresponding increase in the number of calculations that need to be performed. Simple animated graphics can be displayed in real time on an electronic display, while the more elaborate simulations can require several hours of processing to generate a single frame. Cartoon animation has always been created frame by frame, with a master animator drawing the *key frames* (for instance,

frames one and five) and an assistant drawing the *in-betweens* (two, three and four).

Applications in film and television

Television has helped to pioneer many techniques of computer animation. Within the programme schedule itself, animated informational graphics made their first appearance in election broadcasts. During election coverage, returns are sent in by telephone or telex, and these numerical data need to be quickly turned into a visual format. At the BBC in London computer graphics made its debut by replacing the 'swingometer', a crude device resembling a voltmeter whose needle was deflected from side to side to represent voting

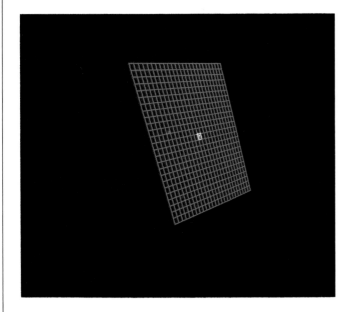

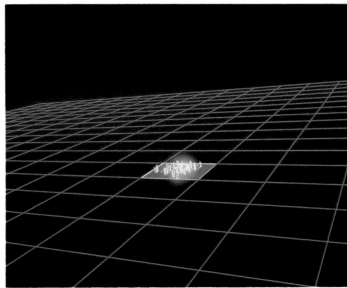

swings from one party to another. Elsewhere, too, new graphics devices were introduced. In Sweden, for example, an early version of Alan Kitching's Antics animation system was used in the 1979 election for generating the smiling heads of the five party leaders. The width of their smiles indicated how well they were doing.

News graphics help to give added impact to a news story, especially when live action footage is absent or irrelevant. Reports on the stock market, retail and wholesale price indices, foreign exchange rates, fluctuations in interest rates and so on are ideal subjects for animated graphic treatment. The work is often required very quickly, sometimes in a matter of minutes. Only a computer graphics system can produce them in time — and even then it requires preparation of standard images and movements well in advance.

Most of the painting systems described in the previous chapter can generate simple graphics for television news. KRON-TV in San Francisco was one of the first local stations to install the Aurora video graphics system. In fact this station has *three* such systems, and uses them regularly for news, sports reports and weather forecasts. Other television companies have been introduced to the techniques of computer graphics through their use of equipment called *character generators.* At first the only function of a character generator was to produce the captions that are superimposed on the screen to indicate the names of people appearing. A wider choice of founts extended their use to end credits and news captions. Eventually a facility for drawing special symbols was added, and the character generator began to evolve into a painting system, complete with a

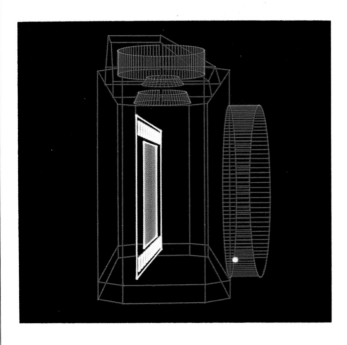

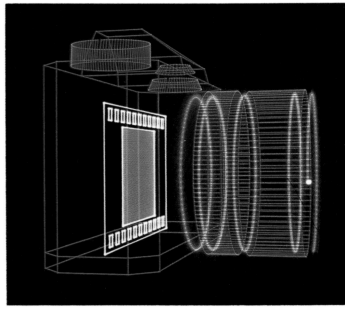

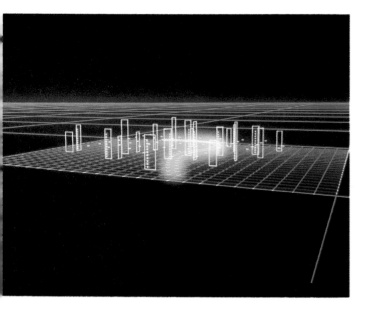

limited animation capability. Now, the Chyron and Vidifont character generators are really dual-purpose machines with many of the characteristics of electronic art systems.

Presenting the weather forecast on television entails the manipulation of quite complex visual data. Atmospheric pressures, wind patterns, and local weather conditions in many geographic areas, all need to be formatted very quickly. Weather satellites send pictures from high above the Earth's atmosphere, but these have to be superimposed on outline maps with lettering and other symbols. Actual forecasting must be accompanied by maps that show conditions as they *will* be, so computer graphics then totally replaces the satellite images.

Further up the spectrum of computer animation are some applications that need more than a simple graphic treatment.

△ **Special effects**
'Special effects' is the term given to film sequences that demonstrate techniques not easily achieved by conventional photography. An example is the extended tracking shot, as seen in these frames from *Cityscape*. The 'synthetic camera' tracks in on the distant city, at the same time rolling over to suggest that the city is tumbling in space

The Moving Picture Company, London, England

▽ **Television advertising 1**
The unique features of a mechanical product can often be best explained by using computer graphics. Here the components of a Nikon camera are effectively displayed by a computer graphic sequence. Ironically, it would not be possible to make a similar image using photography

The Moving Picture Company, London, England

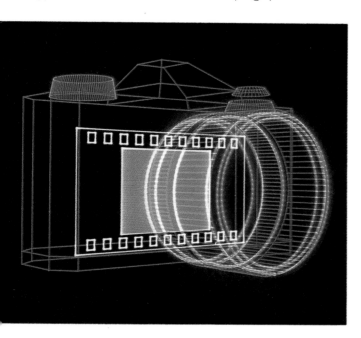

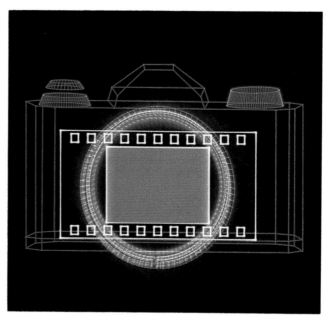

Much of children's programming is cartoon animation. This is so popular on television that demand has for many years exceeded supply. At the same time production of top-quality cartoons by conventional methods has become prohibitively expensive, forcing animators to reduce the technical quality, for example by restricting the amount of movement of the characters and by using the same picture unaltered for three frames at a time. This tends to give a jerky result – though even the better animators in former times used pictures twice. Many animators are now experimenting with computer graphics systems that have been specially developed for this type of work, automatically carrying out the hard labour of in-betweening. Such tasks as inking and colouring also lend themselves to computer assistance.

Realistic simulations have found two major applications on television. The first is in *network identification*, a highly prestigious production task commanding a substantial budget. The symbol of a television network is its hallmark and, like a piece of advertising, it appears frequently and becomes associated with the product. In this case the product is the whole TV schedule, so nearly all the major television corporations renew their animated logos at regular intervals. In the 1980s NBC, ABC and CBS in the United States; the BBC, London Weekend and ITV Channel Four in the United Kingdom; RAI in Italy; NHK in Japan; and Rede Globo in Brazil have all commissioned the latest techniques of computer simulation. It has been the perfect application for them, since all the symbols are geometric in design and their animation is thus well within the capabilities of a medium still in its infancy. The lengthy processing demanded by fully-shaded three-dimensional animation has been sup-ported by high budgets, the expense of several thousand

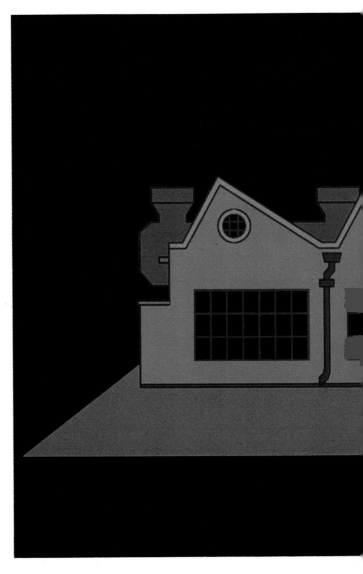

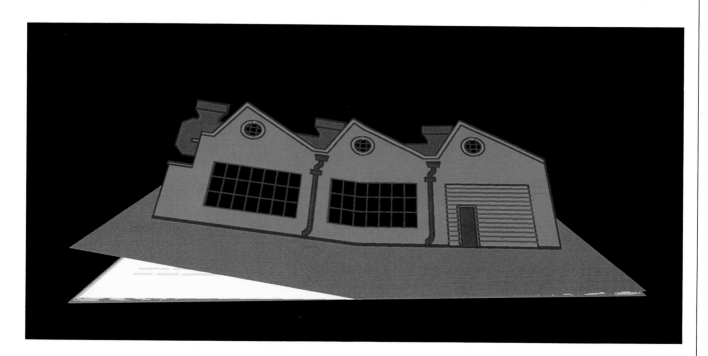

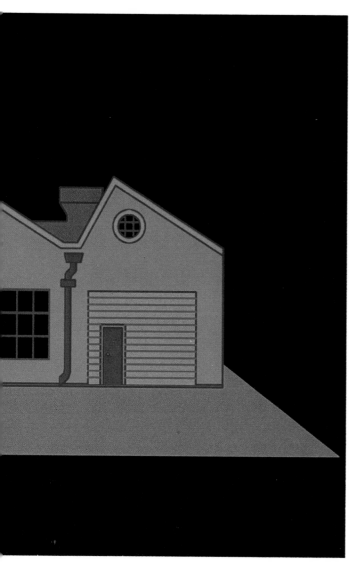

◁ △ **Television advertising 2**
A sequence from a Norwich Union insurance company commercial: Electronic Arts has pioneered the use of computer-generated imagery in commercials on British television. Working with DEC/VAX computers and custom-built frame buffers, they use an adapted version of the MOVIE animation package from Brigham Young University, Utah. Each frame of the film is recorded by a Dicomed digital camera

Electronic Arts, London, England

dollars a second being justified by the fact that network symbols are seen many times each evening by millions.

Important news, sports and current affairs programmes on television have been given opening title sequences made with the same techniques. Costs are gradually coming down, and it will not be long before shows on local stations or even those made for industrial video networks are able to use graphic simulations.

Some of the most significant advances in the creative use of the new techniques have been made in television *commercials*. Advertisers like to be associated with anything that is new, and each fresh development in computer simulation has been pressed into service by a handful of 'high-tech' production companies. Frequently effects have been achieved — particularly with vector graphics — that the computer experts had scarcely believed possible. Now, producers such as Robert Abel & Associates, Moore Graphics & Film and Bo Gehring Associates in Hollywood; Digital Effects and Feigenbaum Productions in New York; Electronic Arts, The Moving Picture Company and Digital Pictures in London; and MTI and TEXNAI in Toyko are taking the techniques of raster graphics to the limit. Some of the most advanced experimental work will continue to be done for television commercials.

◁ ▽ **Television advertising 3**
Two images from a television commercial for TRW, a Los Angeles-based high-technology corporation. The animated vector sequence was made on an Evans & Sutherland Multi Picture System II

Robert Abel & Associates, Hollywood, California

▷ **Television advertising 4**
One of the leaders in the field of three-dimensional computer-generated animation for television commercials is Sogitec Audiovisuel, a division of a French flight simulation company. Shown here are frames from animated sequences, generated on systems originally developed for flight simulation but subsequently adapted to this new application
1 *Histoire à la une*, a television opening, T.F.1, France
2 *Renault 'Electronic Now'*, from a short motion picture, M.C.A.V., Renault, France

Sogitec Audiovisuel, Boulogne, France

1

2

Finally, at the top of the spectrum in this survey of animation applications, there is the cinema feature film. Since all realistic simulations are necessarily film-based it is not surprising that motion-picture producers have tried them. Yet by 1984 only one major film, Disney's *Tron*, had contained more than a few minutes of computer-generated effects. The simulations for *Tron* were subcontracted to four specialist computer animation companies, which called upon practically every available graphics technique to make the sequences. Many of these were *matted* (combined) with live action. For Disney, it was a triumph of art direction but not a great box-office success. As a consequence only one other major studio, Lucasfilm, has invested heavily in computer animation. An example of their work was the exploding planet sequence in the film *Star Trek – Wrath of Khan*, made by the Lucasfilm subsidiary Industrial Light & Magic.

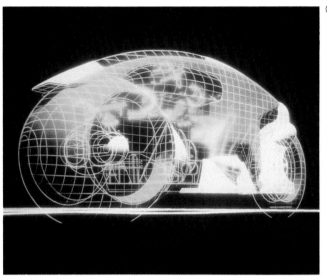

1

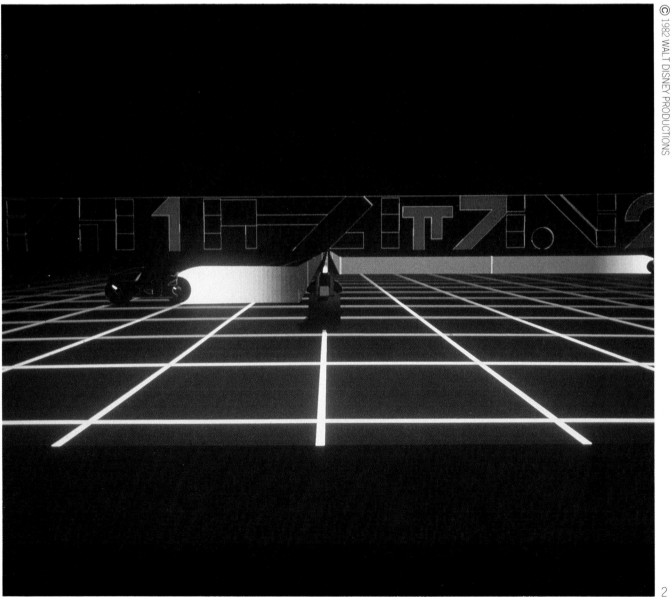

2

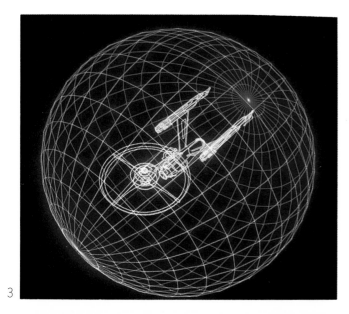

3

4

◁ △ **Computer graphics in movies**
TRON was the first feature film to make extensive use of computer-generated effects. The images shown opposite depict some of the digital models that were animated for the film. On this page are two images used in the motion picture *Star Trek – The Wrath of Khan*: they were created on an Evans and Sutherland Multi Picture System II, using a CSM colour display
1 Futuristic motorcycle, dissolving from wireframe to solid
2 Motorcycles racing across the grid
3, 4 Fictional screen displays from the flight deck of the *Starship Enterprise*

1, 2 *Walt Disney Productions, Burbank, California*
3, 4 *Evans & Sutherland, Salt Lake City, Utah, and Industrial Light and Magic Company, a division of Lucasfilm, California*

Animatics

The least sophisticated types of film and television graphics are often called 'animatics' to distinguish them from cartoon animation and simulations. An animatic consists of just a few frames, perhaps three or four, continuously cycled, 1-2-3, 1-2-3, etc. This image is held on the screen for several seconds, or long enough for the audience to absorb the information contained in it. It is normally inserted into a production containing live-action video, and its purpose is often to explain a process or a concept that requires both movement and a diagrammatic treatment. News bulletins are the main application, but there are many others in educational and training programmes where such an approach is very helpful. Demonstrations of the direction of flow in chemical refineries; of the circulation of ocean currents; or of repetitive mechanical processes such as the action of an automobile engine demand an analytical, diagrammatical treatment which can be well supplied by the technique.

To create animatics, a painting system must have an animation facility allowing the operator to make several images in register. Registration is essential because not all of the elements of the image will move, and those that remain stationary must not be seen to jump out of alignment. This is easily accomplished in computer graphics since the stationary elements can be retained as the basis for the succeeding image. On some systems, such as Logica's Flair, simple *colour cycling* can create a 'flow' effect in one single image. Building the images is done by using all the techniques available on a painting system.

The playback of animatics presumes the use of a medium that can reproduce motion. Once the playback medium has been chosen, the images must then be transferred to it from the computer memory. There are many options.

○ Slides: audio-visual presentation with computer-controlled slide projection; images are photographed by registration camera systems

○ Slides-to-video: subsequent transfer to videotape/cassette by aerial image transfer; an aerial image is one that is formed in space, e.g. projected, rather than on a screen

○ Film, 16 mm/35 2mm; transfer by film recorder which scans the image line by line

○ Videotape: transfer with RGB-to-video conversion

○ Videodisk: subsequent transfer from videotape

○ Computer disk: playback of real-time animatics direct from disk-loaded RAM memory

○ Still store: playback from large buffer memory containing many different frames

This is a wide choice of playback media, although the last two methods are listed more for completeness than

△ ▷ **Animatics**
Short sequences of animation in which a picture is given some intrinsic movement are called *animatics*. These images by Spectrum Art Works, designed on a Cromemco graphics computer with FORTRAN software, are stills from animatic sequences in which water falls into the chasm below, the ship sails out to sea and snow falls gently

Spectrum Art Works, Telluride, Colorado

practicality. Presentation requires an accompanying soundtrack which needs a medium, such as film, video or slide/sound, to synchronize it with the visuals. In live television, however, the presenter is the voice-over and images can be more easily originated from a computer memory.

Cartoon animation
By extending the techniques of animatics, and bringing to it the skills of traditional animation, computer graphics can greatly automate the production of cartoons.

Traditionally, the animator works to a pre-recorded soundtrack. An analysis of the soundtrack is prepared, giving the animator precise timings for lip movements and other actions. Cartoon characters will have been developed by a designer. Making them move is then the specific task of the animator. He begins by making pencil sketches on separate sheets of translucent paper, held in registration by a *peg bar*. These contain the key positions of the characters: the beginnings and endings of movements, with enough in-betweens to show if the movement will work.

Pencil sketches are then filmed, one at a time, on an animation rostrum. In this *pencil test*, hundreds of frames are recorded, but their timings are largely based on the experience of the animator. Here comes the first application of computers in traditional animation. Instead of filming the pencil test, the cameraman records it on a video-based system with computer control. The computer can be used to

vary the timings between one frame and the next, thus indicating precisely the best timings for each sequence. Playback from video, unlike film, is instant. These animation aids, developed by companies such as Lyon Lamb, have become almost universal in animation studios.

The next stage in the conventional animation process is that a background artist paints a large background picture, many times the size of the individual pencil sketches that are being completed by the in-betweeners. The sketches are traced on to transparent acetate 'cels', and then, by another artist, opaqued with colour on the reverse side so that the black outlines remain sharp. An exposure guide is written to explain the assembly of cels and backgrounds, and the required camera movements. Both cels and backgrounds can be moved independently across the rostrum in any direction. The camera can be raised and lowered and, with a multiplane camera (invented by Disney in 1936), several

planes of cels can be photographed simultaneously, creating depth effects in the movement plane.

To this exacting art, computer graphics experts – primarily at Cornell University and New York Institute of Technology – have brought a degree of automation. In this approach the fundamental idea is to retain the traditional qualities of hand-drawn animation while automating the purely mechanical aspects of it.

The first step is to assist the process of transferring drawings to cels. This is done by scanning the drawings into a raster-based system, using a video scanning camera connected to a digital frame buffer. Coloured backgrounds, too, can be entered by making multiple passes for red, green and blue components, using optical filters. Drawings are now held in the buffer as pixel data, and they can be filled with colour by using a *cel opaquing program*. This is similar to a normal set of 'colour fill' algorithms, but with the difference that each colour has a cel opacity value, indicating the extent to which it can obscure the colour behind it. The use of computer graphics to opaque cels electronically can speed up the process tenfold.

The next stage to be automated is the 'filming' itself, in this case, by merging the 'cels' one at a time with the backgrounds. With all the frames held digitally there is little option but to carry out the frame assembly process in the computer, but there are several advantages in doing so. For example, the number of *cel levels* is no longer limited by the physical thickness of acetate, nor will the bottom cel level be less bright than those above it. Camera movements are also virtually limitless, and all the techniques of the multiplane film camera can be simulated. Final merged frames are then recorded by a film recorder, the end product being, as in traditional animation, a strip of film. The quality of the movement still depends on the quality of the hand drawings, but in all other respects the computer has delivered an excellent result with a great reduction in labour.

Manipulation of the type described above requires a powerful minicomputer, such as a VAX 11/780, together with a comprehensive set of software routines specially written for the animator. Hanna-Barbera Productions in Hollywood has supported the development of these techniques, using them regularly for broadcast-quality animation.

Not all animators are willing to accept computer graphics techniques, especially when their own conventional methods have been fine-tuned over many years. This is particularly true when the computer is used for automating the in-betweening. 'There *are* no in-betweens,' says top character animator Richard Williams. It is a lesson that has been passed on by Art Babbitt, Grim Natwick and other great Disney animators. Their argument is a good one. As Chuck Jones has pointed out, the word animation comes from the Latin *animare*, meaning 'to impart life'. A good animator must

▷ **Experimental films**

These images have been taken from three experimental films that were being made at Ohio State University in early 1984. They were photographed directly off an RGB monitor using a 640 × 480 × 32 frame buffer designed and built by Frank Crow and Marc Howard. All the objects are described as polyhedra and were generated using the data generation system 'dg', developed by Wayne Carlson
1 *Gator Dreams*, a film by Judy Sachter
2 *Eye-Kiss*, a film by Judy Sachter
3 *City of the Future*, a film by John Donkin

Computer Graphics Research Group, Ohio State University, Columbus, Ohio

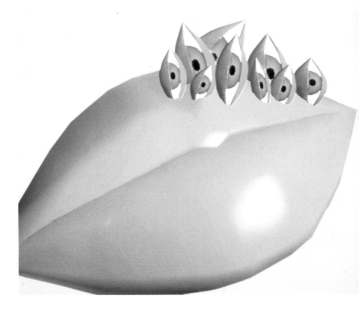

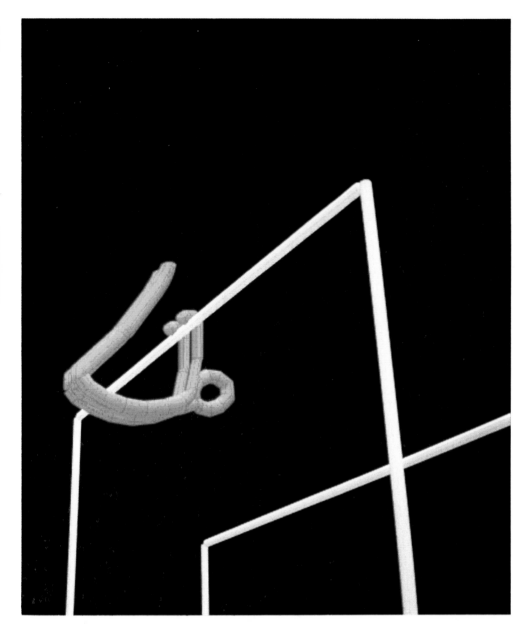

◁ **Three-dimensional interpolation system**
This frame from the animated sequence *The Uneven Bars*, by Susan Van Baerle, demonstrates the use of three-dimensional key frame animation for motion control. The gymnast's motion is controlled using a three-dimensional interpolation system called *twixt*, developed by Julian Gomez. The conventional animation technique of *in-betweening* can thus be calculated automatically not only for cartoon drawings but also for solid objects

Ohio State University, Columbus, Ohio

breathe life into his characters, and he can do it only by manual skill, not by mechanical in-betweening. Notwithstanding this, graphics experts at Lucasfilm and elsewhere have devised some ingenious methods of automating the in-betweening process. In some cases they have succeeded in eliminating the mechanistic look, producing surprisingly good results.

The most fruitful technique involves the use of *moving point constraints*. These are additions to the key frames and they specify the curves in time and space which constrain the trajectory and dynamics (path and speed) of points within the key frames. In this way, the total dynamics of the moving figures may be taken into account. The method is less mechanical than previous automatic in-betweening routines, which did not take into account the fact that cartoons are two-dimensional representations of three-dimensional move-

ments. With moving point constraints, the animator specifies the moving points and the computer works out the relationship of these to the images, calculating a *patch network* which determines the shape of the intermediate frames. The in-betweening routine then takes over and the lines are drawn.

An alternative method of automatic in-betweening is *skeleton animation*, in which a matchstick figure is manipulated by the animator, fixing the positions of the character's arms, legs, feet, etc., in each key frame. Such a skeleton framework can be drawn very quickly, creating a figure like a cardboard cutout with hinged limbs, and dots at the hinge points. Then, in Alan Kitching's phrase, 'the machine faithfully fits the flesh to the bones.' With either type of in-betweening, movements can be 'cushioned' (slowed) or accelerated, just as in traditional animation.

▷ **Animation**
Transformational animation allows the artist to describe sets of independently moving objects, as seen in these images of a butterfly in motion. They were created on a Data General ECLIPSE system and a Ramtex 9100 graphics display terminal, with Stephan Keith's SKY 4 program

Stephan R. Keith, Oakland, California

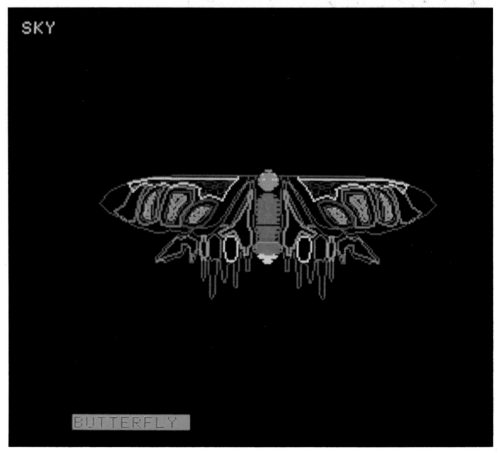

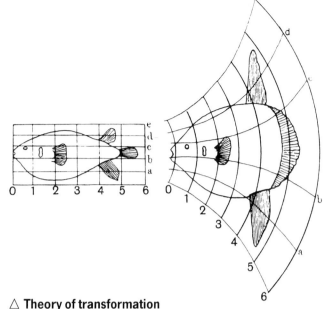

△ **Theory of transformation**
Thompson demonstrates how the shape of the sunfish (right) can be derived from that of the porcupine fish, a related species, by the distortion of the network of coordinate points

'On Growth and Form', D'Arcy Wentworth Thompson, 1917

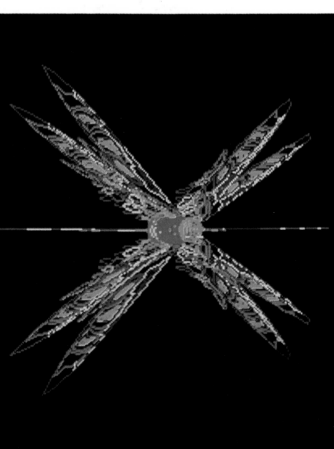

In-betweening leads almost imperceptibly into the subject of *transformations*. Computers are very good at making transformations, which is why this technique has often been confused with proper in-betweening containing the correct trajectories and dynamics. A computer can transform any line drawing into any other line drawing. If the two images are very different, the lines will become meaningless during the period of transition. For example, you could transform a portrait of Hitler into a picture of a Volkswagen, and the moustache would gradually turn into the front bumper. But the midpoint would be a jumble of lines. Such transformations were used in an ingenious film, *Dilemma*, made by John Halas and executed by Computer Creations in Indiana. But their potential is rapidly exhausted because of the meaningless transition.

However, if there is a mathematical relationship between the two images, computer transformations are truly effective. The next question for the animator is therefore whether objects in the real world have a mathematical relationship to each other; to which the answer, unexpectedly, is yes. The biologist D'Arcy Wentworth Thompson published his theory of transformations, *On Growth and Form*, in 1917. He showed how the shape of one species can be seen to derive from the shape of another, related species. For example, Thompson noted how the shape of a sunfish could be derived from that of the very different-looking porcupine fish by plotting the first shape on graph paper and then distorting the network of coordinates until the shape of the second fish was exactly reproduced. 'There is,' conjectured Thompson, 'something, an essential and indisputable something, that is common to them.'

Until recently biologists have largely ignored Thompson's observations of natural forms, but computer animation experts are paying attention to them. If there is a mathematical relationship between shapes, computers can simulate the growth patterns of nature. In a sense, this is an extension of cartoon animation, although it still needs to be explored more thoroughly.

Precise transformations of outline drawings require a vector graphic treatment for the highest quality results. All of the preceding examples in this section have been concerned with raster systems, using pixels and solid colour. But vector animation can be obtained very inexpensively, using a simple procedure. All you need to do is take pen plotter output and film it. Here is an example of an actual project, showing how this is done.

For the television series *Music in Time*, producers were looking for a sequence that would show hundreds of violins floating in mid-air – as if coming out of the screen towards the viewer from a distant point at the top left-hand corner of the screen. In keeping with the title of the series, the violins also had to appear to be playing in time to the music on the soundtrack. The problem was too complex for conventional animation, so the producers turned to computer graphics.

They turned, in fact, to the Middlesex Polytechnic in England, where a graphics program called PICASO has been developed by Dr John Vince and his colleagues. PICASO (with one 's') stands for Picture Computer Algorithms Subroutine Oriented, and it enables the user to manipulate graphic images on the computer. It is a powerful package, with hundreds of subroutines that can be called upon to solve a particular transformational problem.

The process of animating the violins took many different stages. First, accurate drawings were made of the model to be manipulated. It was necessary to digitize only one violin, entering the coordinate points into the computer. Several *instances* of the violin could then be taken, as many as might be needed. The computer calculated the different sizes and positions of the image that would be required at each point in the sequence. In the same way, the movements of the bow were calculated to correspond to a time analysis of the music. The final and most difficult step was in putting the images on to film.

In order to preserve the resolving power of the computer the animators had no choice but to use plotter output. An alternative system such as a film recorder is often beyond the budget of a polytechnic. So the resulting images were drawn, one frame at a time, on sheets of paper that were held by an animation peg bar (for registration) taped to the surface of the pen plotter belt. The images were then photographed on an animation rostrum; colour was fed in optically; and the whole sequence ended up as a strip of film.

This application of the pen plotter is highly effective,

though very time consuming. Similar films have been made at art schools and universities where a project may last for several months. In commercial animation the application is more limited. But powerful vector displays from Evans & Sutherland or Vector General can create such sequences in real time, even allowing interactive control.

Realistic stimulations

Either vector or raster systems, or a combination of the two, may be used for making realistic simulations. Raster is now the preferred display because it can more easily handle solid blocks of colour. In order to create solid surfaces with a vector system you have to draw lots of vectors very close together. Realistic simulation is therefore completed in raster, although the movements of wireframe objects may very well be planned in vector.

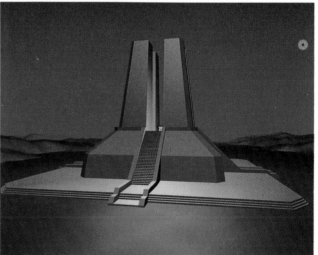

2

3

1

Planning and executing a realistic simulation demands four stages of production: *preliminary modelling, motion direction, full modelling* and *rendering.*

In order to plot the movements of an object in the intended sequence, a preliminary model must be made of it. The object itself might be, say, a racing car that will make a figure-of-eight movement in perspective on the screen. A stand-in model is constructed in outline, using relatively few polygons to describe the shape to the computer. It will be in three dimensions, so coordinate data specifying a front plane (x,y) and a depth plane (y,z) must be entered. In practice it is most convenient to work from original scale drawings made on graph paper, showing the front, back, sides, top and bottom of the car.

The stand-in model is used for making *motion tests.* An animator who works out the movements in realistic

◁ △ **Digital scene simulation 1**
The leading exponents of realism in computer imaging are at Digital Productions in Los Angeles. With their Cray-1 supercomputer, Gary Demos and John Whitney Jr have developed computer software that can match the resolution of photography. The chief application for their work is in motion pictures and television commercials
1 *Self Portrait:* using the Cray to draw itself was the idea of Steve Williams, formerly at the Lawrence Livermore Laboratory – an institution that also has a Cray supercomputer. The data base for this picture has been consistently refined over a long period. Says Williams: 'If time permits, I'll continue to refine it clear down to the nuts and bolts level.'
2 *Composite:* the 'hallmarks' of father and son – John Whitney Sr's familiar *Harmonic Function* above John Whitney Jr's *Cray Temple*
3 *Cray Temple:* echoing the futuristic design of the Cray computer, this image was one of the first to be made at Digital Productions

Digital Productions, Los Angeles, California

simulations uses techniques similar to those of a live action director. He controls the point of view of the 'camera', the positioning of the 'lights' and the movements of the 'actors' in their three-dimensional environment. The use of a real-time vector system is very helpful here. With so many variables it can take several attempts before the movements are right.

Pre-programmed routines can greatly assist the motion director in finding appropriate paths for the objects. For example, an 'explosion' effect can be created by making components of the object automatically fly away from a central point. Or objects can track in towards each other until they meet exactly. Great precision is possible, making the techniques very suitable for showing highly-engineered products in action.

While the motion direction is being completed, the model can be refined to its full level of detail. Since the purpose of realistic simulation is to show the surface appearance of the object rather than its structure, the model need be no more detailed than is essential for creating a crisp image. Areas subjected to extreme close-ups need to be more fully modelled than those remaining in the distance.

Gradually the data base is assembled by digitizing coordinates from drawings or photographs; by adding to the primitive elements (lines and shapes) directly on the screen; and by using the techniques of *procedural modelling* which require only the entering of a number of input variables. If procedural modelling is available, the computer might already be able to draw, say, wheels of racing cars. The operator would simply need to specify the size and type.

Working with a high-resolution raster display, and now equipped with the specifications of the motion direction program, the operator can move on to *rendering* each frame. Rendering is done automatically, in accordance with program instructions written in a *script*. The script supervises both the model manipulation and the motion directions, and provides the routines necessary for all the polygonal descriptions — that is, the changes in shape and size of the outlines.

Camera viewpoints, specified in the script, will determine which surfaces are hidden and which are visible. These are calculated by the computer for each polygon, except on those occasions when one complete object is concealed behind another. Then, to save processing time, the operator can 'switch off' the hidden object completely.

Many algorithms have been written to *shade* the objects, the most effective being the ray tracing routines already described in 'Techniques and Hardware', p 60). Colour and intensity must be calculated for each pixel, in every frame, and for each of the light sources. The frame can be built in a piecemeal fashion, matting those parts of the image that have already been rendered.

Edge definitions can be improved by anti-aliasing techniques, bringing quality up to the standard of 35 mm film.

The result of all these routines is a film sequence, recorded from digital data by a film recorder. Realistic simulation constantly strives to match or exceed the capabilities of conventional filming. Unless there are some real benefits being gained, the whole process can merely be repeating what might be done more easily by live-action or motion-control (one frame at a time) photography.

Yet the results speak for themselves. At their most elaborate, realistic simulations include not only three-dimensional objects in motion but also complete environments in which the objects can move. At Digital Productions, in Hollywood, Gary Demos and John Whitney Jr have developed some of the most sophisticated software for what they call Digital Scene Simulation. Running on a powerful Cray-1 computer, the programs have been used for creating simulations for commercials, feature films, and industrial applications. An early version of the software even simulated a human figure: a juggler in a top hat and evening dress, who kept hundreds of spheres, cubes and pyramids aloft, while he appeared to rotate in space. It was a very convincing image, and it demonstrated the remarkable potential of this approach to computer animation.

Future developments

Computer animation, as we have seen, is advancing on a very broad front. While many of the techniques are being developed for automating traditional animation, others, such as Digital Scene Simulation, are evolving into a new and unique artform. Despite the difficulties of rendering realistic scenes by mathematical descriptions, the latter is surely the more exciting approach.

In the short term, realistic simulation in motion pictures is limited by high costs and slow rates of production. Competitive techniques such as computer motion control, in which the movements of cameras and physical models are controlled by a computer, currently have cost and speed advantages over simulation. Yet in the long term, perhaps before the end of the century, this will change. Most of the theoretical problems of describing objects to the computer, and of making them move, have been solved. The world of computer animation awaits a new generation of more powerful computers that will process realistic simulations in minutes rather than days.

Meanwhile, we can expect to see more computer-generated inserts in motion pictures: short, dramatic sequences that realize 'unfilmable' moments of the action. There is no reason why these inserts should be limited to science fiction films, although their capability of rendering surreal images is ideally suited to science fiction subjects. As John Whitney Jr has said: 'Our challenge is to represent "the mundane" – the everyday street scene. When we can do this, we can then create any scene that we care to imagine.'

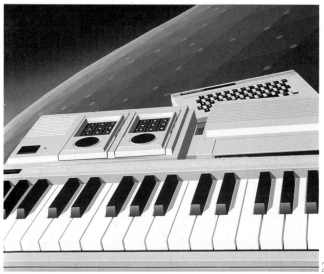

◁ △ **Digital scene simulation 2**
1 *Devo Hat*: a simulated plastic hat tumbling forward, used as a backdrop for the rock group Devo
2 *Mattel Keyboard*: made for a television commercial, this ultra-real computer image shows how digital scene simulation may on occasion be an alternative to conventional photography

Digital Productions, Los Angeles, California

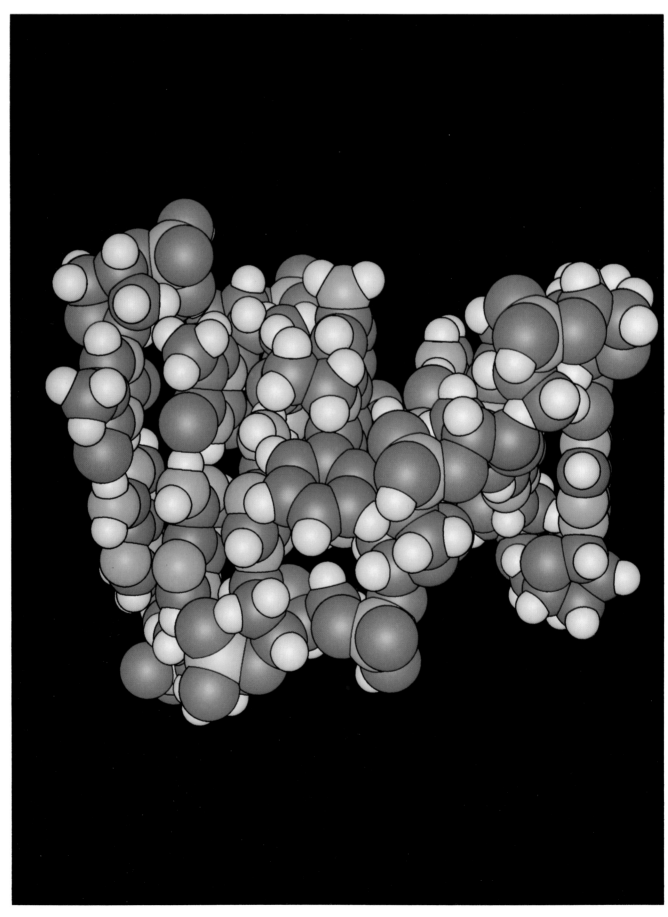

THE

SCIENCES

As a tool for scientists the computer graphics system has become virtually indispensable. It may eventually acquire the same kind of universal application that the slide rule once had, before the invention of the calculator. However, systems that are sufficiently powerful to make them truly useful to scientists are still remarkably expensive, not least because special programs must be written for individual applications. Unlike the slide rule, the graphics system is a group tool rather than a personal one. In most universities hardware and programming are centralized in a graphics facility staffed by computer experts. To these facilities the scientist brings problems that may, he thinks, have graphic solutions. Increasingly this graphics approach is yielding results, and it will not be long before there is a big demand for more personalized systems.

Molecular modelling

One of the widely-publicized applications has been in the field of *molecular modelling*: the use of graphics has coincided with some spectacular developments in molecular biology.

For years scientists had been making three-dimensional models of molecules so that the relationships between their atomic components could be more easily pictured. As long as the molecular structures under examination were relatively simple, the construction of these physical models presented no problem. Then, in the 1950s, the structure of DNA

molecule which carries genetic information was discovered: a long and complex double helix resembling a twisted ladder with 'rungs' of pairs of amino acid molecules arranged in sequence. This caused a surge of interest in the scientific community, leading to the elucidation of many other highly complex protein molecules.

But scientists were now faced with an altogether more complex problem of representation. Making models out of physical materials such as metal and plastic was no longer a satisfactory method of representing molecular structure. The convenient modelling of *macromolecules* such as proteins could only be done on a computer graphics system.

The work of applying interactive graphics to this task was begun at MIT in 1964. Even at this early stage it was possible to rotate the model in real time – an essential facility if

◁ ▷ **Molecular modelling 1**
1 Tomato bushy stunt virus
2 Path of the polypeptide chain of the alpha subunit of haemoglobin (indicated by the yellow tube; the heme molecule is in red)

1 *Nelson Max, Lawrence Livermore Laboratory, Livermore, California*
2 *Michael Connolly, Scripps Clinic and Research Foundation, La Jolla, California*

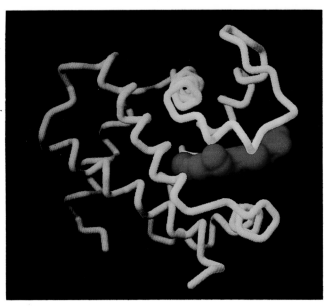
2

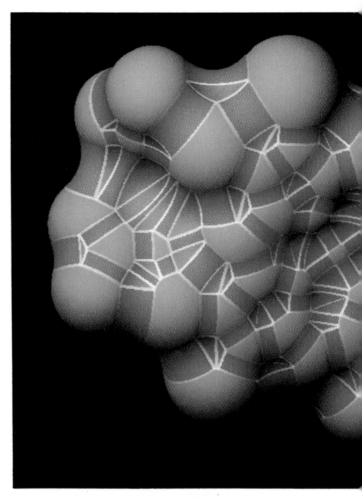

▽ ▷ Molecular modelling 2

Scientists portray the structures of complex molecules by building models of them. Whereas this could once be done only by making physical models out of such materials as wood or plastic, computer graphics is now widely favoured. It allows for much greater manipulation and adjustment of the model – showing how structures change when molecules are combined. Building the structures on an interactive graphics display, the research biologist can describe the intricate shapes of organic molecules using a variety of standard graphics techniques. Shown here are examples of raster and vector systems, both of which are widely used. The raster image (1) was displayed on an AED 767. The vector images (2, 3) were displayed on an Evans & Sutherland Multi Picture System II

1 Heme molecule: convex surface – green; saddle surface – blue; concave surface – red
2 DNA molecule: twelve base pairs
3 Trajectory of a probe sphere as it rolls over a small molecule

Michael Connolly, Scripps Clinic and Research Foundation, La Jolla, California

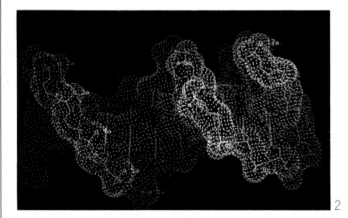

2

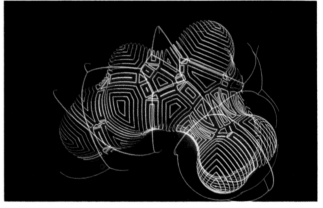

3

visualization is to be enhanced. However, the early systems had a number of limitations which must sometimes have made the operation of them a frustrating experience. Molecules interact at their surfaces, and thus surface representation is an important feature of the model. Yet vector systems do not readily lend themselves to this application. Their wireframe models are excellent for showing structure, but less satisfactory for surfaces.

At the University of California, San Francisco, Professor Robert Langridge and his colleagues overcame the problem.

They developed software that allowed surface representation by the generation of dot-patterns on a vector system. The complete program could not only display several interacting molecules, but it could also monitor the *stereochemical* activity (involving changes of shape) that was taking place.

With the rapid improvement of raster graphics in speed and resolution, the display of molecular models in raster became a reality more recently. These techniques are now moving towards real-time displays, on which the model can be manipulated through an interactive interface.

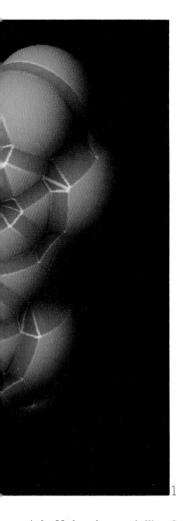

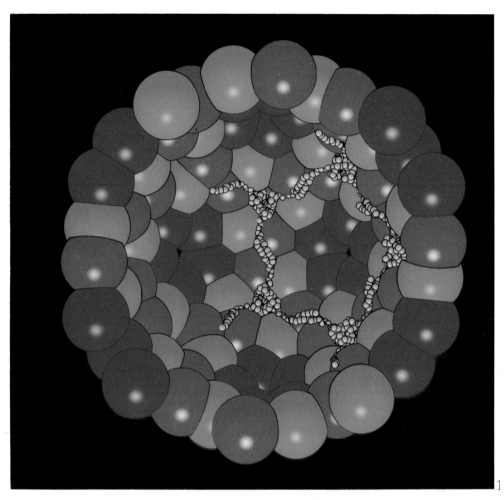

△ ▷ Molecular modelling 3
Nelson Max's spectacular models were constructed on the Cray-1
1 Six DNA base pairs, with the drug ethidium bromide added
2 Twenty RNA (ribonucleic acid) base pairs

Nelson Max, Lawrence Livermore Laboratory, Livermore, California

In this field, Nelson Max at Lawrence Livermore Laboratories has laid the groundwork for real-time molecular modelling using raster techniques, although at the time of writing the high-resolution images still have to be scanned on to film, one frame at a time. Max's models, produced on the massive Cray-1 computer, are among the most striking of all computer-generated images. Their complexity is equalled by their clarity: surely a breakthrough for molecular biology.

This first example of scientific graphics applications shows an aspect of representation that is of great importance to present-day science: the dynamic model. Processes in nature are not properly represented by static illustrations, nor are they accurately reflected in merely mechanical models. Molecular modelling, although only one branch of scientific enquiry, demonstrates that the manipulation of images by a computer is an effective means of describing the interactions of structures. It is very possible that this increased ability will lead to a greater theoretical understanding.

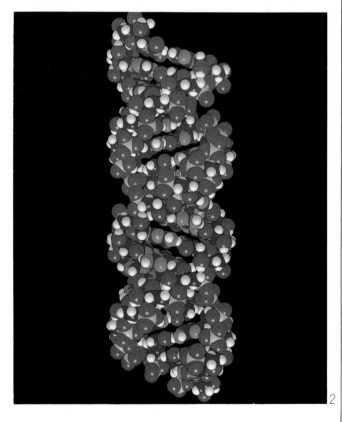

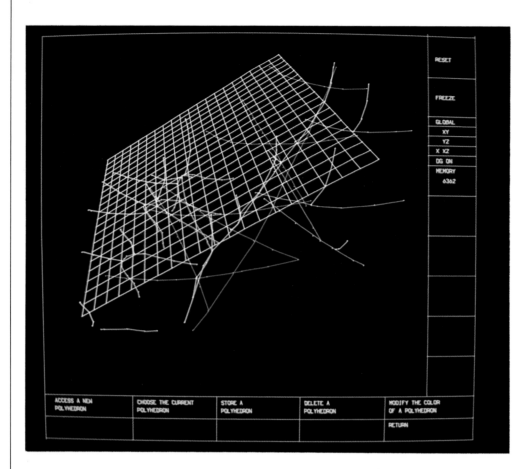

RESET

FREEZE

GLOBAL
XY
YZ
X XZ
DG ON
MEMORY
6362

| ACCESS A NEW POLYHEDRON | CHOOSE THE CURRENT POLYHEDRON | STORE A POLYHEDRON | DELETE A POLYHEDRON | MODIFY THE COLOR OF A POLYHEDRON |
| | | | | RETURN |

◁ **Seismic data analysis**
In this picture, taken directly from the colour shadow-mask display of the Multi Picture System II, fault lines are depicted beneath a grid that represents the Earth's surface. Colour is used to identify lines on a common fault plane

Evans & Sutherland, Salt Lake City, Utah

Cartography

Itself a form of representation, cartography is an example of a science that needed computer graphics techniques long before they became available. One of the tasks of a cartographer is to take a curved surface such as that of the Earth and represent it on a flat surface. In mathematical terms this is a translation from non-Euclidean to conventional Euclidean geometry, and it is not easily achieved without complex projections. Yet computer graphics can perform the transformation with relative ease, and at great speed, once the system has been programmed to do it.

A particular graphics application in cartography is the display of information by making contour maps. Contour lines on a relief map connect points of equal elevation. Conventionally, they are drawn as though seen directly from above. One continuous loop lies inside another. But if you imagine the viewpoint shifting to one side, so that the surface is seen at an angle, the effect becomes one of viewing a three-dimensional 'landscape' marked with horizontal bands. When the viewpoint moves a full 90 degrees from its original overhead position, the loops of the contours should vanish completely, leaving a series of horizontal lines representing a cross-section of the territory.

This kind of manipulation of contour maps can be done with computer graphics. Consequently, the contour map can be used to generate vivid perspective views of a region suitable for displaying a whole range of geographical information. Statistics can be given an immediate geographical framework by relating them to computer-generated maps. Not only the height of the land, but also levels illustrating statistics of the eating and drinking, breeding or buying habits of the world's population can be displayed in contours using computer graphics techniques.

One enormous advantage common to all computer mapmaking is that a master map of an area, stored in the memory, can be used as the basis of any number of maps, at any scale and showing any selection of features for any purpose. The type and position of a feature – contour, telephone box, underground pipe or property boundary – are recorded in digital form for instant recall.

Maps were once made only from data collected by surveying and measurement. More recently they have been constructed directly from photographs. The process of turning a photograph into a map is called photogrammetry: a technique in which stereo views of a terrain are used as a basis for making a two-dimensional contour map. One refinement of the technique is to take account of the distortions in the original photographic images. These are caused by tiny imperfections in the lenses of the stereoscopic cameras. Only a computer can work at this level of detail.

The images are converted to digital data. Corrections for lens distortions can then be carried out by the computer

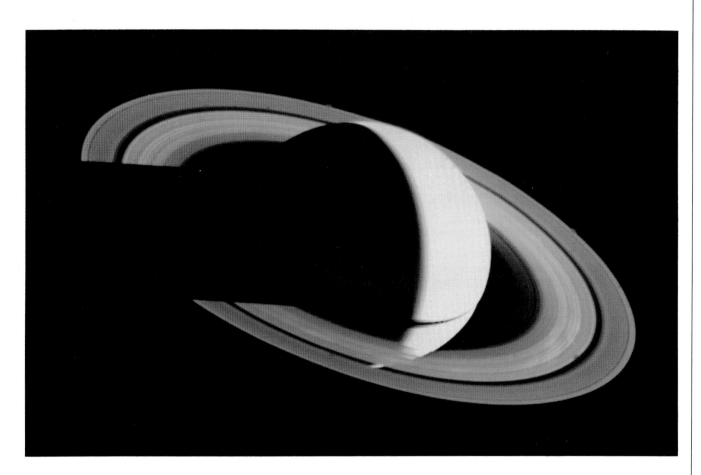

automatically. With the appropriate programming it can also perform many other enhancements to the images, such as sharpening their edge definition and removing unwanted 'noise'. Collectively, these techniques are called *image processing*, and their application is by no means limited to making maps of the Earth.

Image processing

Image processing technology has been instrumental in handling and interpreting the data sent back by the space probes, ever since Mariner 4 was launched in 1964 with an all-digital imaging system aboard. The lunar and planetary missions conducted by NASA over the past 20 years have opened up a vast new geographical territory that can be mapped only by *remote sensing*.

Mariner 9 was the first spacecraft to be placed in orbit around another planet. From Mars, it sent back over 7000 images during its operational period. But the orbiting of a planet is not always a scheduled part of the voyage. If a spacecraft simply passes in the vicinity of a planet, digital cameras will capture a wide-angle scan of the surface. This alternative technique was used in Mariner 10 when its trajectory carried it past Venus and Mercury. In these and in all other cases the images are scanned line by line for transmission back to Earth. Colour pictures involve the use of three colour filters, each picture being scanned separately.

△ **Image processing 1**
This backward glance at Saturn was taken by Voyager 1 on 16 November 1980, after it passed the planet on its voyage through space. Digital data were interpreted to produce this striking image, in which a portion of Saturn's rings is obscured by the planet's shadow. Voyager 1 continues its journey, and will reach true interstellar space (beyond the solar system) in 1990. It is travelling in the direction of the constellation Ophiuchus

Jet Propulsion Laboratory, Pasadena, California

Ten years after Mariner 4, the Viking missions to Mars returned an astonishing volume of data. Every single image from the Viking orbiter (and in all there were over 100,000 images sent back) contained as much data, measured in bits, as had been returned by the entire Mariner 4 mission. During the intervening years many advances in image processing had been made, and the capacity to process data had grown to meet the demand. This was chiefly the result of experience gained closer to home with earth-orbiting systems.

The first LANDSAT earth-orbiting spacecraft was launched in 1972 and remained operational until 1978. LANDSATS 2 and 3 followed, together with SEASAT in the late 1970s. A number of weather satellites, TIROS and NIMBUS, and the GEOS synchronous satellites have provided data on a daily basis for weather forecasting, while other (less publicized) spacecraft return information for military applications.

Image acquisition from spacecraft is carried out by *digital imaging sensors*. There are many types of these remote sensing systems currently being used in space. Those that have *vidicon tubes* project the image on to a photosensitive surface where it produces a small buildup of electric charge. An electron beam scans it line by line, and fluctuations in the electron beam current indicate the light intensity of the image. *Facsimile systems* scan the external scene line by line, using a scanning mirror that sends the image to light-sensitive diodes in the base of the camera system. Thirdly, *charge-coupled devices* are becoming widely used in remote sensing. These consist of arrays of cells that accumulate electric charges proportional to incident light when exposed directly (but via an optic system) to an illuminated scene.

All of these remote sensing systems acquire digital data in one or more regions of the electromagnetic spectrum. *Multispectral imaging* can acquire data in spectral bands to which the human eye is insensitive. But whether the system senses in the ultraviolet, infrared, microwave or X-ray regions, the output data are of the same general type, and represent the image as a two-dimensional array of numbers. In other words, remote sensing provides data for image processing that can be manipulated on raster displays.

The overall quality of the images before processing is dependent upon the number of pixels that resolve them (*spatial resolution*), and the number of bits per pixel that are available to indicate intensity values (*radiometric resolution*). Deep in outer space, the optic system delivers an analog image which is sampled by the sensor, giving a fixed number of discrete values. In order that the desired spatial resolution is attained, sampling must be performed at twice the frequency of interest. For example, if you want to see images

1

as small as 0.2 mm in the focal plane, you would have to sample at every 0.1 mm for them to appear in the digital data. If you then want to see the brightness and colour of the images, you must allow enough bits per pixel to describe them. Three bits per picture element can indicate seven discrete levels of intensity; eight bits can indicate 256 levels. There is, however, a trade-off between the size of the pixel array transmitted from space and the number of spectral bands that can be accommodated. Spectral, spatial, and radiometric resolution are the three parameters of remote sensing. When all three are set at a high level, it can take a very long time to transmit each picture.

Once the image data have been received, processing begins. Computer graphics techniques are applied with the aim of improving the images or adapting them to specific applications. The techniques fall into two categories: *subjective* processing and *quantitative* processing.

Subjective processing is a trial and error technique carried out with interactive displays, and involving the subjective judgment of the operator. Images can be greatly changed by subjective processing, and to the untrained eye may seem to bear little resemblance to the originals. The contrast range may be extended; contours may be introduced by a technique known as *bit clipping*, breaking up the picture into

◁ ▽ **Image processing 2**
The pictures transmitted from deep in space are not photographs but digital images. They have to be assembled back on Earth by interpreting the digital data.
A vidicon camera aboard Voyager 1 was the imaging system used in collecting data for these pictures of Jupiter's Great Red Spot. The distance on the planet's surface from top to bottom in both pictures is 24,000 km (15,000 miles). The Great Red Spot, a huge storm system on Jupiter, is nearly three times as big as the Earth. Although the individual pixels comprising the images are too small to be seen, each one has been allocated a digital intensity value, ranging from 0 (representing black) to 255 (representing white). Colour is obtained by passing the input image through three (or more) spectral filters, thus separating it into its spectral components. Each component is digitized separately
1 The image is assembled, and the end result is a realistic picture that is a close approximation to what an astronaut might see from an orbiting spacecraft
2 The picture has been manipulated using image processing techniques in order to bring out details that would not otherwise be seen. Here the shapes of the cloud formations have been enhanced by exaggerating some of the colours

Jet Propulsion Laboratory, Pasadena, California

2

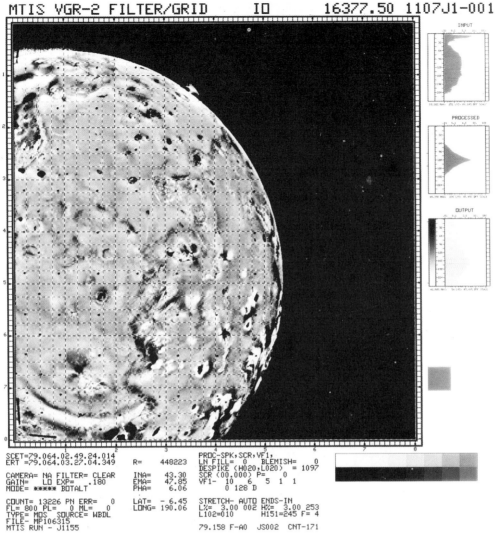

MTIS VGR-2 FILTER/GRID   IO   16377.50 1107J1-001

INPUT

PROCESSED

OUTPUT

SCET=79.064.02.49.24.014   PROC-SPK,SCR,VF1,
ERT =79.064.03.27.04.349   R= 448223   LN FILL= 0 BLEMISH=   0
                                  DESPIKE (H020,L020) = 1097
CAMERA= NA FILTER= CLEAR   INA= 43.30   SCR (00.000) P=   0
GAIN= LO EXP= .180   EMA= 47.85   VF1- 10   6   5 1 1
MODE= ***** BOTALT   PHA= 6.06   0 128 D

COUNT= 13226 PN ERR=   0   LAT= - 6.45   STRETCH- AUTO ENDS-IN
FL= 800 PL=   0 ML=   0   LONG= 190.06   L%= 3.00 002 H%= 3.00 253
TYPE= MOS SOURCE= WBDL   L102=010   H151=245 F= 4
FILE- MP106315
MTIS RUN - J1155   79.158 F-A0   JS002 CNT-171

△ Image histograms

To the right of this image of Io (one of Jupiter's moons) are examples of image histograms of the kind that are frequently used in image processing.

The top ('input') histogram shows the normal distribution of digitized intensity within the image. Below it is a graphic representation of the contrast variation being introduced by the operator. The third histogram, labelled 'output', indicates the adjusted contrast range. In the image itself we can clearly see a volcanic eruption, silhouetted against the blackness of space

Jet Propulsion Laboratory, Pasadena, California

several subregions, each containing a complete intensity range from black to white; *filtering* techniques can separate high-frequency contrast components of the image, showing local variations as opposed to gradual transitions; *bit slicing* can isolate particular intensity levels within an image; *false colour* can be introduced so that more than the (approximately) 32 discrete grey levels resolvable by the human eye can be seen; *colour compositing* can merge, for instance, gravity-field and elevation data into a single colour picture; *image ratioing* uses colour to reveal small variations in a multispectral image.

The operator is helped in the interactive tasks of subjective enhancement and analysis by the use of *image histograms*. These are graphic representations that show the distribution of digitized intensity in each image. The number of intensity levels (0–255, for example) are shown in the horizontal axis, plotted against the number of pixels at a given intensity. This reveals the range of intensity levels within which the operator can most usefully apply enhancement techniques to distingush between levels, and thus extract the maximum of information.

◁ **Remote sensing**

The LANDSAT-D Earth orbiting satellites contain thematic mappers developed at the Santa Barbara Research Center of Hughes Aircraft Company. Orbiting the Earth every 100 minutes at a height of 681 km (423 miles), the remote sensor scans a swath 185 km (115 miles) wide. NASA's Goddard Space Flight Center, in Maryland, processes over 100 scenes a day from LANDSAT-D, each of which shows 34 250 sq km (13,225 sq miles) of territory. Ground resolution in these images is fixed at 30 × 30 m (33 × 33 yd) pixels.

Data are received and recorded on high-density tape, before being corrected for geometric and radiometric distortion. Image processing techniques, such as these, help to reveal much greater detail than would be obtained by direct photography. Final output is laser-scanned film. The image shown here is of Chesapeake Bay, on the East Coast of the USA, captured by LANDSAT-4. Colour is not realistic, but has been varied to clarify the differences between urban (light blue) and rural (red) areas. Since the thematic mapper obtains values for each of seven spectral bands, many such variations are possible.

In the picture, Baltimore is visible at top centre, with Washington DC at centre left. If you compare the picture with a street-map of Washington, you can soon distinguish features such as the Capitol Building, the Pentagon or the Lincoln Memorial

United States Department of the Interior, Geological Survey, EROS Data Center, Sioux Falls, South Dakota

Quantitative image processing is generally non-interactive and relies on preprogrammed routines that are based on mathematical models. The correction of lens distortion and cartographic projection (mentioned above) are two examples, but there are many others. One of the most important is called *multispectral classification*. In this technique the spectral components of the image can be classified precisely – revealing, for example, the types of vegetation on the surface of the Earth or the mineral deposits on Mars. Each individual pixel can be colour coded so that it will be displayed as a specific colour after it has been assigned a category by the computer. In this way *thematic maps* are produced, showing large areas of land in artificial colours, with blue for water, red for urban areas, etc. They have become familiar from LANDSAT imagery.

The technology of digital image processing is helping researchers in many branches of science. For the geologist it provides a new tool for determining the composition of the Earth's crust. For the forester it indicates the types and distribution of forest cover over relatively inaccessible areas of the Earth. And for the agricultural scientist it shows the different types of land use and alerts him to any sudden changes caused by fluctuations in global weather patterns.

Equally important, image processing is a source of new technology for many other computer graphics users. A technique developed for enhancing images for scientific purposes may very well have an application in graphic design, animation, or any one of the applications being surveyed in this book. It has prompted the development of high-quality electronic imaging, bringing raster displays to the forefront of graphics technology.

Medical sciences

The applications of computer graphics in medicine are no less varied than those in other sciences. Three of them are given here as examples: CAT scanning, chromosome karyotyping and surgical planning.

The CAT scanner is universally known as an important diagnostic tool. CAT stands for *computerized axial tomography*. Its function is to construct enhanced three-dimensional images of the human body, or parts of the body. There are now systems that work on several different principles, some of them using X-rays to see through organic tissue, others using *ultrasound*: high-frequency sound signals. In either of these methods, beams are directed through the body from multiple directions in a scanning motion, typically by rotating a scanning head around the patient. The result is not a normal image but a highly complex sequence of digital information relating to time as well as position. From this information the computer constructs an image of the cross section of the part of the body scanned – as opposed to the view through it obtained by conventional methods. Of the computer graphics techniques that are employed, geometric transformations, colour manipulation, edge detection and image enhancement are among the most significant.

One example of how the CAT scanner has changed medical diagnosis is in the detection of senility. When a physician is called upon to decide if a patient is suffering from a form of dementia (the clinical term for such a condition) he must discover whether there is a loss of brain cells, resulting in atrophy and a corresponding increase in the size of the brain's ventricles (internal cavities). By making a visual comparison between the ventricular size of the patient's brain with that of a healthy person of a similar age, the physician can determine whether senility is present.

Before computer graphics in the form of CAT scanning was available, the only method of discovering the size of the ventricles was by subjecting the patient to a painful test. This previous technique was called pneumoencephalography, which, as its name suggests, consisted of the injection of air into the brain's ventricles. Air displaced the heavier cerebrospinal fluid in the top portion of each ventricle. But to see the lower portion, the patient had to be physically turned upside

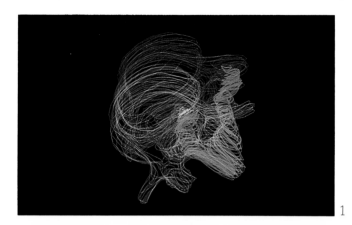

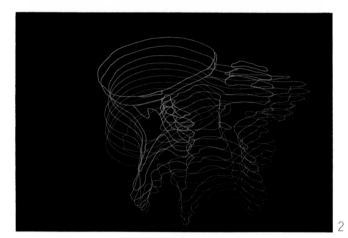

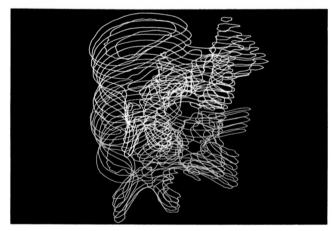

1
2
3

down. The unfortunate person would be left in this position for up to half an hour. Now CAT scanning has replaced this older and somewhat barbaric method.

A second medical application for computer graphics is in the process known as *chromosome karyotyping*. Here, the analysis of chromosome samples gives some vital clues in the detection of disease and genetic defects. This can be done by using some of the pattern-recognition techniques of image processing.

First, a microscope photograph of the chromosomes is taken, and the resulting image is converted to digital format.

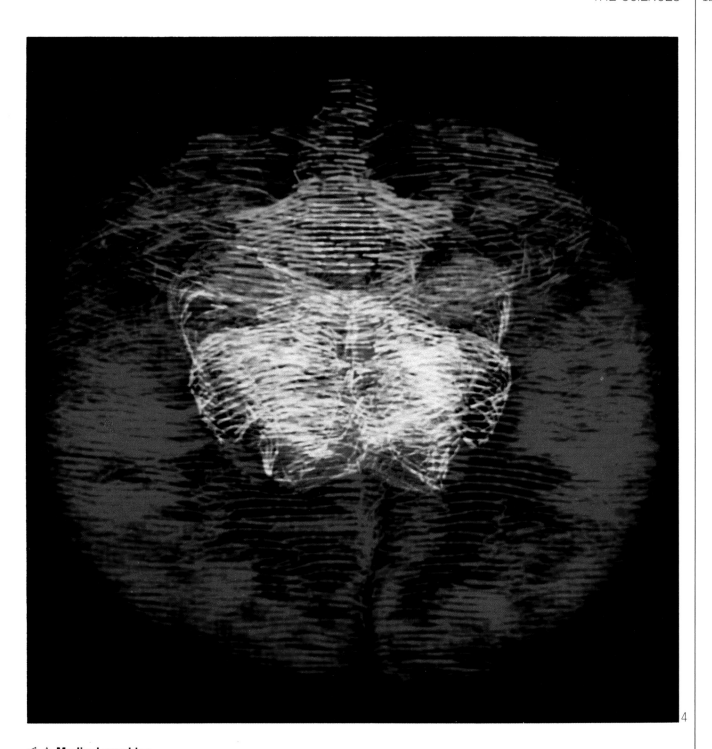

4

◁ △ **Medical graphics**
As a diagnostic tool, computer graphics is now prominent in many
branches of medicine. Its ability to show complex structures in three
dimensions makes it invaluable to doctors and researchers
1–3 Lumbar vertebrae models, made by Dr Steiner
4 A direct frontal perspective of the human brain, showing the
cerebellum, brain stem, cerebral cortex, ventricles and basal ganglia.
Colour filters were used in photographing the image from the E & S
Picture System II monochromatic display

1–3 *Digital Effects, Inc., New York, New York, and Rutgers Medical*
School, New Brunswick, New Jersey
4 *Evans & Sutherland, Salt Lake City, Utah, and University of California,*
San Diego, California

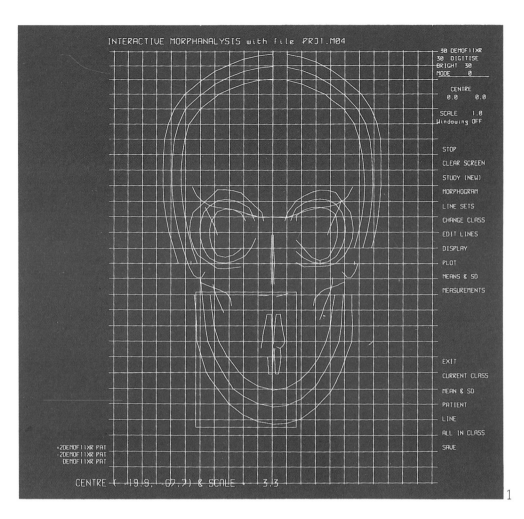

Each chromosome can then be isolated as an individual object. The previously 'confused' image is thus converted to a 'clear' computer graphic image. Once this stage has been completed, comparisons can be made with a data base of standard chromosome shapes, and the classification of the samples performed automatically. Not only does the technique save time in diagnosis, it performs the task more accurately than can be achieved using human judgment unaided by computation.

The third application of computer graphics in medicine to be included here is in *surgical planning*. When a surgeon performs a delicate operation, such as the correction of a skull deformity, he must know in advance exactly what he intends to do. While he can rely upon X-rays and CAT scans to show him what material he must deal with, these pictures do not give any indication of what may be the consequences of surgery. Ideally, the surgeon needs a three-dimensional model of the skull as it is before – and as it will be after – the operation. This can be done by using the interactive modelling techniques that are commonly employed in computer-aided design.

Computer graphics in pre-surgical planning has been used at the University of Manchester in England, and at the Washington University Medical Center in the United States. In the second instance, surgeons entered information derived from CAT scans into a standard CAD system at the McDonnell Douglas Aircraft Corporation, in order to produce a three-dimensional image of a baby's skull. The baby in question was suffering from an irregular growth pattern, the left side of her skull being normal but the right side growing at a slower rate.

The cerebral cortex of the human brain grows rapidly during the first three years of life. Plates of the skull move apart to accommodate the growth. In this case the surgeon had already decided to loosen the area where the seams between plates had prematurely fused. But when he saw the three-dimensional computer model he realized that by making an additional bone graft he could achieve a more symmetrical result.

The manipulation of visual data prior to surgery can be carried out interactively on a graphics display. Values are given to the differences in tissue density, and these can be indicated on the screen in different colours. One structure can be superimposed on another. A part of the body can be seen from all angles, and transformations of the model can simulate the removal or addition of tissue.

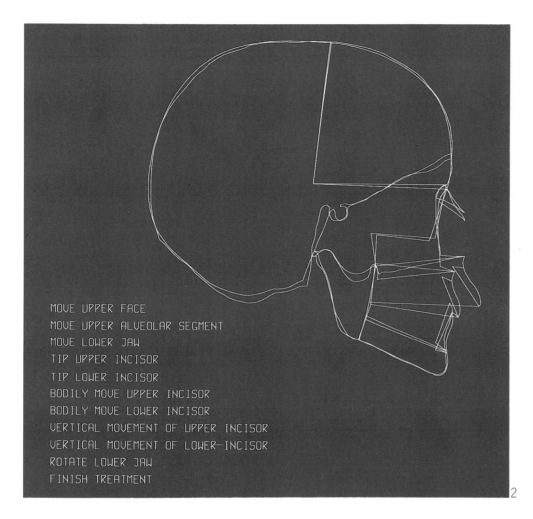

```
MOVE UPPER FACE
MOVE UPPER ALVEOLAR SEGMENT
MOVE LOWER JAW
TIP UPPER INCISOR
TIP LOWER INCISOR
BODILY MOVE UPPER INCISOR
BODILY MOVE LOWER INCISOR
VERTICAL MOVEMENT OF UPPER INCISOR
VERTICAL MOVEMENT OF LOWER INCISOR
ROTATE LOWER JAW
FINISH TREATMENT
```
2

All of these techniques will eventually become an integral part of pre-surgical practice in hospitals. It is another example of how computer graphics can assist in making judgments before any irrevocable action is taken.

The changing nature of science

In an essay, 'The Discovery of Form', Dr Jacob Bronowski made the point that moden science is no longer chiefly a search for numerical measurements, but is more concerned with topological relationships. Having discovered many of the component parts of matter, scientists are now engaged in modelling the structures that are formed by them.

To this end (or to this beginning) computer graphics is proving to be a central tool. It has greatly extended the uses of photography; has enabled large amounts of data to be formatted into convenient visual imagery; has reinstated geometry to its position of eminence; and has brought time-saving techniques to a whole range of disciplines. Above all, it is helping science move from its analytic phase, when it considered the external world as functioning on merely mechanical principles, to a phase of synthesis which is bringing with it much greater understanding of the complex structures and systems of the universe.

◁ △ **Anatomy and orthodontics**
The Computer Graphics Unit at Manchester University is a graphics resource centre for researchers in such diverse disciplines as physics, geology, archaeology and medicine
1 In this morphanalytic investigation of cranial deformities, carried out by the anatomy department, outlines are digitized from X-ray photographs of patients. These are then analysed with the aid of a vector display. The picture shows three outlines: the mean and +2 and −2 standard deviations from the mean for a front view of twenty patients
2 The orthodontics department has developed software that can help create a treatment plan for a patient. After a patient's skull has been X-rayed and digitized it is displayed on the screen along with a mean skull, obtained by averaging over many X-rays of persons of the same sex and similar age. The program also permits a simulation of the treatment a dentist may undertake. At the bottom left of the plot a list shows the options. When a suitable treatment plan has been formulated it may be saved for subsequent comparison with another X-ray of the same patient

Manchester University, Manchester, England

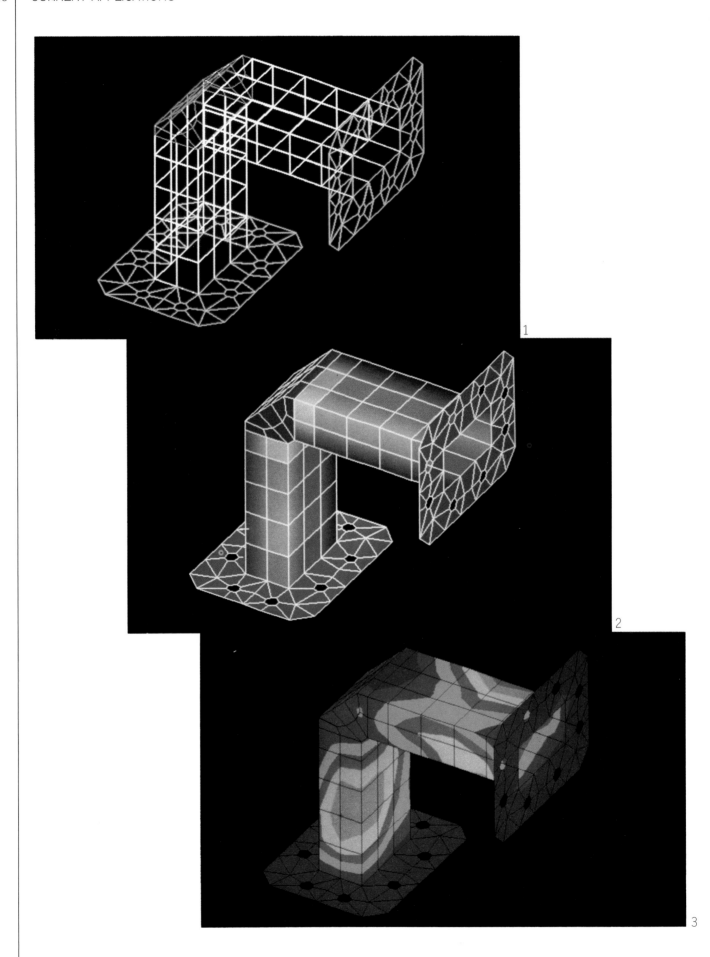

1

2

3

INDUSTRY

Computer graphics is a central factor in what has become known as the Second Industrial Revolution. After its introduction in the 1960s, graphics technology first found a ready acceptance in electronic engineering. The techniques then spread rapidly to other areas, offering benefits not only to the designer at his drawing board but also to the operators of industrial processes. Graphics displays showing the status of complex equipment in oil refineries and chemical plants soon began to take the place of more conventional instrumentation. In factories and power stations throughout the world, the dial was giving way to the video screen.

Industrial applications can therefore be clearly divided between these passive and interactive uses. Whereas designing a product with a computer requires interaction between the designer and the system, the monitoring of industrial machinery is a passive role for the graphics display. It performs this role with great efficiency throughout industry, providing information that can be read at a glance by technicians. For manufacturers the sale of such displays represents a significant proportion of their turnover. But for industry as a whole it is the introduction of interactive graphics that has had the more far-reaching implications.

CAD and CAM

In mechanical and electronic design, the use of computer graphics comes within the scope of CAD, computer-aided design. In manufacturing, where numerical control machinery has been operating for some time, the computer has given birth to CAM, computer-aided manufacturing. If one puts these two activities together, the result is either CAD/CAM or

◁ **Structural analysis 1**
Engineers build finite-element models to determine the distribution of stresses in physical structures. By using computer graphics techniques an engineer can display the results of analysis with greater clarity. For example, colour-coding those parts of a model exhibiting specified ranges of stress gives an immediate picture of structural characteristics. These images of a waveform antenna were produced with SUPERTAB software
1 Early stage in the modelling, without hidden-line removal
2 Surfaces indicated by colour and hidden surfaces removed
3 Output display of analysis results

General Electric CAE International, Inc., Milford, Ohio

CADCAM (that is, with or without the 'slash') depending upon how optimistic one is about the potential for integrating the new technologies.

In reality, CADCAM is still barely more than a dream in the eye of the visionary industrialist. It implies the full-scale introduction of robotics in all the manufacturing processes needed for a given set of products. In its purest form, CADCAM would consist of a designer and a 'black box' factory — in the engineer's sense of 'black box', a device which produces a certain result without one having to take any account of its internal workings. Raw materials would be put in at one end, along with computer designs for a new product. Finished products would come out at the other end, neatly packed and ready to ship. It is an attractive idea.

Some progress has been made towards turning this dream into reality. New products, for instance, must be tried and tested before being put into production. But with computer simulations even the need for prototypes is obviated. A design can be put through its paces on the computer and its performance accurately assessed. Realistic computer graphics can show exactly what the product, or each component of the product, will look like. The whole manufacturing process can itself be analysed on the computer, thereby ensuring that each stage of production is coordinated with every other stage. Integration is gradually taking place, and there is no theoretical reason why CADCAM should not become a reality in the near future.

In present-day industry, computer-aided design is conventionally grouped into four functional categories. These are: *geometric modelling, engineering analysis, kinematics* and *automated drafting.*

Among experts, there is some argument over these categories, and it is often claimed that CAD itself is chiefly limited to automated drafting alone. Certainly, the mechanical drawing of plans forms a major part of the CAD industry, as does the mechanical drawing of 'as-builts', a term that refers to drawings describing a finished construction after all modifications. But CAD is also linked closely to the other function areas where computers now play a major role. As David Evans has said: 'Graphics are the clustered models — the communications links between people and a model.'

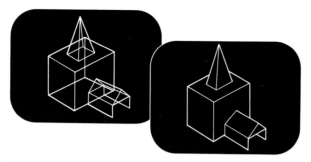

△ Hidden-line removal

By applying special computer algorithms, the user can automatically remove hidden lines: shown in the left-hand diagram is a complete wireframe model; to the right, the hidden lines have been removed

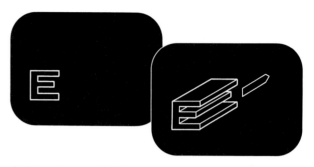

△ Extrusion modelling

Three-dimensional objects of consistent cross-section can be created by extending or *extruding* the two-dimensional wireframe image into the next dimension

Geometric modelling

The industrial designer uses an interactive graphics system to construct a *geometric model*, representing the size and shape of the object to be manufactured. This model becomes a part of the application data base. Whenever the designer wants to modify it, he recalls either the whole object or a relevant detail, and makes adaptations or additions.

Objects may be defined by their edges, their surfaces or their volumes. There are thus three types of geometric model: *wireframes*, made of interconnected line segments; *surface models*, defining the entire outside geometry of the object; and *solid models*, representing the actual volume of

the object in the computer. They are listed here in an ascending order of sophistication, with solid models having been developed most recently.

Geometric models are not necessarily three-dimensional. While all of those mentioned above are indeed three-dimensional representations, models can also be two-dimensional for describing flat objects, or '2½-D' for describing parts that have a constant section, such as tubes without any side-wall details.

Wireframes are the simplest models in the three-dimensional category, but they can be very confusing. Although they show surface discontinuities they make no differentiation between inside and outside surfaces. They simply contain a network of lines: the basic skeleton of the object without *hidden-line removal*. But once the lines that would normally be hidden from view are automatically removed by a special algorithm, the surfaces are revealed by implication.

Full surface definition requires another approach, especially when curved surfaces are involved. Suppose, for example, that the designer wants to represent a turned object such as the stem of a table lamp. Not only would this

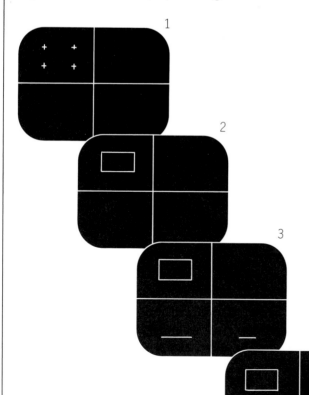

◁ Split-screen modelling

In this sequence of six steps, a simple three-dimensional wireframe model is created by the use of a split-screen display. Four screen sections simultaneously show top, front, side, and isometric views of an object under construction. The user specifies four vertices (1), and instructs the computer to draw lines between them (2). The image is then projected into the other views (3). When a third dimension is added (4), it is displayed as a wireframe in isometric projection. By specifying points above the block (5), the operator adds a sloping 'roof' to the model (6)

◁ **Ambiguity of wireframes**
Wireframe models are not always easy to read at a glance. The central box could, for example, be open at the top or at the front and back, and there are other interpretations. Hidden-line removal clarifies the designer's intentions

be difficult to do by connecting many vectors together, it would also be hard to describe the shape accurately to the computer. Both goals have to be achieved: *representation* for viewing by the user, and *description* of the object in mathematical terms. So the designer calls on a *surface-element* function, a shape-drawing routine that he will find in the menu of a typical CAD system. In this particular example, he will need a function called a 'surface of revolution'. He represents the central axis of the table lamp by drawing a line segment. Then he draws a curved line depicting the outline curved shape of the lamp's stem. By selecting the 'surface of revolution' function, the designer attaches it to the two line segments, and the vector system responds by displaying a three-dimensional image that shows the object as a network of finely-drawn lines. The called routine has interpreted the command by revolving the curved line around the straight-line axis. To the operator the resulting image looks as though it has been turned on a lathe. To the computer, it is defined as being an arbitrarily-curved object whose cross-section is always circular, though of varying diameter.

A CAD system has many of these surface-drawing functions. Indeed, the whole geometric model can be constructed from them. A simple *plane* can be defined by connecting two parallel line segments with several parallel lines at right angles to them. A *tabulated cylinder* creates a curved plane between two parallel and curved line segments. A *fillet surface* can connect two planes with a curved transition. Most widely used are the *free-form sculpted surfaces* that can both describe and represent general surface shapes, such as those required for automobile bodies. In this case, a network of *patches* displays the shape of the object. Yet the computer knows that the patches are not flat, and that points within an individual patch may be at varying distances from an adjacent plane.

△ **Techniques of solid modelling**
The object may be created by *constructive* representation (left), using solid primitives. Alternatively, with *boundary* representation (right) each surface of the object must be defined

Solid modelling is a quite different method of creating a three-dimensional geometric model. Here the designer deals with solid primitives: spheres, cones, cylinders and pyramids. The theory behind one approach to solid modelling is based on the fact that even very complex volumes can be represented by combining and subtracting these various primitive shapes.

The advantages of solid modelling have made it the subject of intensive research in recent years. For example, the mass properties of the object can be more easily calculated, and cross sections more easily taken. But the

▽ **Surface types**
In boundary representation surface types must be readily accessible. They are shown on the display as ruled lines or as patch networks, but the computer recognizes them as continuous surfaces

PLANE   TABULATED CYLINDER   FILLET SURFACE   SCULPTURED SURFACE

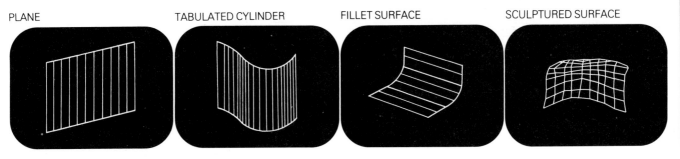

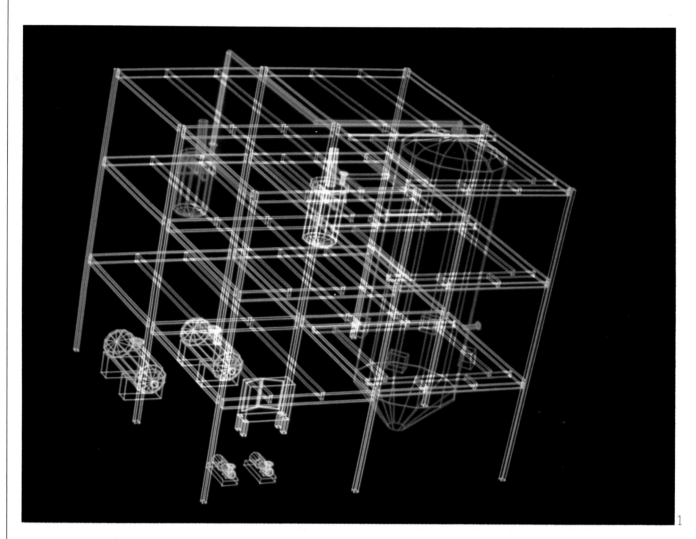

1

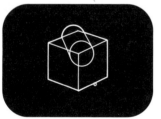

BLOCK AND CYLINDER

DIFFERENCE

INTERSECTION

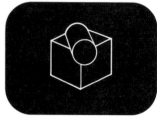

UNION

△ **Combining and subtracting basic shapes**
Complex objects can be constructed using the Boolean operations

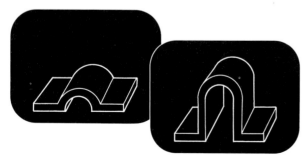

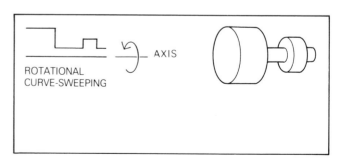

ROTATIONAL
CURVE-SWEEPING

AXIS

△ **Tweaking**
Selective distortions can be achieved by tweaking faces of a solid model.
Corrections are computed to maintain the integrity of the object

△ **Sweeping**
Adopting the lathe-turning principle, the user of a solid-modelling system can
create an object by rotating a linear shape around a central axis

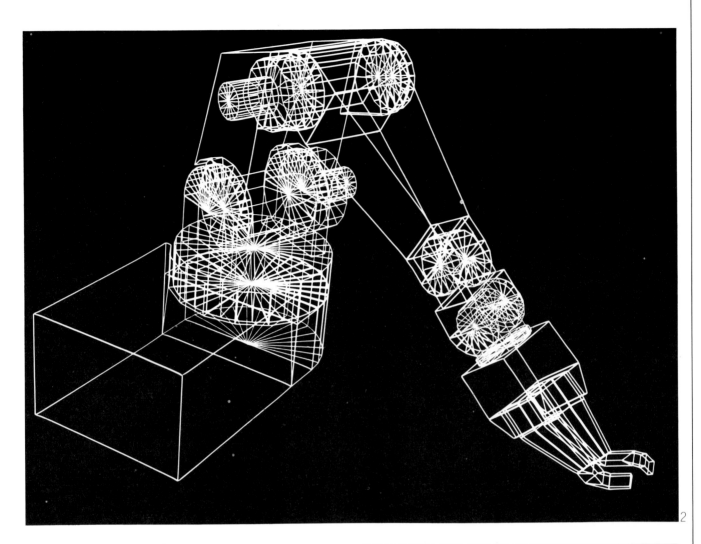

techniques require powerful processing, restricting their use – in the early days of solid modelling – to universities and large corporations. Another factor delaying their widespread adoption by industry was the need for fast high-resolution displays, without which the model cannot be represented in block colour. Once raster systems became available at greatly reduced cost, many solid modelling packages came onto the market. SYNTHAVISION is perhaps the best known, developed by the Mathematical Applications Group, Inc. (MAGI). Others are: ROMULUS, from Cambridge University, England; COMPAL, from the University of Berlin; and PADL, from the University of Rochester, New York.

Engineering analysis

Whether the geometric model is a wireframe, a surface or a solid model, its usefulness does not end when the basic design of the product has been completed. The computer design can be used in the next functional category: engineering analysis. Here the geometric model forms the basis for a *finite-element model* (FEM) for stress analysis.

The technique of analysing structures by the finite-element method is now almost universal practice in engineering. A

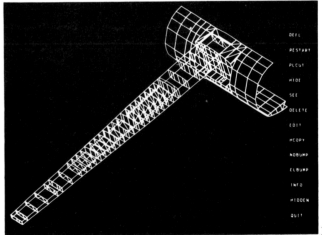

◁ △ **Computer-aided design**
1 Three-dimensional model of a chemical manufacturing facility which allows a designer to reconfigure the various components
2 Robot design displayed on the PS 300 computer graphics system
3 Lockheed C-130 Hurricane wing and fuselage (hidden lines removed)

1,2 *Evans & Sutherland, Salt Lake City, Utah*
3 *with Lockheed, Georgia*

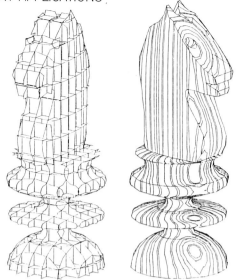

△ **Solid modelling**
Chess pieces: one shows a hypothetical structure, reduced to finite elements; the other shows the piece modelled from a simulated block of wood

Cambridge Interactive Systems, Cambridge, England

By graphically simulating stresses on the finite-element model, the engineer can actually observe their impact and take note of the results. Computer graphics techniques have made this possible. Elements can be colour coded according to their degree of deflection from a normal 'at rest' position. The colours indicate the areas of maximum stress, revealing how the structure will perform in reality, or even under stresses beyond any real ones, as when a bridge model is subjected to winds and traffic loads far in excess of those it is likely to bear, so that safety margins may be built in. Alternatively, the new FEM can be superimposed on the original model in a different colour. Any deflection in its shape, after simulated impact, can again be seen at a glance.

Yet even with computer assistance, the construction of FEMs could be a lengthy and expensive process. If every structural transition is represented by a single *node*, the mesh will be correspondingly complex. Some further methods of automating the procedures have therefore been devised.

In some cases the nodes can be derived directly from the geometric model; in others they may be automatically digitized from engineering drawings. Simplifying the mesh by using *isoparametric* elements is a widely-accepted technique. In a conventional finite-element model, nodes occur only at the corners of the shape being modelled. However, those objects that are curved require an alternative approach. Isoparametric elements have additional nodes at their midpoints, enabling the engineer to specify the stresses more accurately. He can choose from a library of elements in order to model a whole range of surface types – for example, using a shell element to represent a thin curved surface, or a bricklike element for modelling thicker material.

An isoparametric model may need only one-third as many elements as a conventional model. With the correct application of all these techniques the time-saving over manual methods can be truly spectacular. Computer-assisted finite-element modelling, with such packages as Central Data's UNISTRUC program, can reduce the time taken to build a small model from ten days to less than one hour.

structure is subdivided into its component parts, and the stresses on each component are quantified. In all structures, from wheelbarrows to suspension bridges, stresses are unevenly distributed. Some parts of the structure have to bear more strain than others, and it is these parts that particularly interest the engineer. He takes the designer's geometric model and uses it to create a *mesh* of elements with which to determine stresses, deflections (bending), centres of gravity, and other structural characteristics.

Finite elements are connected at points, called *nodes*, forming the mesh or *grid* of lines that comprise the finite-element model. Individual elements of the intricate mesh have certain deflection characteristics that can be expressed as a mathematical equation. The set of equations, when solved, will indicate the behaviour of the whole structure.

Kinematics

In computing it is a small step from analysing static designs to examining moving designs. In the function category of kinematics, CAD has found a most exciting application.

Kinematics deals with the dynamics of a model. Most products have some moving parts: a hinged flap that can easily interfere with some other component; a crankshaft that might scrape against a piece of metal housing if some last-minute modifications are made. The engineer must find ways of avoiding such errors.

The path taken when a moving component is extended throughout its range can be plotted by a computer and replayed on a display. In cases where there is a choice of

ELEMENT TYPE	LINEAR	PARABOLIC	CUBIC	LINEAR-PARABOLIC	LINEAR-CUBIC	PARABOLIC-CUBIC
AXISYMMETRIC	◇	◇	◇	◇	◇	◇
PLANE STRESS	◇	◇	◇	◇	◇	◇
FLAT PLATE	▣	▣	▣	▣	▣	▣
THIN SHELL	▣	▣	▣	▣	▣	▣
SOLID	▱	▱	▱	▱		▱

DISPLACEMENT ORDER

△ **Isoparametric elements**
Structural Dynamics Research Corporation, Milford, Ohio

ways in which the object can move, for example if a pivot can be positioned at one point or another, the engineer, interacting with the computer, can discover the optimum *motion path* by entering appropriate data through the keyboard. This is particularly useful when he has to choose between a variety of complex linkages to achieve the desired motion of the component. Again, weeks of normal work can be reduced to a few hours of computer simulation.

The uses of kinematics can be extended, once the techniques have been thoroughly mastered. Industrial designers will be able to devise products that are more compact or contain a greater number of moving parts. There are many applications for kinematics in the field of robot design, where hundreds of mechanical components and linkages are made to function within very restricted spaces.

Automated drafting

In terms of the number of users, automated drafting is the largest of the function categories. Indeed, CAD might once have stood for computer-aided drafting instead of computer-aided design. Even today, the acronym CADD (for design *and* drafting) is still sometimes used.

Automated drafting is the preparation of working drawings by pen plotters or other output devices, acting on the instructions of a computer. The output medium is normally paper or Mylar film, and the resulting *hardcopies* are used by people on the manufacturing side of industry.

Engineering drawings or 'blueprints' have always been necessary to the manufacturing process, and it was inevitable that the introduction of computers into product design should have increased the demand for hardcopy output. The computer's ability rapidly to calculate multiple views of an object and draw images of it in various projections is of great help to the manufacturer. Yet, in the long term, working drawings may disappear altogether. If CAD and CAM are to be fully integrated, all the paperwork must be eliminated.

Such a fundamental change might not be welcomed by everyone in industry, but it is thought to be within the capabilities of the new technology. By the year 2000 industry may be in transition, moving towards a time when *all* data are handled electronically. The sharp increase in the number of working drawings may be symptomatic. But until there is complete integration between designing and manufacturing, automated drafting fulfils a vital role.

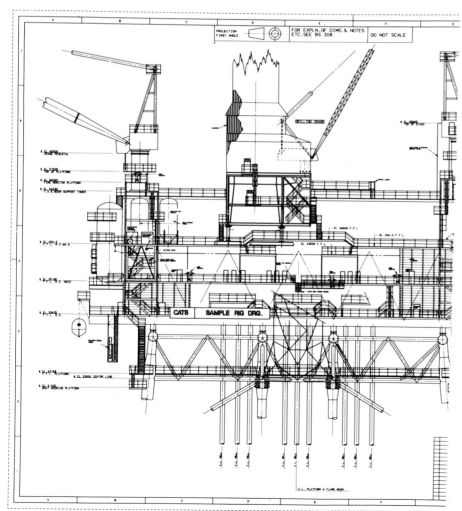

◁ **Automated drafting**
Both pen plotters and electrostatic machines are widely used in automated drafting. Shown here is a typical example: a plot produced directly from the computer by a Versatec 8236 electrostatic plotter. Although electrostatic plotting in colour (developed first by Versatec) has been available since 1983, the vast bulk of automated drafting is in black and white. Quality of drafting can be varied according to the application.
A preliminary plot preview, such as that illustrated here, is more quickly produced on an electrostatic machine. For this type of output, picture data must be rasterized: i.e. converted to data describing the picture in terms of horizontal lines. However, higher-quality pen plotting, in which 'random' lines (verticals, diagonals, etc) can be drawn with clean strokes of a pen, remains a popular technique for making final engineering documents

Versatec Electronics Limited, Newbury, Berkshire, England

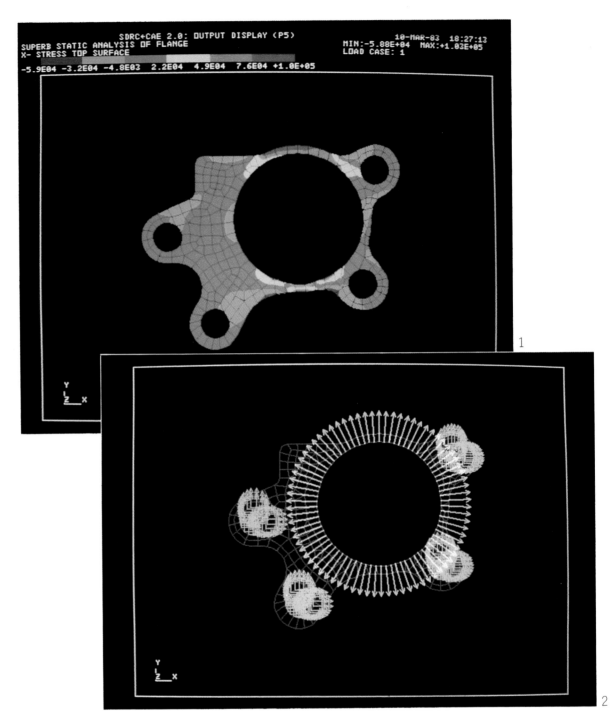

SDRC+CAE 2.0: OUTPUT DISPLAY (P5)
SUPERB STATIC ANALYSIS OF FLANGE
X- STRESS TOP SURFACE
10-MAR-83 18:27:13
MIN:-5.88E+04 MAX:+1.03E+05
LOAD CASE: 1

-5.9E04 -3.2E04 -4.8E03 2.2E04 4.9E04 7.6E04 +1.0E+05

1

2

To the human eye, computer plotter output is a far more precise representation of graphic detail than the electronic display. Plans, on paper, contain more information in a given area than even the highest resolution video screen, and offer it in more convenient and portable form. Plans are also relatively cheap to produce once the initial equipment has been installed. Consequently the working drawing will not be relinquished until computer graphics displays can equal hardcopy output in clarity, convenience and cost.

In comparison with conventional drafting by manual techniques, automated drafting is extremely fast. A new plan can be generated at approximately five times the manual speed; a second plan with revisions and changes might be produced at 25 times the manual rate. Today's draughtsman must familiarize himself with computer technology.

The pen plotter is not only faster than a human draftsman, but it performs its task of drawing plans with greater accuracy. An automated drafting system can make additions to a drawing that would normally be added by hand. For example, crosshatching can be entered in appropriate places at the touch of a button. Text and symbols may be inserted by using an 'intelligent' pen plotter that will interpret

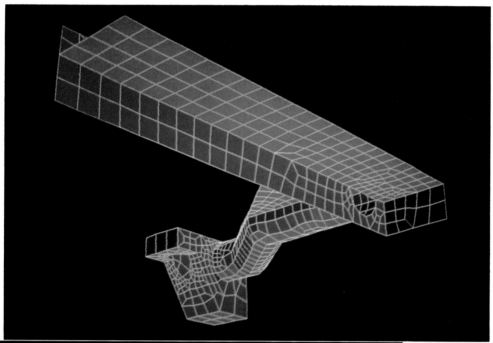

3

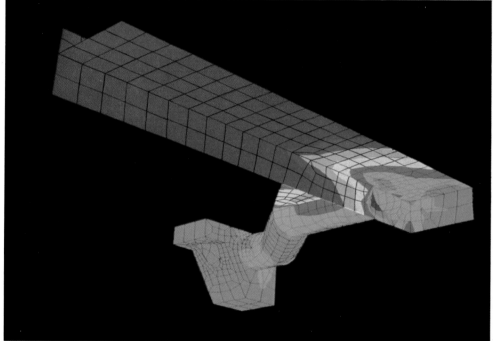

4

computer commands for these additions. Likewise, dimensional information can be added, and the images themselves can be scaled up or down at will.

Automated drafting is often the first step taken by a company on its way towards a full implementation of computer-aided design. But piecemeal introduction of computers into industry has not, over the years, always been beneficial. The full benefits of CAD will be realized only when products are conceived, parts manufactured, and assembly undertaken solely by electronically-controlled systems; and at present few manufacturers contemplate such a radical move.

◁ △ **Structural analysis 2**
Data for building a finite-element model may be taken directly from the original geometric model constructed on a CAD system by the design engineer. Subsequent work with the finite-element model tests whether a product will perform as the designer intended. Now the characteristics of the materials to be used become a key factor in the computations
1, 2 Gear housing plate, showing (1) cast and machined components, and (2) a structural analysis of the plate
3, 4 Rear axle of an automobile

General Electric CAE International, Inc., Milford, Ohio

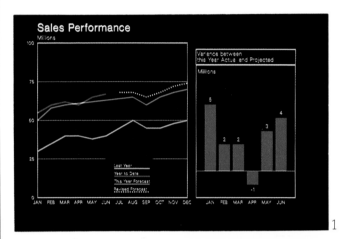

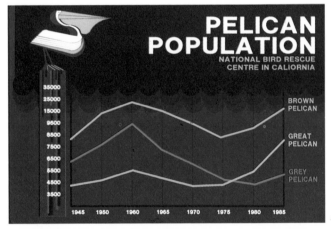

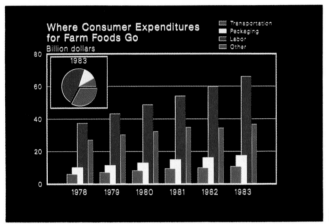

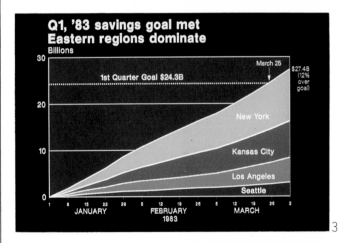

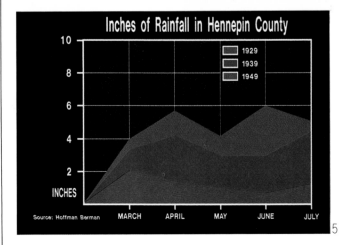

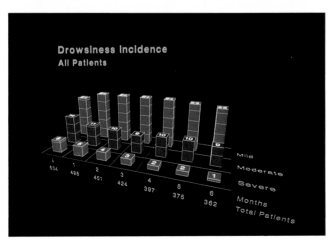

BUSINESS

An acceptance of word processing by all strata of people in business has helped to familiarize nearly everyone with the presence of computers in the office environment. This has surely paved the way for the placement of special-purpose graphics systems alongside the telephones, typewriters and other essential items of business equipment. Like word processing, the technology that enables images to be manipulated with the same facility as words has become readily accessible to the non-expert user.

The production of computer-generated images for managers and executives, for sales and marketing people, and for financial analysts, comes under the generic title of *business graphics*. It is a huge application area and, since 1980, has been the fastest-growing sector of the computer graphics industry.

At the outset it is important to make a distinction between two very different types of business graphics. Unless this distinction is drawn, any attempt at implementing graphics systems in the office will be severely hindered by a lack of clearly-defined goals. The two types are *analytical* and *presentation* graphics. They serve quite different functions within the more general context of business communications.

Analytical graphics

Each day people in business are faced with the prospect of taking decisions. Must we raise the price of product X? Should we open an office in St Louis? Can we offer a larger discount to bulk purchasers? Such questions need to be

◁ **Statistical graphics 1**
Statistics are rarely the most exciting information that we encounter, yet they are essential to business, science and industry. Although computer graphics can never guarantee to save us from drowsiness (mild, moderate or severe) when we attempt to absorb statistics, it can present the information with clarity and visual appeal

1 *Sales Performance*, Integrated Software Systems Corporation (ISSCO), San Diego, California
2 *Where Consumer Expenditures for Farm Foods Go*, ISSCO, San Diego, California
3 *QI, '83 Savings Goal Met*, ISSCO, San Diego, California
4 *Pelican Population*, Sheridan College, Ontario, Canada
5 *Rainfall in Hennepin County*, Dicomed Corporation, Minneapolis, Minnesota
6 *Drowsiness Incidence*, ISSCO, San Diego, California

answered before action is taken. They occur frequently in business. In order to answer them, managers must examine all the data relevant to each question. Consequently very large quantities of data must be available to them.

But how, and in what form, can the data be made available? Since the widespread introduction of computers to businesses the sheer quantity of facts and figures has grown exponentially. At the same time the quality of information has been slowly improved. For example, if a sales manager is considering raising the price of product X, he can run a program on the computer that will estimate the potential impact of this price increase on the sales of the product. An up-to-date list of figures could be printed out in a matter of seconds. But then the manager would have the task of examining them in a strictly linear fashion before he could draw any firm conclusions. Both the time gained by having a computer to deliver the appropriate set of data, and the precision gained by having it 'massage' the data according to predetermined routines, may easily be lost when the manager comes to evaluate the resulting information.

Increasingly, the solution to this problem is the use of *analytical graphics*. With these computer-generated images, information is given a visual format. Instead of lists of figures being the raw material upon which the manager bases his decisions, now charts and graphs will contain exactly the same information. They can be read at a glance, and they are prepared automatically by the computer. Because they provide a basis for decision making, these analytical graphics are often called *decision-support graphics*.

The method of making them may differ from conventional data processing in that the graphics display can now be permanently *on-line* to the company's financial data base, allowing even the most recently entered data to be interrogated. This interactive style of processing, so characteristic of computer graphics, can be expensive in business applications. It is not necessarily more effective than batch processing but it is undeniably more convenient. It has become very popular in the United States and has found acceptance among the larger corporations in Europe.

Instantaneous access and system flexibility are currently the most important features in decision-support graphics systems. Unless these features are available on the main-frame computer, individual managers usually build their own data bases on personal computer systems, so that, provided they are meticulous, up-to-date information is constantly at their finger tips. Analytical graphics can therefore either be grafted on to existing computer systems or introduced as a separate entity, with its own CPU and graphics workstation.

Two other general characteristics of analytical graphics are the variety of output media on which they can be placed, and their restricted area of circulation. Most of the output devices listed in 'Techniques and Hardware' (p 50) may be used for analytical graphics. But whether the computer-generated charts and graphs are reproduced electrostatically, photographically, or by some other hardcopy technology, they rarely leave a company's own offices. They are designed primarily for internal consumption.

Presentation graphics

Presentation graphics are distinguished by the wider audience for whom they are produced. They are often much more elaborate in their design, and they are usually custom-made for individual business presentations. They may be destined for audiovisual shows, company reports, or printed advertisements. Besides taking the form of conventional charts and graphs, presentation graphics may include full-blown illustrations, painted by top graphic designers using conventional or computer-aided tools. These 'high-impact' graphics are always in demand no matter how appealing their counterparts, the analytical graphics, have become. Unique and original solutions to the problems of presenting factual information are sought after, since now the elements of persuasion and aesthetic quality are considered at least as important as factual content.

Presentation graphics are primarily intended to enhance someone's reputation: either that of the company through sales, marketing or public relations, or the reputation of an individual executive who is staging a high-level presentation to senior management. They are more pictorial, more entertaining and inevitably far more expensive (on average) than analytical graphics.

Charts and graphs

Charts and graphs may be produced in high resolution and be well up to presentation quality standards, but the majority of them are in medium- or low-resolution graphics. For purposes of analysis, the visual quality of the images, while still important, is not the prime criterion. The chief concern of the programmer must be to design software in such a way that the businessman can obtain all the information he requires. The user must be able to set the parameters for each chart, calling on routines that will arrange the data into a format that is clear, readable, and appropriate to the task.

Broadly speaking, there are *five* basic chart formats: pie, column, bar, line and dot. They are not necessarily interchangeable. Information that is properly expressed by a line chart will not automatically be suited to, say, a pie chart. Selecting the correct chart type is normally the responsibility of the user, although systems can be programmed to produce a daily set of figures in a tried and tested format. A brief survey of the different formats should therefore be worth studying.

All the various types of chart and graph are concerned with making *comparisons*. Their main function is to enable the business manager to see comparisons at a glance.

Pie charts are used for showing a breakdown of component amounts that make up a total of 100 per cent. Here, the comparison is between the relative proportions of each amount.

Column charts show comparisons between quantities over a period of time. Rather than setting several 'pies' side by side, the display now shows a series of vertical columns.

Bar charts are column charts turned on their side — but normally without a timescale, since we tend to interpret the horizontal axis as representing a progression in time. The horizontal bars in a bar chart make a straightforward comparison between quantities, and they are often grouped in pairs to make a more meaningful pattern.

Line charts are most appropriate for showing trends. A whole table of figures can be reduced to a single curve in which any fluctuation will be apparent. Normally, time is in the x axis and quantity is in the y axis.

Dot charts are among the most sophisticated formats used in business graphics. Patterns emerge from them that might not otherwise be noticed. For example, individual transactions can be plotted in a sales chart in which a vertical dimension represents sales, and the horizontal axis represents the size of the discount. If there is a correlation between discount and sales volume, it will emerge from the distribution of dots on the screen.

With these five basic types of chart most of the financial data, sales figures and market trends of the commercial world can be represented. If we were to judge them solely by their aesthetic appearance they would not seem to be particularly important, nor even worthy of great attention. Yet nothing could be further from the truth. Not only is their production becoming a multi-billion dollar industry but they are also already being used in such vast quantities that their design and appearance are rapidly becoming a matter of some considerable urgency.

There cannot be any universal standardization of business graphics formats. However, the great variety of styles, shapes, line widths and colours is certainly confusing to people in business. In attending meetings and reading reports, executives are assailed by garish colours, eccentric founts, assorted

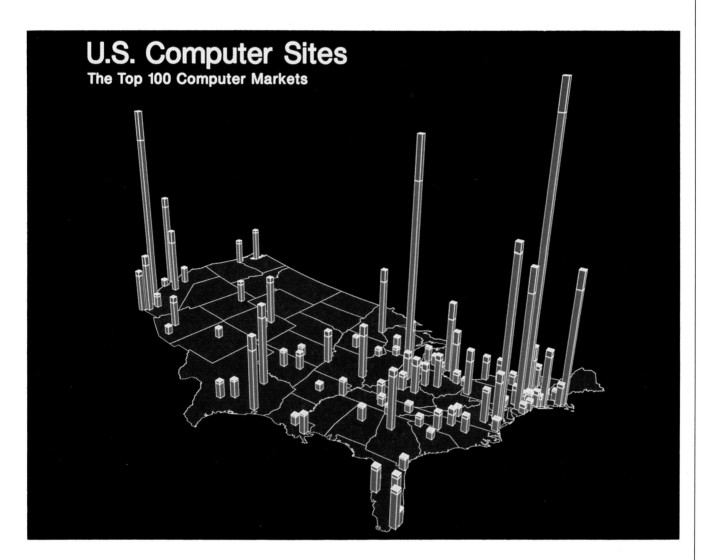

U.S. Computer Sites
The Top 100 Computer Markets

backgrounds, and (worst of all) unsuitable combinations of the different kinds of chart. It is a little like reading a newspaper that has been printed in a haphazard variety of typefaces, or laid out in different styles. While there is no immediate solution to this problem, experiment may eventually give way to habit, and business graphics may settle down to a smaller number of acceptable variations.

Production techniques

Analytical and presentation graphics may share the same display technologies, but they differ in their production techniques. The nature of analytical graphics demands special attention in production, while for presentation graphics greater attention is paid to display (see 'Display', p 141). Although simple pictorial graphics can be made on a good painting system, decision-support graphics can be produced only on systems designed for that purpose.

△ ▷ **Statistical graphics 2**
Produced with DISSPLA and TELL-A-GRAF mainframe software
Integrated Software Systems Corporation, San Diego, California

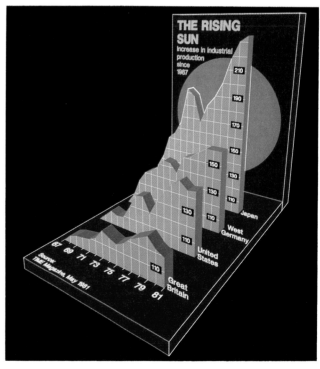

THE RISING SUN
Increase in industrial production since 1967
Source: TIME Magazine, May 1981

Analytical graphics may be generated on a mainframe computer with the addition of a suitable graphics package. For some years the market leader in this software has been ISSCO (Integrated Software Systems Corporation) of San Diego, who seized the opportunity of adding graphics capabilities to the mainframes that handle financial data in large corporations.

Long before established data processing companies realized the market potential of graphics, ISSCO brought out two packages, DISSPLA and TELL-A-GRAF, which enabled managers to obtain presentation-quality decision-support graphics from existing data bases. The second of these packages established a continuing trend towards making business graphics software easy to use by clerical and executive staff. It is worth noting that in 1977 the sophisticated TELL-A-GRAF package could run on only a mainframe costing over a million dollars, whereas the same package can now be put onto a microcomputer costing less than $10,000.

Since many people need access to the graph-making facilities of the computer, terminals are distributed throughout an organization. With 'intelligent' terminals, data can be downloaded from the mainframe to a local graphics workstation. Access to hardcopy devices is shared, with electrostatic or laser printers meeting the heaviest demands of many different users.

Alternatively, a company may take a more individual approach, with standalone systems tailored to the needs of individual departments. Keeping the production of decision-support graphics completely separate from a company's central data processing facility appeals to many managers. An extraordinary variety of standalone systems is now offered by suppliers. These fall broadly into two categories: those that are based on a general-purpose computer with graphics software, and those in which the graphics capability is built into the hardware of the system. Both will perform similar functions and both help the executive to produce decision-support graphics at what is just a mere fraction of the cost of having them drawn manually by a commercial artist.

Regardless of the system being used, the business manager expects good picture quality even in day-to-day support graphics. Many standalone systems provide only low-resolution images, and the danger is that these will find their way into company reports, audiovisual shows, and into other media where low resolution is inappropriate. Executives who use these systems may well see images such as the illustrations in this book, and ask: 'Why can't we get images like these?' But the descriptions already given of graphics displays and output devices should be sufficient to show why the highest-quality images are not necessarily available to everyone who owns a computer.

Now that the *personal computer* has become more powerful it is able to support some excellent business graphics software. Dozens of packages are available for Apple, IBM, and Commodore machines. For example, the following will all run on the IBM PC: BPS Business Graphics (Business and Professional Software); Chart-Master (Decision Resources); Graphwriter (Graphic Communications); Fast Graphs (Innovative Software); dGraph (Fox & Geller); PFS:Graph (Software Publishing Corporation); and 1-2-3 (Lotus Development Corporation).

Before investing in any graphics software, the personal computer user should compare the packages carefully. Not all will run on his machine, and there are many other points besides. For example, some programs will automatically convert from linear to logarithmic scaling of values, whereas others will not. If this is a feature that is required, the prospective user must choose accordingly. Again, a graphics program may offer a wide choice of founts, but others may be more limited. In some programs colour choices can be specified by the user; in others they are selected automatically. Although it is desirable to have as many features as possible – including automatic and manual scaling of data values, fixed and movable page positions, and the facility to vary the size of a graph – there is always a risk that the more versatile packages will be more difficult to operate. A purchaser should certainly use the software before buying it.

It is quite feasible for a business manager to become familiar with analytical graphics on a personal computer before committing his company to investing in a larger system. Many of the same facilities are available, although personal computer packages are rarely as comprehensive and will certainly not give the highest resolution. But a trial period with a smaller machine can help the manager decide whether business graphics are as beneficial as their reputation suggests. At the very least, he will be able to generate some decision-support material to help him make up his mind!

Decision-support graphics often contain highly confidential information, and must therefore be produced under controlled conditions within the office. However, presentation graphics can be supplied by an *outside service bureau*. Using a bureau is another good way of getting started with business graphics, since the financial commitment is relatively small.

In the United States the pioneer of the presentation graphics bureau has been General Electric with its Genigraphics computers. These versatile machines produce slides and other forms of hardcopy with full pictorial content and a more limited range of typographic detail. They offer an extremely high resolution (4000 lines) which is sufficient for large-screen projection. Transparencies can be designed and printed in exact register for projected sequences in which additional components of an image are added with each successive slide. A set of, say, four of these cumulative images, presented by a dual-projector unit with dissolve control, can explain a complex message that would be too condensed if it were packed onto a single slide.

Display

Both presentation and analytical graphics can be viewed directly on a VDU; placed on to hardcopy such as paper; used as visual aids in overhead projection; or interwoven into more sophisticated audiovisual presentations. A modern *presentation room* in a large corporation is equipped with:

○ Film and slide projection facilities
○ Overhead projectors
○ Video monitors, or large-screen video projection
○ Random-access slide projection
○ Computer-controlled multi-image slide-shows with play-back of synchronized soundtracks

Eventually, all of these systems may be replaced by a single flat-panel display fed with still or moving images by wholly digital means. The marriage of video to computer graphics technology is likely to produce this necessary simplification.

At the time of writing, the sector of the audiovisual industry that deals with photographic slides (and their projection) is approximately the same size as the entire computer graphics industry. By 1990 it will be dwarfed by it. As electronic displays begin to match the quality of photographic images they must eventually displace most of the electromechanical devices of slide projection. The changeover will take many years to complete, although it is expected that companies will continue to find uses for photographic slides until well into the next century.

Slides will tend to linger as a popular medium because they are reassuringly tangible, long-lasting, easily sortable, and still relatively simple to produce on familiar equipment. The lecturer or business executive, clutching his trays of speaker-support slides, can be seen at any hour of the day in New York or London as he hurries to a conference.

It might seem impossible that anything so ubiquitous as the slide could be easily replaced; yet there are other reasons for expecting it to be. In recent years computer graphics may have boosted the use of slides beyond their previous level, but the sheer quantity of images now being produced for business presentations cries out for wholly electronic methods of production and display. A large corporation may produce 100,000 slides a year, all of which require cataloguing and storage under controlled conditions. Slides have to be transported from one office to another, and from one country to another – and this is accomplished not at the speed of light but at that of a freight-handling company. Slides are easily damaged by dust, damp and heat, and they are not infrequently dropped by the executive when he hands

them over to the projectionist just before beginning his presentation.

All this could be avoided if an entire sequence of speaker-support images could be held in digital form on a small microcassette, approximately the size of an after-dinner mint – and already this is technically possible. High-quality digital images can be stored in a remarkably compact space. One thing is lacking: an effective means of displaying them on large screens. Video projection does not match the picture quality of slide projection, though a single light-beam video system may be several thousand times as expensive. Large audiences need large-screen projection: the distance between the screen and the last row of seats should not exceed eight times the height of the projected image.

Display solutions

Clearly, some guidelines are needed for finding the best solutions to the problems of displaying presentation graphics. The four variables are *room sizes, image quality, equipment availability* and *convenience.* Each one of these has to be taken into account. A businessman who travels to address a large convention carrying just a small video cassette may very well be trading-off image quality for convenience, unless first-rate facilities await him at the other end.

The following methods are usually considered suitable for audiences (and, by implication, rooms) of given sizes.

AUDIENCE SIZE	DISPLAY METHOD
500 plus	Computer-controlled xenon-lamp slide projection
250–500	Computer-controlled tungsten-lamp slide projection
20–250	Large-screen video projection
1–120	CRT video display

The value of presentation graphics

Studies have shown that the use of visuals in business presentations considerably enhances the audience's opinion of a speaker's performance. In a famous study done at the Wharton Business School student presenters played the role of marketing experts and argued opposing viewpoints, some of them using graphic assistance, others not. Those who made use of overhead projection won their point 67 per cent of the time; equally important, they were able to convince the audience in 28 per cent *less* time than those who were not using any form of visual aid.

This is an impressive endorsement of business graphics, whether or not they have been generated by a computer. A business executive now has to 'project the right image' (in more ways than one) if he is to shine on the lecture circuits.

FUTURE APPLICATIONS

This book has surveyed a cross-section of computer graphics applications. In the opening pages, a graphics expert was quoted as saying that there seems to be 'no field of human endeavour that cannot be enhanced by the application of computer graphics.' By now, Dr Diment's contention may strike the reader as being somewhat more reasonable than perhaps it appeared to be.

Yet our survey has concentrated only on the most prominent applications of computer graphics. A sceptical reader may still be compiling a long list of 'fields of human endeavour' where application of the new techniques might seem to be highly unlikely, if not impossible. What about politics, for example? Or archaeology? Or gardening? In fact two of these have begun to use computer graphics, and for the third it is only a matter of time.

Computer graphics is already playing a political role – at the very highest levels of power. The Central Intelligence Agency rarely gives a presentation to the President of the United States without the support of computer-generated analytical graphics. ISSCO mainframe software has been adapted to the purpose. Those not privy to these meetings cannot know how the graphics are used, but one could imagine that the relative strengths of overseas military commitments are more easily assessed when they are set out in visual form – and the arguments put forth are more persuasive. Thus even the balance of world power can be and, one suspects, *is* being expressed in computer graphics.

Archaeologists piecing together the fragments of past civilizations are finding that techniques of computer imaging can help them classify ancient pictographic and alphabetic symbols. At Manchester University, for example, twelfth-century Ethiopian manuscripts have been deciphered in this way. The technique is similar to that of chromosome karyotyping already described (p 122), but in this case the pattern-recognition routines are applied to identifying individual letters of a language. The letter 'A' might be written in a hundred different ways, but the computer can quickly decide whether the mark represents an 'A', or some other letter.

Gardening poses more of a problem; but it is not difficult to invent quite a plausible application, and one that might very well be used in the near future. Computer graphics is often most useful when the computer is performing non-graphical tasks in addition to generating pictures. This would be true if a gardening model were created on the computer. Growth rates of plants, local weather conditions, distributions of light and shade, seasons of the year, and type of soil would comprise the variables of the model. The graphics display would show the garden in full colour, taking into account not only the choice of plants, but also the other variables that

would influence the garden's appearance. Such a system would allow a person not only to choose flowers and shrubs that could be grown, but to visualize the effect of combining different kinds, and to preview the result of these options for any month of the year. This is a purely hypothetical application, but there is no reason why such a service should not one day become available.

Yet there is no need to search too diligently for unexpected or esoteric applications. They will all evolve naturally as computer graphics becomes familiar to a wider range of users. The medium is infinitely adaptable, and it will be applied whenever a potential benefit is perceived.

One such benefit has been found in sports training. As already mentioned, realistic simulations can help skiers and racing drivers to rehearse their races by interacting with dynamic displays. Other athletes – indeed, *all* athletes – can benefit from watching graphic analyses of their physical movements, and such techniques are already beginning to be used. For example, by viewing a 'matchstick model' derived from slow-motion photography, a discus thrower can observe the motion paths of hands, limbs, pelvis and shoulders as he tries to perfect his action. This type of graphic analysis, where all the joints of the body are pinpointed on a display, is far more revealing than slow-motion photography by itself.

The dangers of computer graphics

Rather than extend the list of applications further, it would be wise to conclude with a note of warning. Technology, by its very nature, is primarily concerned with *how* tasks are performed, not with whether they should or should not be performed in the first place. Computer graphics is no exception, and not all graphics innovations will necessarily be beneficial to society as a whole.

In particular, the introduction of computer graphics into primary education needs to be examined with great thoroughness and with a full awareness of the potential power of the medium. The outlook in this direction is threatening, not least because of a brilliant and persuasive book, *Mindstorms*, by Professor Seymour Papert of MIT (Basic Books Inc, New York, New York, 1980).

It is Professor Papert's contention that computers are not being used effectively in education. They are being used, he says, to 'program the child'. Instead of allowing a child to explore what he calls 'Mathland' (the world of mathematics) on his own, and at his own speed of discovery, computers are being made to imitate all the bad habits of conventional classroom education. They conduct didactic dialogues, posing questions and then evaluating the child's responses. Professor Papert believes that it is preferable to allow the *child* to ask the questions, and to this end he and his colleagues have devised an ultra-rational program called LOGO.

LOGO simulates a logical environment for the child to explore. It is an interactive system, with one of its central features being a graphics display that contains a picture of a small turtle. This symbol is a computational 'object-to-think-with', having the mathematical characteristics of a Euclidean point (a location with no dimension), but with the additional property of direction. It can be moved only in the direction in which it is facing.

Sitting in front of the graphics display, the child can put the turtle through its paces, making it walk around the screen to trace out various geometrical shapes. He or she soon discovers that complex and highly satisfying patterns can be generated by instructing the turtle to perform certain sequences of movements. A circle, for instance, can be made by telling the 'animal' to take one pace forward, turn a little, take another pace forward, turn a little, etc. With each step, the 'turn-a-little', if always equal, will ensure that the turtle arrives back at its starting place. However, the child also discovers that by making the 'turn-a-little' more exaggerated with each step (by adding a steady increment) he ends up with a spiral rather than a circle. Thus the child begins to acquire mathematical understanding by his own efforts.

Make no mistake, LOGO is highly effective. A more ingenious method of indoctrination can scarcely be imagined. But our new-found ability to confront a child with a completely logical environment may not be as harmless as it appears. The idea behind it is to extend the 'rapid learning years' of infancy – the years when language and perception are acquired – into later life, perhaps even throughout school and university. This, in itself, is an attractive idea – but unless the techniques of 'learning environments' are applied simultaneously to other subjects, we should be placing too great an emphasis on mathematics at the expense of alternative skills. Unwittingly, Professor Papert is programming the child by singling out mathematics (his own subject) as being the most important route to knowledge. Computer graphics, which is based on mathematics, lends itself most readily to this purpose.

Another danger, this time inherent in computer graphics, is the distance that it places between the human operator and the real world. By enhancing sight at the expense of touch we may literally be *losing touch* with reality. An extreme manifestation of this is the advent of push-button warfare, in which destruction can be inflicted by remote control. Television viewers may recall the 1981 BBC *Horizon* programme on computer graphics, which also appeared in the *Nova* series in the United States. It showed naval training exercises in which operators were taught to fire at computer images of ships. But how many viewers remember that the target being used was a representation of HMS *Sheffield*, a

ship that was actually destroyed by remote control some months after the programme was aired? It is a chilling reminder of the destructive power of technology, and of the potential role that computer graphics may play in persuading us to unleash this power.

Putting distance between ourselves and the world by relating to images may not in the long term be beneficial to us. The tools of high technology, computer graphics among them, are the most effective that have been developed. They could be used to turn most of the natural world into a wholly artificial environment. Far from being representative of a clean and non-polluting 'post-industrial' revolution, high technology may simply enhance our ability to build factories, destroy landscapes, upset delicate ecosystems, and create an urban wasteland – all at a distance and by remote control.

This is the biggest danger posed by the new techniques: the danger of substituting an artificial reality for reality itself. Whereas the manual creation of images, by drawing and painting, recreated the world according to a language of *representation*, and whereas photography, film, and television record *traces* of the real world, computer graphics enables us to *simulate* reality. It is a power that could easily be abused. Already, so-called 'photographic reality' can be simulated, as the pictures in this book amply demonstrate. Thus, a news report on television could even now easily be totally fabricated, and an expert viewer could not tell that the events depicted never took place in actuality.

Many operators of graphics systems become alarmed at the relentlessly cerebral demands of the medium. Artists, in particular, are drawn away from their primary activity – experience of the real world – and are lured into concentrating their attention on the image: on the non-reality which is now so much more easily fabricated. Just as the word processor has little to offer the serious novelist, except perhaps a measure of convenience, so the graphics system has relatively little to offer the fine artist. As Kimon Nicolaides has said: 'There is only one way to draw and that is the perfectly natural way. It has nothing to do with artifice or technique. It has nothing to do with aesthetics or conception. It has only to do with the act of correct observation, and by that I mean a physical contact with all sorts of objects through all the senses.' (*The Natural Way to Draw*, Houghton Mifflin, Boston, Massachusetts, 1969). For further discussion of the graphics computer in the fine arts see p 146.

Those traditions in the arts, continued and taught by Kimon Nicolaides, contain an approach to knowledge that is far removed from the structuralist theories of Professor Papert. Despite the almost universal application of computer graphics to 'every field of human endeavour' – indeed, *because* of it – we must try to counterbalance the illusions of technological power with a new-found reverence for natural phenomena.

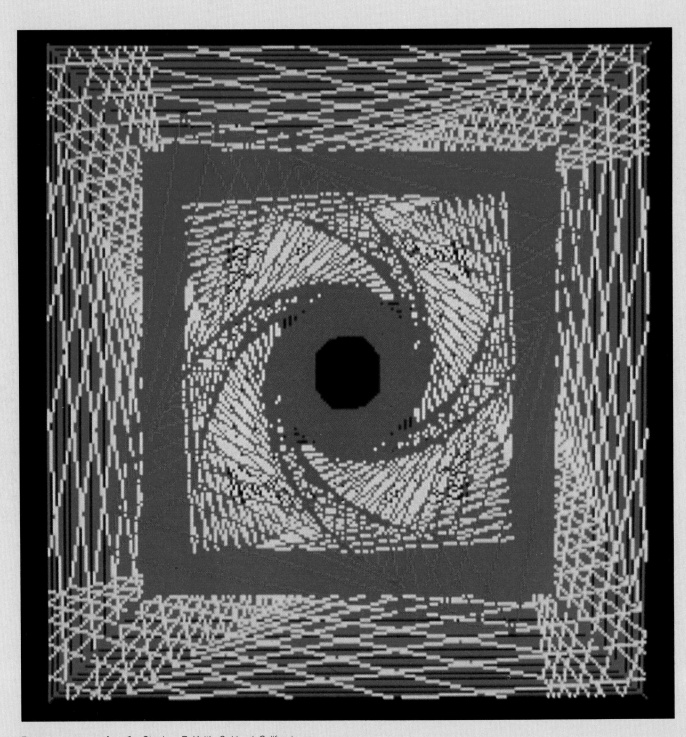

Pattern generation 1 *Stephan R. Keith, Oakland, California*

APPENDIX: COMPUTER GRAPHICS IN THE FINE ARTS

To the art historian the advent of computer-generated 'paintings' poses something of a problem. Artists who use computers will frequently claim that the electronic system is simply another tool – much like any other that would be found in their studios. Yet if this is true, there is an implication that the artist uses it merely to reveal what he has already visualized imaginatively. In fact, the computer by its very nature tends to contribute rather more to the work being created than is generally admissible in fine art. Unlike the applications of the computer in graphic design and illustration, where it is clearly the servant of the artist, in many works that have found their way into art galleries the computer has apparently become the master of the artist.

However, in the highly fragmented world of twentieth-century fine arts we have to accept that the computer offers almost unlimited opportunities for experimental activity. The search for new forms, new materials and new tools has led artists to explore many branches of technology with interesting, if not entirely convincing, results. This drive for originality may one day be seen as an expression of neurosis: an exaggeration of the individuality of artists to counterbalance the collective enterprise of science. In the meantime, several artists have made genuine efforts to come to terms with our new technology and adapt it to serve their own creative needs.

△ **Computer art 1** *Paul Jablonka, Tucson, Arizona*

▽ **Computer art 2** *Martin Kahn, Berkeley, California*

△ **Computer art 3** *Paul Jablonka, Tucson, Arizona*

▽ **Pattern generation 2** *Frank Dietrich, Chicago, Illinois*

Foremost among artists who have used the computer as a tool is John Whitney Sr, an American film maker who has gained an international reputation for his experimental animated films. Mr Whitney's work has derived largely from his desire to construct visual patterns – an equivalent to the sound patterns of music. He was also keenly aware, when he first visited Europe in the 1930s, that he wanted to make use of the tools of the twentieth century. With a conventional movie camera he tried to expand the expressive vocabulary of film, although he eventually dismissed the technique as being too mechanical for his purposes. It was unable to reproduce the dynamic patterns that he had in mind. He imagined a whole new artform in which one could manipulate abstract visual elements with the same facility and control as the composer can manipulate sound.

John Whitney Sr's quest for such an artform is significant because, in a sense, he was anticipating the techniques of computer graphics. Without the rapid evolution of computing, his efforts would have been doomed to failure. Long before dynamic graphics displays were available, he began to explore the possibilities of linking a computer to a film camera, controlling the movements of both the camera and the objects being filmed. These experiments led to the development of motion-control cinematography – techniques now prominent in the special-effects industry.

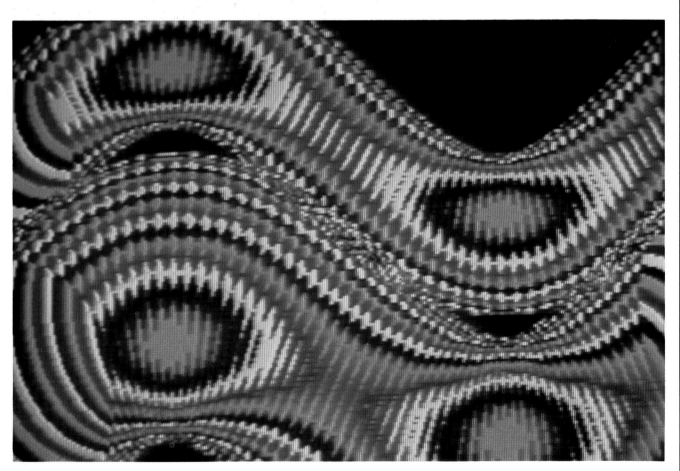

Despite the practical applications of his work, Mr Whitney's personal vision of a new artform has remained largely unfulfilled. While he has shown convincingly that geometrical progressions of dynamic patterns have certain similarities to music, he has not incontravertibly demonstrated that these compositions can stimulate our emotions as music does. Although a graphics display can provide an environment in which abstract shapes and colours can be both generated and set in motion, it is still not an instrument to be 'played upon'. The first task of an artist who wishes to make 'visual music' must be to *create* his own instrument – by programming the machine to allow a suitable range of visual effects to be accessed at will.

Hundreds of artists other than Mr Whitney have used the computer as a tool, but they have, on the whole, been less visionary in their approach. Many have tended to accept the formal tradition of art as the creation of static objects that can be displayed in a gallery or reproduced in books. For them the computer is an accessory – a drawing or painting aid – rather than the central means for both the creation and the display of their work. Indeed many artists begin using computers simply because they become fascinated by the unusual geometries and intricate patterns that can be generated. The continued popularity of abstract art has allowed such computer-assisted paintings to be gradually accepted by the art world. A few artists have even had their work displayed in major museums.

A factor that may have a negative influence on the reactions of critics and other arbiters of taste is the sheer

△ **Mathematical art**   *Kerry Jones, Huntsville, Alabama*

quantity of work that can be produced with computer assistance. Yet much of this work is not entirely lacking in recognizable 'qualities' – particularly when seen in the context of twentieth-century painting. For example, a person with little or no aesthetic sensibility, using an appropriately programmed graphics system, could easily produce paintings bearing a striking resemblance to those of, say, Piet Mondrian, the Dutch abstract painter. And furthermore, the

◁ ▷ **Art school graphics**
Sheridan College was the first major art school to offer a course on computer graphics with a properly equipped studio. These images were made by students in 1983, the first year of the studio's operation

Sheridan College, Ontario, Canada

▽ **Pattern generation 3**
An infinite variety of patterns can be generated using computer graphics. This facility is now applied to designing textiles, wallpapers and carpets – indeed to anything that bears a pattern. The examples in this section, however, were made for no specific application

Sheridan College, Ontario, Canada

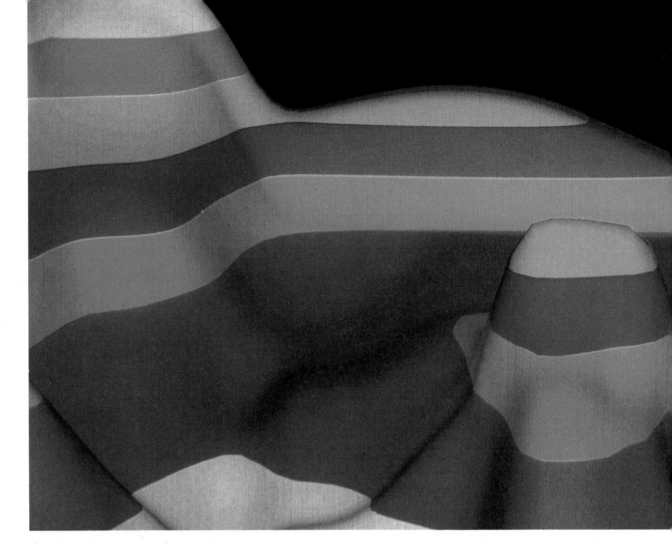

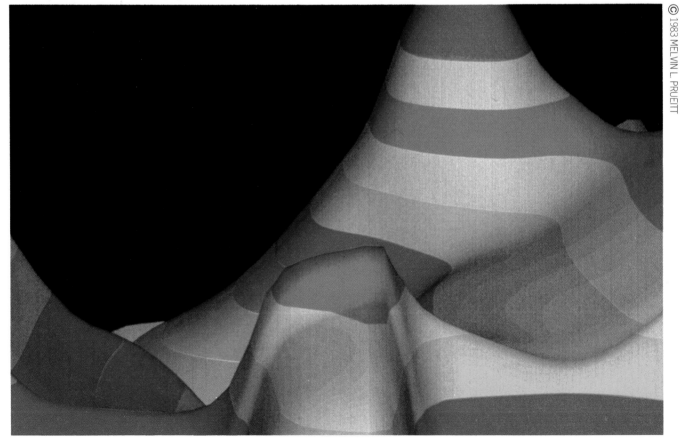

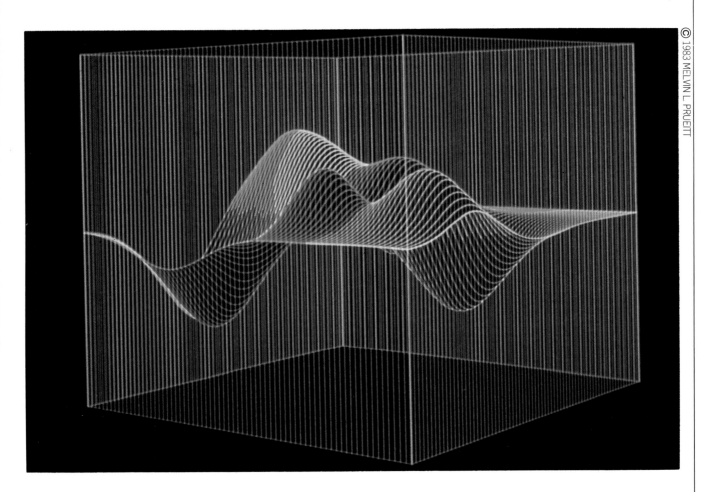

computer artist could generate something resembling the entire *oeuvre* of Mondrian in just a few hours, and one can seriously speculate whether many experts would be able to tell the difference. It is quite possible that the rise of the computer will eventually erode the reputations of some of the modern masters of abstract art.

For today's generation of artists there is little doubt that the computer represents a big challenge. It is a difficult tool to master. Computers have little use until they are given specific tasks to perform. There can be no general-purpose computer with a ready-made program for assisting the fine artist. This would be a contradiction in terms for it would mean that the programmer must know *in advance* exactly what the artist wants to achieve. In the fine arts each person who chooses to work with computers must be prepared to learn how to program the machine so that it will perform the functions required.

In the early days of computer graphics, when there were no painting systems or other conveniently packaged application software, American artists such as Ken Knowlton, Lillian Schwartz and Larry Cuba became deeply involved with the mathematics of computer imaging. Others, such as David Em who frequently uses the powerful software developed by Dr Blinn at the Jet Propulsion Laboratory, Pasadena, California, have found creative opportunities by adapting the

◁ △ **Experimental computer art**
Science becomes art in Melvin Prueitt's high-resolution contour modelling. With colour-fill, shading and hidden-line/surface removal, these images, remind us of mathematics' aesthetic aspect

Melvin Prueitt, Los Alamos National Laboratory, Los Alamos, New Mexico

CB

work of scientists to their own ends. Yet in art schools today the installation of special-purpose graphics computers has allowed students to bypass the complex mathematics of graphics programming altogether. Indeed, unless one is already familiar with the methods of individual artists, it is now extremely difficult to assess the extent to which they have mastered the tools of their trade. Traditionally, by examining the end result one could gain a good idea of the skill involved. This is no longer true.

Most of the artists included in this portfolio section have become highly expert at graphics programming. Most of them work for computer corporations or are engaged on graphics research in universities. In the work of each of them one can detect not only a fascination with mathematics but also a sheer delight in the aesthetics of complex geometries and colour combinations. Computer art requires this unique range of skills. It demands a sensitivity to the formal aspects of painting and an ability to cope with the intricacies of computer programming. The 'ideal' computer artist might have a degree in mathematics, a knowledge of computers and a keen desire to create images. Perhaps this is why there are relatively few artists producing good work.

$9\ 30\ 79$

◁ △ **Computer art 4**
1 *Grass: Series 1*
2 *Structure Study: blue, red, brown, black*

Colette and Jeff Bangert, Lawrence, Kansas

Colette and Jeff Bangert of Lawrence, Kansas, have succeeded in producing work with real artistic qualities by combining their individual skills. Colette is more inclined towards the visual arts, whereas Jeff Bangert has a knowledge of computing. Together they find unique solutions to aesthetic problems that interest them. The result has been a body of work containing some striking images, particularly those that reveal the artists' interest in observing the world around them. This is, alas, unusual among artists who use computers: the machine frequently tends to intervene and impose its own structures on an image. Yet in the Bangerts' 'Grass' series, for example, there is certainly a feeling that the real world has been examined and transformed.

With the equipment and techniques described in this book an artist certainly has access to a considerable range of visual effects. There is now, too, a vast, powerful capacity to manipulate complex geometries using the unique characteristics of the computer. This is amply demonstrated here in the work of Dr Melvin Prueitt and Paul Jablonka – two American artists whose images make full use of the computer's 'uniqueness' and could not be achieved in any other way.

But it must also be acknowledged that some of the primary benefits of the computer have no relevance in the fine arts. Speed, which is so essential in the applied arts, is one example, another is the ability to accomplish routine tasks with the help of automation – no task is strictly routine for the fine artist. There is also the ever-present danger that this complex technology can distract artists from their true vocation. Neither the inner world of feelings and imagination, nor the external world of appearances and perceived reality receive sufficient attention if artists are struggling to master the tools of their craft. Like most technological developments, the graphic computer is an ambiguous gift: its benefits are almost exactly counterbalanced by its disadvantages.

GLOSSARY

Cross references are indicated in italic.

Accuracy aids In CAD, pre-programmed techniques that allow a designer to achieve positioning accuracy on an interactive display, e.g. a *grid constraint*

Additive colour mixing Producing colours by mixing red, green and blue light

Address A character, group of characters, or other bit pattern that identifies a particular storage location in a computer memory

Addressable point Any screen position which can be expressed in *device coordinates*

Address space The area defined by the coordinate system representing the internal digital limits of the display device

Aiming symbol A movable *screen cursor* on a display screen

Algorithm A series of instructions or procedural steps for solving a specific problem

Aliasing Unwanted visual effects, especially jagged lines and edges (*jaggies*) in raster images, caused by improper sampling techniques

Alphanumeric (Having) letters of the alphabet, together with numerals and symbols: as on an alphanumeric keyboard or display monitor

ALU Arithmetic Logic Unit. The component of a *CPU* that performs arithmetic and logic operations

Analog Class of computers operating on the principle of manipulating a continuously varying physical analogy of a problem to be solved

Anti-aliasing Techniques that reduce *aliasing* in computer graphics images

Batch processing A non-interactive type of computer processing in which all the input data are entered before any output is received

Beam penetration CRT A *vector display* system which produces colour by varying the strength of an electron beam directed at a screen coated with (typically) both red and green phosphor layers

Belt-bed plotter A pen plotter which uses a wide continuous belt for holding the paper

Benchmark A task used for measuring the performance of a computer system

Binary digit The basic unit of the binary system of counting, expressed as either '0' or '1'

Bit One binary digit

Bit depth In a *frame buffer*, the number of bits available for representing colours or intensity levels. A frame buffer 8 bits deep can store 256 colours

Bit map In raster systems, a buffer that stores the image as an array of *pixels*: a *frame buffer*

Boundary fill Filling a region with colour by switching to a new value all pixels that are bounded by other pixels having boundary values

Boundary representation One of the main methods of *solid modelling*, in which the object is described by its geometry and topology

Boxing The use of bounding boxes to select particular entities on a computer graphics display

Brush In computer painting, a marker that draws a line or pattern on the display surface

Buffer An electronic memory in which data can be stored temporarily and subsequently released

Byte A fixed number of bits, usually 8, treated by the computer as a single group

CAD Computer Aided Design. The term, though general, is normally reserved for engineering and architectural applications of computer graphics

CADCAM Computer Aided Design/Computer Aided Manufacturing

CADD Computer Aided Design and Draughting

CAE Computer Aided Engineering

Cartesian coordinates The x,y (horizontal and vertical) coordinates that specify the position of a point on a plane, and the x,y,z (horizontal, vertical and depth) coordinates that specify a point in a cube or spatial volume

Chip Colloquial but universally-used expression for a microprocessor; more precisely, the unpackaged wafer of silicon which incorporates a micro-electronic circuit

CIM Computer Integrated Manufacturing

Clipping The division of *primitives* in *world coordinate space* which overlap the boundary of a rectangular *window* onto that space

Clock pulses Electronic pulses which control the timing of all circuits in a computer

COM Computer Output Microfilm. A type of high-resolution film recorder which turns computer output into photographic images

Colour look-up table A small piece of memory (often within a *frame buffer*) which contains colour content values

Colour scanning The analysis of full-colour images into the subtractive primaries (cyan, magenta and yellow) and black, used in making colour separations for printing

Command language The set of rules by which a user and a computer system conduct their 'conversation' in *interactive* computing

Compiler A computer program that converts the source code of a computer language into machine code for processing

CNC Computer Numerical Control. The control of machine tools directly from instructions given by a computer

Configuration A particular selection of computer equipment, including a host computer, peripherals and interfaces, which will work efficiently together

Constraints Types of *accuracy aids* that force interactive input into regular patterns. They are most often used for achieving exact correspondence of newly-entered points, lines or shapes with existing points, lines or shapes on the screen (and, more importantly, in the data structure itself)

Coordinates An ordered set of absolute or relative data values which specify a location. See *Cartesian coordinates*

CPU Central Processing Unit

CRT Cathode Ray Tube. A television vacuum tube (and associated electronics) for converting voltages into a pattern of images on a phosphor-coated screen

CSG Constructive Solid Geometry. One of the chief methods of *solid modelling*, using solid *primitives* and Boolean operators to construct complex solids

Cursor A position indicator. It can be a symbol on the screen (a *screen cursor*) or a hand-held device for entering coordinate points (a *hand cursor*)

Cut and paste An interactive technique for moving items to new locations on the screen

Data base A collection of interrelated data, stored for serving one or more applications in the most convenient manner

Data tablet The flat working surface used for the input of coordinate information. Also called a digitizing tablet, it is used with a *stylus* or a *hand cursor*

DBMS Database Management System

Device coordinates Coordinates which represent the area (or volume) that can be displayed by a display device expressed in a coordinate system defining the digital limits of the device

Device drivers Specialized programs, often embedded in hardware, that interface between physical devices (e.g. a data tablet/stylus) and their specified logical mode of operation

Digital-to-analog converter An interface that converts digital data into analog (continuous signal) form

Digitize To input an image (or model) into a computer by converting it into coded signals which can be stored and processed electronically

Digitizing tablet See *data tablet*

Disk A random access magnetic storage medium. Floppy disks are relatively small and portable; hard disks store more data

Display list A list of display instructions in a graphics computer, containing detailed data which specify items to be drawn on the display surface

Display surface The part of a computer graphics display device (such as a CRT or pen plotter) which actually displays graphical data: i.e. the screen itself or the plotting surface

Dot matrix printing A hardcopy output technique in which characters or graphics are printed from a two-dimensional array of dots

Dragging An interactive technique for repositioning an image on a screen

Drum plotter A pen plotter in which the paper is rotated on a drum while the pen moves along the opposite axis

DVST Direct View Storage Tube. A vector CRT device (made exclusively by Tektronix) in which the image is held in a storage grid in the display device

Electrostatic printer/plotter Output device that delivers raster images by depositing patterns of negative charges on plain paper surfaces. The patterns are then coated with positively-charged toner

Emulation The use of software and/or hardware to make a computer system behave as though it has the operational characteristics of a different system

Endpoints In vector graphics, the points that specify each end of a line segment

Event An action by the operator of a graphics system, such as pressing or releasing a *stylus* switch, that produces an input

Extents (Conceptual) lines, rectangles or solids that separate or surround individual polygons or segments. They are *not* displayed on the screen, but are devices used by graphics programmers

Extrusion An interactive modelling technique in which a further dimension can be added to an existing definition, e.g. a line can be extruded from a point, a plane from a line, and a solid from a plane

Facets In three-dimensional modelling, polygons that comprise the surface of a computer-generated object

False colour Colour which is added to monochrome images by transforming intensity values into colour values

FEM Finite-Element Model. A computer model used by engineers (and often derived from the designer's geometric model) to determine (for example) stresses on a structure

Field In television and raster graphics, one complete scan of the picture image from top to bottom

File A collection of data stored in a computer memory, usually for a specific purpose

Filter A mask: a bit pattern which alters another bit pattern

Firmware Computer programs stored in PROMs (programmable read-only memories) which can be replaced but not reprogrammed by the user

Flat-bed plotter A pen plotter in which the paper (or film-based material) is held on a flat drawing table traversed by one or more pens in a pen carriage

Flat panel displays Visual display units (VDUs) which most often use technologies other than the CRT in order to reduce the bulk and power requirements of the VDU, e.g. *liquid-crystal displays* and *plasma panels*

Fractal geometry The description of intermediate shapes whose dimensionality need not be a whole number. Fractal dimensionality can express degrees of irregularity – and hence is used in computer graphics for generating realistic simulations of natural formations, such as mountains, coastlines, etc.

Frame buffer A solid-state memory in a computer graphics system which holds a matrix of digital values corresponding to the pixel pattern displayed (or about to be displayed) on the screen

Frame grab Temporary storage of a video frame for later manipulation on a graphics computer

Gate A switch in an electronics circuit

Geometric modelling The creation of a computer model that is defined primarily by its shape and spatial layout

Graphics standards Agreed specifications which define the common interfaces between computer graphics systems or subsystems

Graphics subroutine packages So-called 'toolbox' systems that enable programmers to build their own application software using pre-written graphics utilities

Grid constraint An *accuracy aid* that causes the screen cursor to jump to the nearest grid intersection whenever a point is entered

Grids Patterns of horizontal and vertical lines, displayed on the screen to aid the user in entering coordinate data

Group technology In CAM (computer aided manufacturing), an aspect of process planning in which the parts to be manufactured are grouped together in families. The computer identifies similarities among thousands of components, thus aiding efficient manufacturing techniques

Hand cursor A hand-held device (often called a 'puck') for inputting coordinate data. It has 'cross-hairs' to identify exact locations and is used with a data tablet

Hardcopy Computer output onto a tangible substrate, such as paper or film

Hidden-line removal The (automatic) removal of those lines that would normally be hidden on a real object by virtue of being obstructed by the front surfaces of the object

Histogram A bar chart, especially one used in *image processing* to show the distribution of intensity values

Hither plane The front clipping plane that defines a finite *view volume*

Host computer The main computer that provides processing power for the terminals and peripherals connected to it

Icon A small representational graphic symbol, frequently used for giving a visual indication of the meaning of a command on a VDU menu

Image processing The science of interpreting digital images by using computers and computer graphics techniques. Most image processing deals with data acquired by remote sensing devices aboard satellites or spacecraft, but the techniques can be used in many branches of science, engineering and the arts

In-betweens In animation, the frames that come 'in-between' the key frames and which smooth the movements of the cartoon figure being animated

Ink-jet plotter A computer graphics output device which sprays the image onto paper, using ultra-fine jets of coloured ink

Input Literally, 'that which is put in', i.e. data entered into a computer system. The word is also used as an ungainly verb: to input

Instance A replication of a subobject, such as a

symbol, taken when more than one image of the symbol is required on the screen at the same time

Interactive Instantaneous (or near-instantaneous) response to a user input. With interactive computer graphics, models and images can be created by the user conducting a 'dialogue' with the computer

Interface A shared boundary. In computing, the boundary between two subsystems or two devices – and hence the device (the interface) that matches these parts of the system

Interpolation Introducing or inserting additional values between the existing values in a series. It is frequently used in computer graphics, especially in colour shading techniques

Interpreter A program that performs operations on a source program in memory, translating instructions one by one and executing them immediately

Iterative routine A program which repeatedly performs a series of steps (iterations) making successive and increasingly accurate approximations until a specified condition is obtained

Jaggies Jagged lines or edges, often found in low-resolution raster displays. They are reduced by *anti-aliasing* techniques

Joystick A physical interaction device: a lever that can be moved in all four compass directions to control, for example, a rotating object on screen, to move the whole image or to position a *screen cursor*

Keyboard A physical input device for entering character strings into a computer

Kinematic programs In CADCAM, visual simulation programs used for solving those design problems which involve moving parts

Light pen A hand-held device that detects light emitted by elements comprising the picture (such as lines or points) on the screen

Line segment In vector graphics, the portion of a line bounded by *endpoints*

Liquid-crystal display A display which uses the unique properties of liquid-crystal molecules to change their orientation when subjected to electrical forces

Lofting An interactive graphics technique in which the third dimension is obtained from a two-dimensional representation – as in elevating the contours of a topographic map

Magnetic tape A storage medium from which information can be retrieved sequentially, i.e. by searching the tape from one end to the other

Map A detailed representation in which the positions of points have a known correspondence to the positions of real or allocated points on the object being represented

Memory planes Subdivisions of a computer memory, usually with some correspondence between the contents of each plane, e.g. a *frame buffer* may have several memory planes, each one holding a complete image for display on a CRT screen

Menu A visual display of various possible commands, being composed of elements such as text, colours and *icons*, to help the user perform a task. They can be implemented on the display screen, on a separate menu monitor, or on a *data tablet*

Micrographics A specific (and non-computer graphics) term, meaning the use of photographically-reduced information for convenient storage, retrieval and examination of records, files and documents. It should *not* be used for describing computer graphics generated on microcomputers

Mirroring Time-saving graphics technique in which the designer draws one half of a symmetrical object, and then uses the computer to draw the other half

Mode A general term, meaning 'one among several alternative methods of operation' – all of which have some common characteristic

Monitor A video display screen which does not have any radio-frequency receiving circuits

Mouse A hand-held interaction device that inputs relative coordinate information. Popularized by Apple Computer, the mouse is chiefly used as a 'pick device' for selecting items from a screen menu, and it can be operated without a data tablet

Object A conceptual graphic unit in an application program. It may be a geometric model (or part of a geometric model) and is described in *world coordinates* in terms of *primitive* functions and attributes

Off-line Unconnected to the central computer

On-line Connected to the central computer and (by implication) under its control

Operating system An integrated collection of procedures that supervises the sequencing and processing of programs in a computer

Origin In a coordinate system, the point at which all the values are at zero

Output devices Devices that draw, print, photograph or otherwise display the images that have been created in the computer

Output pipeline A conceptualization of what happens when successive transformations are performed on an object description in order to produce an image of the object on a screen

Panning Moving the displayed portion of the image to the left and right, thus revealing further portions of the image

Parallel transmission In data transfer, a method in which all the bits of a byte (usually 8) are transmitted simultaneously over parallel communication lines (such as a ribbon cable in a computer)

Parameter A 'variable' that remains constant under one set of circumstances but varies when the circumstances are changed

Passive graphics Non-interactive graphics, as, for example, in the applications of instrumentation and process control – where the operator is simply receiving visual information

Pattern recognition The recognition of shapes and patterns by machine systems

Pen plotters Computer-driven line-drawing output device that produces high-quality plots on paper or film. It is a random-scan device in that its pens can move directly between any two points on the surface. See *flat-bed, drum* and *belt-bed plotters*

Peripherals External items added to a computer system, for example, graphics peripherals such as plotters, printers, display units, etc.

Persistence A measurement of the time taken for a phosphor's output of light to decay to 10 per cent of its initial *phosphorescence*

Phosphors A class of substances giving off light when acted on either by radiation or by certain chemicals

Physical device coordinates Device dependent coordinates to which output *primitives* are finally transformed for display on a particular output device

Pixel Short for 'picture element', being the smallest addressable point of a raster image. Popular matrices of pixels are 512×512 and 1024×1024

Plasma panels Gas discharge displays which typically use cells of neon gas trapped in thin panels for displaying electronically-generated images

Primitives Basic graphical entities, such as points, line segments and polygons, that can be geometrically orientated in a two- or three-dimensional world

Procedural modelling Time-saving methods for constructing computer models whereby the object geometry is not defined directly but is represented as a procedure, e.g. a staircase is created with three input variables: height, width and stair type

Programmed function keyboard An auxiliary keyboard, usually containing 16 or 32 pushbuttons, which, when pressed, generate user commands

PROM Programmable Read-Only Memory

Puck A hand-held digitizer, also called a *hand cursor*

RAM Random Access Memory

Random scan A term used for describing display devices which allow the drawing of *vectors* between specified *endpoints*

Raster The pattern of horizontal lines traced by the electron beam in an ordinary television or raster graphics monitor

Raster scan The horizontal scanning pattern of a raster display. Also, that class of graphics equipment in which the image is held as a pattern of horizontal lines (and subdivided into *pixels*) and which is distinct from random scan (vector) devices

Ray-tracing A technique for creating realistic computer images by tracing rays from viewpoint to light source (i.e. the reverse path of light rays). It calculates both hidden surfaces and shading – but tends to be slow, requiring lengthy processing by the computer to generate the image

Read/write head In magnetic storage devices, an electromagnet which reads (gathers data) and writes (deposits data) on the storage medium (tape, disk, drum, etc.)

Refresh The process of renewing the image on the display surface of a refresh tube, typically 30 or 60 times a second

Register A short-term store for digital data in the central processing unit (CPU) of a computer system

Resolution A measure of the ability to discriminate between the smallest separate parts of an object or image. In computer graphics, 'resolution' may refer to screen or to data base resolution. With raster graphics, screen resolution is determined by the number of available *pixels* on the display – whereas in vector graphics it is determined by the *spot size* of the electron beam. In hardcopies, resolution is best expressed as the number of discernible line pairs per mm (or inch)

Response time The time taken for a system to respond to a user action

RGB Red, Green, Blue. An RGB monitor is driven directly by an RGB colour input signal which is fundamentally three monochrome signals separately driving the CRT's red, green and blue electron guns

ROM Read-Only Memory

Routine A computer program, or, more often, a part of a program

Rubberbanding A line-drawing technique in which an 'elastic' line is extended from one (or more) point(s) to wherever the movable *screen cursor* is positioned

Run-length encoding A technique for encoding information (particularly raster image definitions) very compactly, taking advantage of the fact that adjacent *pixels* often have the same intensity values

Sampling The process of obtaining a series of discrete instantaneous values of a signal at specified intervals

Scaling Finding the appropriate degree of enlargement or reduction of an original image and subsequently using the graphics computer to execute the operation

Scan conversion The process of converting a stored definition of an image into a *pixel* array that approximates to the original definition. Vector images must be scan converted for raster monitors

Screen cursor An indicating symbol (usually a small cross) generated by the display hardware and moved by the user around the screen area. Its position on the screen can be made to correspond to the position of a hand-held input device, such as a *stylus* moved across a *data tablet*

Scrolling Moving all the displayed information on a screen vertically (and sometimes horizontally also)

Seed filling Filling a bounded area with colour by switching just one pixel (or very few pixels) to the chosen shade

Segment A named portion of the display list, defining a display item

Shadow mask The perforated screen in a CRT which is interposed between the electron guns and the phosphor screen so that accurate alignment with the respective red, green and blue phosphor dots is achieved

SIGGRAPH Special Interest Group on (Computer) Graphics: a branch of the ACM (Association for Computing Machinery) in the USA. Also, the (colloquial) name of the annual conference and trade show held by this group

Signal A detectable impulse (e.g. in voltage, current, magnetic field, or light) by which information is communicated

Sketching Freehand drawing of lines and colours with an interactive display

Software packages Computer programs supplied 'off-the-shelf' on disks, complete with reference manual, application notes, and often including special circuit cards, starter files and other accessories with a specific (but not *too* specific!) computing application

Solid modelling Creation of three-dimensional objects which (unlike *wireframes* and *surface modelling*) can be guaranteed to be unambiguous representations of the objects' structure

Specular light Directional light from a specific source that reflects directly off the surface of an object without entering it

Spot size In *vector displays*, the diameter of the focused electron beam on the display surface

Standalone system A self-contained computer system which is not linked to a larger computer

Stroke display An alternative name for a CRT vector display

Stylus A pencil-shaped graphical input device, used in conjunction with a *data tablet* to enter data and commands into an interactive graphics system

Subroutine A set of instructions in a program which can be entered via a branch instruction

Subtractive primaries Cyan, magenta and yellow. These colours are the exact complements of red, green and blue – and, when mixed, produce black. They are always used in colour printing and are often called the 'pigment primaries'

Surface modelling One of three broad categories of three-dimensional modelling, the others being *wireframe* and *solid modelling*. In surface modelling, the surfaces of objects are defined by connecting surface elements to the edge model

Tablet menu A selection of user commands that are implemented on a *data tablet* for easy access

Terrain models Semi-realistic three-dimensional models of landscapes, containing accurate topological features together with approximate representations of buildings, trees and other smaller objects

Texture mapping The mapping of digitized surface textures onto a surface

Thematic mapping The production of colour-coded maps by using multispectral classification algorithms

Three-dimensional digitizer A piece of digitizing equipment for taking coordinate data directly from a physical three-dimensional object (such as an architectural model) rather than from engineering drawings

Touch panel A physical interaction device that allows a user to indicate a position on a screen by touching the screen surface. Touch panels are transparent and are mounted directly in front of the display

Track ball A physical interaction device that is most often used for *panning* and *scrolling* the picture across the screen

Transformations Changes applied to model and image representations by using mathematical techniques which are executed automatically by the graphics computer

Tree A hierarchical arrangement of data into a structure similar to an upside-down tree

Triad A group of three. In video, a triad is specifically a group of three dots: one each of red, green and blue, thousands of which comprise the surface pattern of a colour raster CRT

Tweaking In CAD, a modelling technique in which the user 'tweaks' a control dial (or other input device), causing a selected shape to elongate on the screen

2½-D An enhancement to a two-dimensional system in which priority values are assigned to displayed objects, allowing them to be overlapped on the screen to produce an effect like pieces of paper on a desk, each partially obscuring the one below

User interface That part of a computer system which determines the ways in which a user can communicate with the computer (and vice versa)

VDU Visual Display Unit

Vector In mathematics, a quantity having direction in space and magnitude – and the line representing it

Vector display A line-drawing display that creates images by drawing vectors (lines connecting *endpoints*) on the phosphor surface of the CRT, using a single focused electron beam which can move at random (up, down, sideways, diagonally, etc.)

Video colorizer A video effects system: usually one having *analog* picture and control inputs

Videotex Umbrella term for all types of viewdata and teletext systems and services

Viewport A rectangular portion of the screen onto which the *window* and window contents are mapped

View volume The space in which objects are seen to exist in a three-dimensional display

Voxel Volume Element. The basic element in some types of three-dimensional imaging systems, especially those used in medical applications. It can be thought of as a 'solid pixel'

Window A rectangular region in unbounded *world coordinate space*, defined by specifying high and low limits along each world coordinate axis

Window-to-viewport mapping The transformation of *primitives* from the *world coordinate system* to the *device coordinate system*

Wireframe A three-dimensional outline image displayed as a series of connected *line segments*, including all the hidden lines

Workstation A configuration of interactive computer equipment, providing facilities for a human operator at an individual work location

World coordinate space The coordinate system in which the geometric model is defined: typically, a right-handed Cartesian coordinate system. An object defined in this 'world coordinate space' must be transformed by viewing *transformations* before an image of the object (from one point of view) can be displayed on a screen

X-axis The horizontal axis in a coordinate system

Y-axis The vertical axis in a coordinate system

Yon plane The back clipping plane that defines a finite *view volume*. See also *hither plane*

Z-axis The axis indicating depth in a coordinate system

Z-clipping Limiting the three-dimensional space in the depth dimension by defining a *hither plane* and a *yon plane*, both parallel to the view plane

Zooming A cinematic-type effect, created by moving the *window* onto *world coordinate space* 'in' and 'out'

BIBLIOGRAPHIES

COMPUTER GRAPHICS JOURNALS AND RESOURCE PUBLICATIONS

Scientific/academic

ACM Transactions on Graphics, Association for Computing Machinery, 11 West 42nd Street, New York, NY 10036 (quarterly)

Color: Research and Application, John Wiley & Sons, 605 Third Avenue, New York, NY 10158 (quarterly)

Computer Graphics and Applications, IEEE Computer Society, 10662 Los Vaqueros Circle, Los Alamitos, CA 90720 (bi-monthly)

Computer Graphics, Association for Computing Machinery, 11 West 42nd Street, New York, NY 10036 (quarterly)

Computer Graphics and Image Processing, Academic Press, 111 Fifth Avenue, New York, NY 10003 (monthly)

Computers and Graphics, Pergamon Press Inc., Maxwell House, Fairview Park, Elmsford, NY 10523 (quarterly)

Harvard Library of Computer Graphics, Harvard University Graduate School of Design, Gund Hall, Cambridge, MA 02138

SIGGRAPH Conference Proceedings, Association for Computing Machinery, Special Interest Group on Computer Graphics, 1133 Avenue of the Americas, New York, NY 10036 (annual)

World Computer Graphics Association, Conference Proceedings, 2033 M Street NW, Suite 250, Washington DC, 20036

Business applications

The Anderson Report, Anderson Publishing Co., Simi Valley Business Park, Simi Valley, CA 93063 (monthly)

Computer Graphics Market Alert, Management Roundtable Inc., PO Box 404, Newton, MA 02161 (monthly)

Computer Graphics News, Scherago Associates Inc., 1515 Broadway, New York, NY 10036 (bi-monthly)

Computer Graphics Software News, Greg Passmore, 910 Ashford Parkway, Houston, Texas (bi-weekly)

Computer Graphics Technology Newsletter, Computer Graphics Technology Co., 1432 Comet Street, Irvine, CA 92714 (monthly)

S. Klein Newsletter on Computer Graphics, 730 Boston Post Road, Sudbury, MA 01776 (bi-weekly)

Engineering applications

CADCAM International, EMAP Business and Computer Publications Ltd., 67 Clerkenwell Road, London EC1R 5BH (monthly)

Design Drafting and Repro Graphics, Syndicate Magazine Inc., 390 Fifth Avenue, New York, NY 10018 (monthly)

General

Computer Graphics World, PennWell Publishing Co., 1714 Stockton Street, San Francisco, CA 94133 (monthly)

Computer Pictures, Back Stage Publications Inc., 330 West 42nd Street, New York, NY 10036 (bi-monthly)

Graphics Network News, National Computer Graphics Association, 8401 Arlington Boulevard, Fairfax, VA 22031 (bi-monthly)

BOOKS ON COMPUTER GRAPHICS AND RELATED SUBJECTS

Allan, John, J., **A Survey of Industrial Robots**, Leading Edge Publishing Inc, Dallas, Texas, 1981

Allan, John J. **The CAD/CAM Glossary**, Leading Edge, Dallas, Texas, 1979

Angell, I.O. **A Practical Introduction to Computer Graphics**, Halstead Press, New York, New York, 1981

Barnhill R.E. and Riesenfeld, R.F., **Computer Aided Geometric Design**, Academic Press, New York, New York, 1975

Booth, Kellogg S. **Tutorial: Computer Graphics**, IEEE Computer Society Press, Maryland, 1979

Calma Corporation, **Interactive CAD Considerations for Architects, Engineers and Constructors**, Sunnyvale, California, 1980

Cardamore, T., **Chart and Graph Preparation Skills**, Van Nostrand Reinhold, New York, New York, 1981

Castleman, K.R., **Digital Image Processing**, Prentice-Hall, New Jersey, 1979

Chasen, S.H., **Geometrical Principles and Procedures for Computer Graphics Applications**, Prentice-Hall, New Jersey, 1978

Chasen, S.H. and Dow, W., **The Guide for the Evaluation and Implementation of CAD/CAM Systems**, Online Publications, Pinner, Middlesex, England, 1983

Conrac Corporation, **Raster Graphics Handbook**, Conrac Division, Conrac Corporation, Covina, California, 1980

Evans and Sutherland Corporation, **Picture System II User's Manual**, Evans and Sutherland Corporation, Salt Lake City, Utah, 1977

Evans and Sutherland Corporation, **PS 300 User's Manual**, Evans and Sutherland Corporation, Salt Lake City, Utah, 1981

Foley, J.D. and Van Dam, A., **Fundamentals of Interactive Computer Graphics**, Addison-Wesley, Reading, Massachusetts, 1982

Freeman, H., **Tutorial: Interactive Computer Graphics**, IEEE Computer Society Press, Maryland, 1980

Giloi, Wolfgang, **Interactive Computer Graphics: Data Structures, Algorithms, Languages**, Prentice-Hall, Englewood Cliffs, New Jersey, 1978

Green, William B., **Digital Image Processing**, Van Nostrand Reinhold, New York, New York, 1983

Greenberg, D. (and others), **The Computer Image: Applications of Computer Graphics**, Addison-Wesley, Reading, Massachusetts, 1982

Hamilton, Edward A., **Graphic Design for the Computer Age**, Van Nostrand Reinhold, New York, New York, 1970

Harrington, Joseph, **Computer Integrated Manufacturing**, Industrial Press Inc, New York, New York, 1974

Jarett, Irvin M., **Computer Graphics and Reporting Financial Data**, Ronald Press, New York, New York, 1983

Judd, D. and Wyszecki, G., **Color in Business, Science and Industry**, John Wiley & Sons, New York, New York, 1975

Kawaguchi, Yoshiro, **Digital Image**, ASCII, Tokyo, Japan, 1981

Kepes, Gyorgy, **The New Landscape of Art and Science**, Theobald, Chicago, Illinois, 1956

Klein, S., **Directory of Computer Graphics Suppliers**, S. Klein, Sudbury, Massachusetts (annual)

Krouse, John K., **What Every Engineer Should Know About ... Computer Aided Design and Computer Aided Manufacturing**, Marcel Dekker Inc, New York, New York, 1982

Krueger, Myron W., **Artificial Reality**, Addison-Wesley Publishing Company, Reading, Massachusetts, 1982

Leavitt, Ruth, **The Artist and the Computer**, Harmony Books, New York, New York, 1976

Levitan, E.L., **Electronic Imaging Techniques**, Van Nostrand Reinhold, New York, New York, 1977

Machover, Carl and Blauth, Robert, **The CAD/CAM Handbook**, Computervision Corporation, Bedford, Massachusetts, 1980

Mandelbrot, Benoit, **The Fractal Geometry of Nature**, W.H. Freeman, San Francisco, 1983

Mitchell, W.J., **Computer-Aided Architectural Design**, Petrocelli-Charter, New York, New York, 1977

Monmonier, Mark S., **Computer Assisted Cartography**, Prentice-Hall, Englewood Cliffs , New Jersey, 1981

Myers, Roy E., **Microcomputer Graphics**, Addison-Wesley Publishing Company, Reading, Massachusetts, 1983

Newman, William M. and Sproull, Robert F., **Principles of Interactive Computer Graphics**, McGraw-Hill, New York, New York, 1979

Paller, Alan; Szoka, Kathryn; and Nelson, Nan, **Choosing the Right Chart**, ISSCO, San Diego, California, 1981

Papert, Seymour, **Mindstorms**, Basic Books Inc, New York, New York, 1980

Pratt, W.K., **Digital Image Processing**, Wiley-Interscience, New York, New York, 1978

Rosenfeld, A. and Kak, A.C., **Digital Image Processing**, Academic Press, New York, New York, 1976

Ryan, Daniel L., **Computer-Aided Graphics and Design**, Marcel Dekker Inc, New York, New York, 1980

Scott, Joan E., **Introduction to Interactive Computer Graphics**, John Wiley & Sons, New York, New York, 1982

Tranimoto, S. and Klinger, A., **Structured Computer Vision**, Academic Press, New York, New York, 1980

Tannas, Lawrence E., **Flat Panel Displays**, Van Nostrand Reinhold, New York, New York, 1981

Waite, Michael, **Computer Graphics Primer**, Howard W. Sams & Co, Indianapolis, Indiana, 1982

Whitney, John, **Digital Harmony**, Byte Books, McGraw-Hill Publishing Company, New York, New York, 1980

Youngblood, Gene, **Expanded Cinema**, Dutton, New York, New York, 1970

Zelazny, G., **Choosing and Using Charts**, McKinsey & Company, New York, New York, 1972

INDEX

The figures in bold type indicate references in the captions to the illustrations.

ACKNOWLEDGMENTS

The author and publisher would particularly like to thank the following people, companies and institutions for their contribution to this book:

Robert Abel; Robert Abel & Associates, Hollywood, California; Maggi Allison; Will Anielewicz; Aurora Systems, San Francisco, California; Colette Bangert; Jeff Bangert; Robert Blalack; James Blinn; Peter Bloch; CalComp, Anaheim, California; CalComp Ltd, Bracknell, Berkshire, England; CAL Videographics, London, England; Cambridge Interactive Services, Cambridge, England; Chartmasters, San Francisco, California; Michael T. Collery; Concept Marketing & Communications, Bourne End, Buckinghamshire, England; Michael Connolly; John Cook; Gordon Cramp Studio; Cranston-Csuri Productions, Columbus, Ohio; Crosfield Electronics, London and Peterborough, England; Peter Dean; Gary Demos; Dicomed (UK) Ltd, Ascot, Berkshire, England; Frank Dietrich; Digital Effects, New York, New York; Digital Productions, Los Angeles, California; John Donkin; Hans Donner; Douglas J. Dunham; Dean Eaker; Yoshio Eguchi; Eidographics, London, England; Electronic Arts, London, England; David Em; Louise Etra; David Evans; Evans & Sutherland, Salt Lake City, Utah; Vicki Fontanes; Sylvia Forcey; Joseph Fornataro; Bruce Fox; Meldon Gafner; Bo Gehring; Bo Gehring Associates; Ken Glickfield; Groupmedia, Chicago, Illinois; Earl F. Hadden II; Donald Harbison; James Hartnett; Peter Hayward; Hewlett-Packard, Wokingham, Berkshire, England; David Hodes; ISSCO, San Diego, California; Paul Jablonka; Jet Propulsion Laboratory, Pasadena, California; Eve Jordan; Martin Kahn; Stephen R. Keith; Malcolm Kerley; Brian Kewell; Robin King; Philip Kipling; Ken Knowlton; Kongsberg System Technology, Maidenhead, Berkshire, England; Lawrence Livermore Laboratories, Livermore, California; Jim Lee; Bob Leemer; Jim Lindner; Peter Lloyd; Los Alamos National Laboratory, New Mexico; Mike Luckwell; John Lyons; Lindsay MacDonald; Nelson Max; Ritch McBride; Douglas Merritt; University of Minnesota; Wendall Mohler; Zsuzsa Molnar; David Moore; Moore Graphics & Film, Hollywood, California; Gwyn Morgan; Wayne Morris; The Moving Picture Company, London, England; Myriad Productions, London, England; Mike Newman; NHK, Tokyo, Japan; Nicolet Instruments Ltd, Warwick, England; Stan North; Guy Nouri; Elaine Obici; Ohio State University, Columbus, Ohio; Penny & Giles Potentiometers Ltd, Christchurch, Dorset, England; Richard Peters; Alan Pipes; Polaroid (UK) Ltd, St Albans, Hertfordshire, England; Nacy Scott Price; Melvin Prueitt; David Ramey; Damon Rarey; Rede Globo, Rio de Janeiro, Brazil; Judson Rosebush; Judy Sachter; Andrew Salanson; Tom Sancha; Vivianne Scott; Scripps Clinic & Research Foundation, La Jolla, California; Sheridan College, Ontario, Canada; Derrick Sherwin; Richard Shoup; Stephen Slingsby; Sogitec Audiovisuel, Boulogne, France; Peter Sorensen; Laurie Spiegel; Lee Stausland; Nicholas Tanton; Richard Taylor; Steve Temple; Terminal Displays Systems Ltd, Blackburn, Lancashire, England; James Teter; Thames Television, Teddington Lock, Middlesex, England; Dave Throssell; Tom Tolnay; Toucan, San Francisco, California; Versatec Electronics Ltd, Newbury, Berkshire, England; WACS Productions, Toronto, Canada; Walt Disney Productions, Burbank, California; Ron Whitfield; John Whitney Jr; John Whitney Sr; Richard Williams; Nick Winton; Randall Wise; David Witte; David Zeltzer.

The artwork was drawn by the following artists: David Mallott 31 bottom, 34 top, 46 top left, 48 left, 56 top, 56 bottom; Orbis Design Studio/Gordon Cramp 10 bottom, 11, 32, 81 top, centre and bottom, 82 top, centre and bottom, 128 top and bottom, 129 top, centre and bottom, 130 centre, bottom left and bottom right; Hugh Schermuly/Stan North 38 top and bottom, 40, 42 top and bottom, 43, 44; Technical Art Services, London 9, 10 top, 29, 30 top and bottom, 31 bottom, 33 right, 34 top, 39 top and bottom.

The author wishes to record his thanks for the considerable contribution to this book made by the designer, Ruth Prentice, and the editor, Mary Davies.